THE PHENOMENOLOGY OF MOODS IN KIERKEGAARD

THE PHENOMENOLOGY
OF MOODS
IN KIERKEGAARD

by

VINCENT A. McCARTHY

MARTINUS NIJHOFF / THE HAGUE/BOSTON / 1978

To the Memory of
C. ERIC SMITH

© *1978 by Martinus Nijhoff, The Hague, Netherlands*
All rights reserved, including the right to translate or to
reproduce this book or parts thereof in any form
ISBN 90 247 2008 7

TYPESET IN GREAT BRITAIN

PRINTED IN THE NETHERLANDS

TABLE OF CONTENTS

Acknowledgements   viii

Key to Abbreviations   x

INTRODUCTION   1

I. IRONY   7

A. Irony and the Concept in *The Concept of Irony*   9
  Preliminary Considerations   9
  Irony as Tool   13
  The Ironic Consciousness   17
  Negative Aspects of Irony   22
  Mastered Irony   27
  The Essence of Irony as an Existence-Stance   29

B. Irony as a Measurement and Tool in the Analysis of the Aesthetic
  Life-View   30

II. ANXIETY   33

A. Anxiety in *The Concept of Anxiety*   36
  Style and Format   36
  Theory and History of Spirit   38
  Types of, and Stances in Relation to, Anxiety   40

B. The Concept of Anxiety in Kierkegaard's Other Writings   47

C. The Idea of Anxiety. The Experience and Structure of Anxiety   48

D. Attitudes toward Anxiety   50

E. Anxiety and the Aesthetic Life-View   52

III. MELANCHOLY   53

A. The Term "Melancholy"   54

B. Melancholy in *Either/Or*   56
  As Reflected in the Structure of Part I   56
  As Described in Part I   60
  Judge William's Analysis (Part II)   66

C. Melancholy in *Repetition* and *Stages*   72

D. Towards a Concept of Melancholy   78

IV. DESPAIR

82

A. Preliminary Considerations 84

B. Despair in *Either/Or* 86

C. Despair in *The Sickness Unto Death* 88
Relation between Anxiety and Despair 89
The Definition of the Self 90
The Four Forms of Disequilibrium 91
Unconscious Despair: the Commonest Form 96
Conscious Despair: the Principal Forms 96

D. The Idea of Despair 100
State and Structure 100
Experience and Act 101

E. Despair and the Aesthetic Life-View 103

V. THE MOODS AND SUBJECTIVITY OF THE YOUNG AESTHETE JOHANNES

106

A. Johannes' Irony 108

Seeking the Ideal 109
Negative and Positive Irony 110
The Stance of Johannes 110

B. His Anxiety 111

Johannes' Essential Anxiety 111
His Stance in Anxiety 112

C. His Melancholy 113

Johannes' Awareness 113
Johannes' *Tungsind* 114
Need for Resolution 114

D. His Despair 116

Johannes' Disequilibrium 116
His Stance: Conscious Despair 117

E. Dialetic of Moods in Johannes 117

VI. THE DIALECTIC OF MOODS

120

A. Defining "Mood" 122
The Four Moods of the Self 125

B. The Crises-Sequence 127

C. Interrelationships 131

D. Function of Moods in Emerging Religious Subjectivity 132

E. Moods and Life-Views 133

VII. FROM VICTIM TO MASTER OF MOODS: TOWARDS THE CHRISTIAN LIFE-VIEW

135

A. Preliminary Considerations 136
The Term "Life-View" 136
Biographical Prelude 137
Philosophy 138

TABLE OF CONTENTS

vii

B. Life-View in *From the Papers of One Still Living* 140

    Background 140
    Theory of Literature 141
    Forming a Life-View 144

C. Life-View in *The Book on Adler* 146

D. Life-View in *Either/Or, Stages,* and the *Postscript* 148

E. Life-View in the *Papirer* 152

F. The Meaning of Life-View 155

G. The Aesthetic Life-View Exposed 157

CONCLUSION   160

Selected Bibliography   162

Index   167

ACKNOWLEDGEMENTS

Søren Kierkegaard might object to this study of his thought. Any scholar must live with the possibility of such rejection as well as his warnings to any pedants who would lay a dialectical hand upon his works. But the young aesthete Kierkegaard would have empathized with the chance origins of this study from wanderings in Mexico with a suitcase and a satchel of Kierkegaard's works. The same peripathetic style has been maintained throughout, with the original manuscript having been written in France, Denmark and California. The present manuscript represents a revision of the work submitted at Stanford University (Stanford, California) in 1974 for the Ph.D. Revisions were carried out in New York and Connecticut and the printed text will emerge in Europe, at the Hague.

Every traveller as well as scholar owes many debts, and in this I am happily no exception. Gracious scholars, readers and critics aided much through conversation and also correspondence. Others provided the wherewithal for the author to set the study down on paper. One is never able to say whose contribution was the more significant. All my contributors were in many ways invaluable and so I thank them simply, sincerely, singly and alphabetically:

Beverly Baldyga, Joachim Bark, Sandra Hatch, Paul L. Holmer, Howard V. Hong, Akiko Kurimoto, Gregor Malantschuk, Kevin McCarthy, Johannes Mouritsen, Philip H. Rhinelander, William J. Richardson, Lucio Ruotolo, and Niels Thulstrup.

But to none perhaps do I owe a greater debt than to Robert McAfee Brown whose humanity and scholarly good-sense were decisive in allowing this study to come to be.

Finally I dedicate this work to the memory of C. Eric Smith, S.J. (1898–1973) of Guelph, Ontario, scholar, linguist and diplomat who inspired my own wanderings in languages, ideas and places.

ACKNOWLEDGEMENTS

ix

Grateful acknowledgement is made to Princeton University Press for permission to quote from *Concept of Dread*, trans. by Walter Lowrie (copyright 1949 © 1957 by Princeton University Press; Princeton Paperback, 1967); *Either/Or*, Vol. I, trans. by David F. Swenson and Lillian Marvin Swenson (Copyright 1944 © 1959 by Princeton University Press; Princeton Paperback, 1971); Vol. II, trans. by Walter Lowrie (copyright 1944 © 1959 by Princeton University Press, Princeton Paperback, 1971); *Repetition*, trans. by Walter Lowrie (copyright 1941 © 1969 by Princeton University Press); *Stages on Life's Way*, trans. and ed. by Walter Lowrie (copyright 1940 © 1968 by Princeton University Press); *Sickness unto Death*, trans. by Walter Lowrie (copyright 1941, 1954 by Princeton University Press; title Princeton Paperback, 1968: *Fear and Trembling* and *The Sickness unto Death*); *On Authority and Revelation: The Book on Adler, or a Cycle of Ethico-Religious Essays*, trans. by Walter Lowrie (copyright 1955 by Princeton University Press); to Princeton University Press and the American Scandinavian Foundation for permission to quote from *Concluding Unscientific Postscript*, trans. by David Swenson (copyright 1961 © 1969 by Princeton University Press; Princeton Paperback, 1968); to Indiana University Press for permission to quote from *Søren Kierkegaard's Journals and Papers*, trans. and ed. Howard V. Hong and Edna H. Hong (copyright 1967 by Indiana University Press); to Stanford University Press for permission to quote from *Johannes Climacus* or *De omnibus dubitandum est*, and *A. Sermon*, trans. by T. H. Croxall; to Harper and Row Publishers, Inc. and Indiana University Press for permission to quote from *Concept of Irony*, trans. by Lee Capel; to Hutchinson Publishing Group, Ltd. and Harper and Row Publishers, Inc. for permission to quote from Gilbert Ryle's *Concept of Mind*; to Harper and Row Publishers, Inc. for permission to quote from Martin Heidegger's *Being and Time*, trans. by John Macquarrie and Edward Robinson.

KEY TO ABBREVIATIONS

ENGLISH TRANSLATIONS OF KIERKEGAARD'S WORKS CITED

CI   *The Concept of Irony*, trans. Lee M. Capel (New York, 1965).

EO 1   *Either/Or*, trans. David F. Swenson and Lillian Swenson with
EO 2   revisions by Howard A. Johnson (New York: Anchor Books,
                     1959), Parts I and II.

R   *Repetition*, trans. Walter Lowrie (New York: Harper Tor-
                     chbooks, 1964).

CA   *Concept of Anxiety* (Dread), trans. Walter Lowrie (Princeton,
                     1967).

SLW   *Stages on Life's Way*, trans. Walter Lowrie (New York: Schoc-
                     ken Books, 1967).

CUP   *Concluding Unscientific Postscript*, trans. David F. Swenson with
                     revisions by Walter Lowrie (Princeton, 1968).

SUD   *Sickness Unto Death*, trans. Walter Lowrie (New York: Anchor
                     Books, 1954).

AR   *On Authority and Revelation*, trans. Walter Lowrie (New York:
                     Harper Torchbooks, 1966).

DO   *De Omnibus Dubitandum Est*, trans. T. H. Croxall (London,
                     1958).

DANISH EDITION OF KIERKEGAARD'S WORKS

All references are to:

S.V., I-XIV   Søren Kierkegaard, *Samlede Værker*, udg. af A. B. Drach-
                     mann, J. L. Heiberg og H. O. Lange. København: Gylden-
                     dalske Boghandel, 1901–1906. I-XIV.

INTRODUCTION

Kierkegaard himself hardly requires introduction, but his thought continues to require explication due to its inherent complexity and its unusual method of presentation.

Kierkegaard is deliberately un-systematic, anti-systematic, in the very age of the System. He made his point then, and it is not lost upon us today. But that must not deter us from assembling the fragments and viewing the whole. Kierkegaard's religious psychology in particular may finally have its impact and generate the discussion it deserves when its outlines and inter-locking elements are viewed together.

Many approaches to his thought are possible, as a survey of the literature about him will readily reveal.[1] The present study proceeds with the simple ambition of looking at Kierkegaard on his own terms, of thus putting aside biographical fascination or one's own personal religious situation. I understand the temptation of both, and have seen the dangers realized in Kierkegaard scholarship. In English-language Kierkegaard scholarship, we are now in a new phase, in which the entire corpus of Kierkegaard's authorship is at last viewed as a whole. We have passed the stages of "fad" and of under-formed. Almost all the corpus is available in English, or soon will be. Perhaps now Kierkegaard can be viewed, understood, and criticized dispassionately and objectively, not withstanding author Kierkegaard's personal horror of those adverbs.

The present study hopes to make its contribution toward this goal. The theme of the present study is little discussed in Kierkegaard literature except by a very few, Professor Paul Holmer of Yale University being among the most notable. The scholarly lacuna is not a little surprising, when one sees the centrality of moods to Kierkegaard's thought. The present study aims then to bring mood and the psychology of moods to the center of Kierkegaard scholarship and to any assessment of Kierkegaard's philosophical anthropology.

Kierkegaard is simultaneously philosopher, psychologist, religious writer and litterateur. The present study respects him as all of these, as

---

[1] Among the recent studies Mark Taylor's *Kierkegaard's Pseudonymous Works* (Princeton, 1975), pp. 3–37, discusses many possible approaches to Kierkegaard and the merits of each.

INTRODUCTION

it focuses on the philosophical anthropology and centers on the meaning and role of moods. It examines each of four cardinal moods in his analysis of the aesthetic life and discerns a dialectic of moods.

Extreme rationalists may be surprised or embarrassed by the choice of moods as a subject for philosophical exploration. Conversely, irrationalists may prematurely rejoice in the choice of such a subject, expecting to find here justification for their own emphasis on emotions and the downgrading of reason. Those who know Kierkegaard realize in advance that there is no justification for either extreme position. Kierkegaard is no irrationalist, no matter his post mortem association with some excesses of existentialism. But neither is he a rationalist who denies the emotions or refuses them consideration. Kierkegaard recognizes the logic of the heart just as the logic of the mind. "Heart" and "mind" are both metaphors, and neither can be strictly localized. And both logics are logics of the whole person.

Kierkegaard takes moods and the emotional life with the utmost seriousness. Thus he walks the line between the Romantics who unduly celebrate them and the intellectuals who shun them. He sees a function of moods in the life of the whole person and sets out to describe, probe, explore, and analyze. The several works emphasized in our own study are those which carry out his project. It is an intensely rational project from beginning to end, completed by the pathos of Christian seriousness.

As a Socratic philosopher, Kierkegaard was concerned that the wisdom of experience be articulated, and so the present study also discusses the category of "life-view" and its relation to the moods. In the course, it shows that the moods represent a rite of passage from childish illusions about the self to mature understanding which is properly a life-view. In addition the movement to maturity, in a mature life-view, at the same time represents the radical change from victim to master of moods. The present study outlines that transformation process, as it traces the development of (religious) subjectivity, first in the abstract (Chapters One to Four) and then in the concrete analysis of the principal character of Kierkegaard's aesthetic writings, who is described by his moods (Chapter Five).

In opening any volume of Kierkegaard's works, one is plunged *in medias res* on every occasion. Characters soliloquize and dialogue, dialecticians unfold their thought. But it is all part of a larger study of the human person and his emerging spiritual potential. Thus, among the purposes of this study are to point out the *whence*, discern the *whither* and explore in detail the *how* of the spiritual-psychological evolution which constitutes the central thesis in Kierkegaard's philosophical anthropology.

In medias res any but the most initiate may be overwhelmed by an excess of points and purposes. Since these are not tangential, their relation to the central thrust of Kierkegaard's thought is discussed. Kierkegaard is thoroughly polemical from beginning to end. The battles

INTRODUCTION 3

are often colorful, intricate, subtle and engaging. The three principal "villains" which Kierkegaard seeks to wound mortally, in the process of constructing his own dynamic theory of the individual's being and evolution, are Romanticism, Hegelianism (as the symbol of what professional philosophy has become) and Christendom. In the material with which we are here principally concerned, Kierkegaard battles the first and second, which in the end he considers identical. Christendom, the third, is more explicitly the target of the "later writings", during which the transition away from pseudonymity takes place.

The movement which we trace begins with the unmasking of an illusory life-view (the aesthetic) and the gradual preparation for the formation of a new, authentic view of life by means of the spiritual growth reflected in a sequence of moods which rise to prominence in the emotional life of the individual. The aesthete represents man under the illusion of having a life-view and attempting to live according to such a view. It is thus in existence, rather than in detached contemplation, where a life-view (or philosophy of life) is tested and in existence too where a new life-view will be formed.

The starting point will be the collapse of the aesthetic life-view, represented by the mood of irony. Irony (Chapter One), as a mood, represents the first conscious breakthrough in the illusion of aesthetic (or non-religious) existence. A sequence of moods follows naturally one upon the other, viz. anxiety (Chapter Two), melancholy (Chapter Three), and despair (Chapter Four), in a series of crises of the personality. Chapter Five attempts to render the moods and their sequence less abstract by applying the general analysis of each mood to the principal aesthetic character of Kierkegaard's authorship, viz. Johannes of *Either/Or*. Chapter Five precedes the discussion, in Chapter Six, of the dialectic of moods and thus reflects the fact that Johannes never, and no individual ever necessarily, makes the full movement into resolution and the construction of a new life-view. Chapter Six articulates a discernable dialectic of moods which emerges in the course of the examination of the scope, directionality, and interrelationships of the individual moods. Chapter Seven explores in detail the idea of a life-view which pervades Kierkegaard's authorship and points out that for Kierkegaard only the Christian religious, towards which the moods naturally direct the soul of man, merits the predicate "life-view" and represents true mastery of the moods. The dialectic of moods and concern with an authentic philosophy of life converge, since the moods constitute preparation for articulating the new life-view.

In the course of the present study, we have of course had to take a position on problems in Kierkegaard scholarship. We have first of all had to decide to include everything written by Kierkegaard, and not merely the "canon" which *The Point of View for My Work as an Author* sets up. For one must view the entire corpus in order to understand the developments of themes as well as the full outlines of Kierkegaard's thought.

4 INTRODUCTION

Even a cursory reading of Kierkegaard would reveal that the material developed here is scattered in fragments throughout the corpus. Thus we reassemble it, working with the conviction that, for Kierkegaard and ourselves, it really does have a systematic unity which can be abstracted from the form of presentation in the authorship. In this, however, we have not allowed ourselves to ignore the pseudonyms who are the purported authors of the works.

The battle has long raged as to whether one has the right to take what the pseudonyms say as the thought of Kierkegaard himself. The two extreme possible positions are either to "erase" the pseudonyms and take everything as Kierkegaard's, or else to accept nothing as Kierkegaard's, as he himself counsels, unless it is published under his name. In our opinion, both extremes must be rejected and a "compromise" struck which is grounded in scholarship, faithful to the intent of Kierkegaard, and representing a realistic reading of the texts. Thus we put to one side the characterizations and "autobiographical" remarks of the pseudonyms, except as contributing to character studies, but we accept the reflections and insights of the pseudonyms as those representing the unfolding thought of Kierkegaard as expressed by pseudonyms with ever-wider perspectives.

There are different levels of pseudonymity, from *Either/Or* to the scarcely pseudonymous *Concept of Anxiety* and *Sickness Unto Death*. These latter are not complicated by the presence of a pseudonymous author who is also a character. In addition, in these instances, the *Papirer* indicate that Kierkegaard nearly published the works under his own name. Thus, the pseudonymity, in these instances, is a formality, before Kierkegaard abandoned pseudonymity, and indeed the thoughts expressed are clearly Kierkegaard's own. In the *Repetition, Stages on Life's Way* and *Either/Or*, certain stances are limited by the life-view of the pseudonymous author. But, the views presented there represent degrees of understanding commensurate with the character's level of personal development. In no case is there question of inconsistency or contradiction. Johannes, Constantine Constantius, Judge William and Frater Taciturnus represent different levels of development and understanding, and the final pseudonym Anti-Climacus provides the final perspective under which to organize the vast array of insights into, and reflections upon, the aesthetic life-view and the conflicting spiritual movement underway in the personality.

This manner of interpretation allows the gathering of insights, but avoids the trap of confusing autobiography and characterization with unfolding ideas about the nature and destiny of the human person.

Terminology and translations have presented their problems. It is hoped that some improvements are offered here upon the efforts of the past, but the present writer too confesses his limitations and frustrations in this regard.

Of course, the root problem is that no language can ever be fully translated, nor certainly any author so closely tied to his mother tongue.

INTRODUCTION 5

Kierkegaard is both translated and traduced. An effort has been made in the present study to insure uniformity of terminology, by correcting existing translations in some instances and re-translating in others, in each instance so indicating. We have adopted the title of a forthcoming revised translation of Kierkegaard's *Begrebet Angest*, viz. *The Concept of Anxiety* (rather than Walter Lowrie's *The Concept of Dread*) and we have adopted the term "anxiety" throughout. We believe that "anxiety" is a more adequate term, and allows uniformity of terminology in other words built upon the Danish root *Angst*.

In instances where no adequate English equivalent has been found, certain terms and phrases are left in Danish and the reader is thus invited to widen his international philosophical vocabulary until a more satisfactory solution is found.

However, not all problems of terminology have to do solely with the differences of language. In many instances, Kierkegaard employs normal terms in special senses, always building on the usual sense but unmistakably departing in order to add essential new content. This is the case in the use of all the key terms in this study, viz. irony, anxiety, melancholy, despair and life-view. In each chapter, the departure from normal meanings is noted and points of linguistics are discussed. Thus, for example; irony, for Kierkegaard, does not merely refer to the tool of discourse but to a stance characterized by an attitude of passionate rebellion and rejection of the phenomenal world, after its illusory nature has been discovered. Anxiety revolves around "nothing" because around oneself and one's possibilities. Melancholy (*Tungsind*) revolves around the religious nature of the personality. And despair has at least four senses: choosing the self, loss of hope, sinfulness, and the taking on of sin-consciousness.

All quotations from Kierkegaard's works are cited in existing English translations, except where otherwise noted. In all instances, the original Danish text is also cited. All references and quotations-translations are keyed to the first Danish edition of the *Samlede Værker* eds. A.B. Drachmann, J.L. Heiberg, and H.O. Lange (København, 1901ff.). In this way, the present study is tied to the Danish text, rather than to any present or forthcoming translation. In addition, however, it will allow cross-referencing to the forthcoming *Kierkegaard's Writings* edited by Howard V. Hong, which will be published by Princeton University Press.

In the last analysis, Kierkegaard's thought is un-apologetically Christian and relies upon Revelation as providing the final perspective toward which the meaning of experience points. Kierkegaard attacks modern Pelagian attitudes, and the parallels with Augustine are readily seen by those familiar with the work of the Fourth Century A.D. Bishop of Hippo. Like Augustine, Kierkegaard flatly denies that the natural man left on his own can "save" himself. Hence his polemic against Romanticism and the hubris of academic philosophy.

The psychology which Kierkegaard describes begins with the natural

6   INTRODUCTION

man and moves through a process of self-discovery. But, for Kierkegaard only the super-natural can, and does, overcome the disharmony in man and reconcile him with himself, after the natural process has been completed. Kierkegaard knows this as a Christian, on the basis of Revelation which he accepts and the grace of reconciliation which he claims to have experienced personally.

The super-natural, however, will not be introduced into the human drama as *deus ex machina*. Rather, for Kierkegaard, it will be portrayed as a continuation which fulfills a natural development, which takes one across the threshold at whose gates one has been pressing. Revelation will be the grace to move forward when one had reached a natural terminus, will be the understanding of that final step and a retrospective upon one's development.

Revelation, then, provides the final perspective in which Kierkegaard's religious psychology (and philosophical anthropology) operates. From within this perspective, Kierkegaard raises a challenge to all those who seek to understand man – to the poets and Romantics, to the philosophers, to the theologians and also to the psychologists, but most of all to the individual. It is a challenge which cannot be taken up until heard more clearly.

CHAPTER I

IRONY

> Ut a dubitatione philosophia sic ab ironia vita digna
> quae humana vocetur, incipit.
>
> – Thesis XV, *Om Begrebet Ironi.*

Irony is the first mood which announces a crisis in the aesthetic life. It indicates a *prise de conscience* and a new attitude toward the actual world around one. In irony, one realizes that beforehand one had been immersed in the world and believed its implicit promise of fulfillment. With the advent of irony one has broken through illusion – in experience – and initially takes up an attitude of negativity, of passionate rejection, of the actuality which deceived.

Irony as existence-stance is clearly an important new use of the term. The unforewarned reader would expect a discussion of irony to point to the dissimulation and cunning associated with the term. In his treatment of irony, Kierkegaard does not neglect these and other aspects. However, he emphasizes the ironist himself, and therefore the essence of irony consists of what irony represents in the individual existing ironist, who manifests irony in his discourse but, more importantly, in all of his existence.

For Kierkegaard, irony is still a tool of discourse, but much more. It is viewed as a consciousness – an ironic consciousness – which represents an insight into the nature of reality, an enlarged perspective upon oneself and one's relation to reality. But at the same time, irony is a mood which alters the perceptions of reality. Irony, as mood, is a filter, as it were, which colors objective reality, as it brings the subjectivity of the ironist into sharp relief. Reality and even the ironist himself are colored with negativity. In its breakthrough to discover the limits of actuality posing as an all-fulfilling infinite, irony, in an initial adolescent enthusiasm, tends to reject all reality – thus the "infinity negativity" of irony about which Kierkegaard will speak. In order to gain equilibrium, without sacrificing the insight and higher consciousness which it represents, irony will ultimately have to negate itself, in what is termed "mastered irony," and thus re-enter into a relation with reality, henceforth to be regarded with circumspection.

The mentions and uses of irony in Kierkegaard's writings are abundant. He himself delighted in the role of ironist in Copenhagen society, as do his pseudonyms for maieutic purposes of their own. Only in *The Concept of Irony*, however, does Kierkegaard discuss the essential

8   IRONY

characteristics, uses, and dangers of irony both in the more normal use
of the term as tool of discourse and as the existence-stance which
indicates an initial overcoming of the aesthetic and the incipient movements of the spirit toward the religious. We here focus on *The Concept
of Irony* in order to understand the mood and consciousness which irony
represents and then to observe the function of irony as a measurement
and critical tool in the analysis of the aesthetic life.

While *The Concept of Irony* is the principal source for an inquiry into
the meaning of irony as an existence-stance in Kierkegaard's thought,
the work does not facilitate the task. Not unlike the older man, the
young Kierkegaard is simply trying to do too many things at one time,
thus making the concept of irony in *The Concept of Irony* anything but a
straightforward exposition. The work was Kierkegaard's dissertation for
the degree Magister Artium (equivalent to the modern American Ph.D.)
and is unfortunately characterized by the over-display of learning so
often found in formal, degree-seeking treatises. While the full title
declares the work to be *The Concept of Irony with Continual Reference to
Socrates*, it neglects to mention Hegel and the Romantics[1] who are
present throughout and are introduced as "whipping-boys" at appropriate points. This work then, as so many others, is thoroughly polemical,
as it sets up Socrates as a model of irony as both tool and existence-
stance and then proceeds to use him as a measure to evaluate the irony
of the Romantics (which he judges superficial and ill-directed). And
since Hegel, in his mentions of Socrates, neglects his irony, Kierkegaard
seizes upon the opportunity to voice for the first time in a published
work his criticism of Hegel and the entire Idealist movement for which
Hegel served as symbol. The work proceeds to develop the concept by
means of setting up contrasts and a mutually negating either-or which
suggests the need for a new context in which the true concept is to be
found (the Socratic and the Romantic positions negate each other, in
terms of providing the concept of irony for modern man, and point to
the Christian).

Kierkegaard's view of Socrates, who is so prominent in the work, may
in the end be a brilliant misinterpretation. Kierkegaard was no classicist.
But whatever the limitations of his scholarship or the correctness of his
interpretation of Socrates, Kierkegaard does arrive at setting forth a
concept of irony whose emphases are both novel and insightful. Our
own concern will not be his interpretation of Socrates, or his evaluation
of the Romantics or even of Hegel, but rather the essence of irony
developed in this many faceted work. In order to arrive at the essence,
however, we will survey the development of the argument contained in
the work. But in the end we hope to step back and behold the concept
of irony, as tool and existence-stance, which the work promises but only
delivers in the elaborate wrappings of sometimes debatable scholarship,
confusing polemics, and a good bit of pedantry. These criticisms are not

[1] For a concise treatment of Romanticism, cf. Oskar Walzel, *Romanticism* (New York:
Capricorn Books, 1966; original edition G.P. Putnam's Sons, 1932).

IRONY 9

meant to undermine the work, whose value and contribution are beyond dispute. Rather they voice the inevitable frustration of the reader who tries to discern the concept of irony in the work and finds himself confronted, even assailed, by a wealth of insights and interpretations marshalled for many purposes, only one of which is the stated aim, viz. the exposition of the concept of irony.

A. IRONY AND THE CONCEPT IN *THE CONCEPT OF IRONY*

PRELIMINARY CONSIDERATIONS

The structure of *The Concept of Irony* is important for at least two reasons. First, because Kierkegaard is a self-conscious author whose style itself is a none-too-subtle element in the material under discussion. Second, because the structure of the work does not, as has been suggested, make access to a "concept of irony" a simple and straightforward matter. In fact, one might go as far as to say that the structure of the work confuses the concept which the title proclaims to be its concern. We propose to examine, then, the structure in order to recover Kierkegaard's points from the structure itself.

Kierkegaard begins and carries on his discussion "with constant reference to Socrates." He advances a thesis and wishes the structure of the work to support it: that Socrates marks the appearance of irony. However, in the course of the study there occur abrupt leaps, across world history, from Socrates to the Nineteenth Century. First is the leap represented by the "Supplement" to Part I. Part I ("The Standpoint of Socrates conceived as Irony") develops the conception, based on an attempt to get at the "existence" of Socrates in the writings of Xenephon (who renders Socrates harmless and boring), of Plato (who renders him ideal), and of Aristophanes (who, in the *Clouds*, renders him negative). As if there has never been another commentary on Socrates since then, Kierkegaard directs a "Supplement" at a modern figure who has treated Socrates, viz. Hegel, but who has neglected Socrates as an ironist and treated him as a moralist.[2] For Hegel, in his treatment of irony, discusses only romantic irony, never the mastered irony of Socrates.

Part II ("The Concept of Irony") reverts to Socrates. However, here too one finds a world historical hiatus in the discussion. For, after Socrates has been defined as the ironist par excellence, a sizable third section ("Irony after Fichte") launches a polemic against another modern phenomenon, viz. the Romantics F. Schlegel, Tieck and Solger (and the Romantic school in general). But when one recalls that these are precisely the men whom Hegel discusses in his treatment of romantic irony, the subtle anti-Hegelian polemic will not be missed. This third section is used to point out the weaknesses of the ironic position as found in modern times – as well as being highly critical of Hegel. The following, and concluding, section ("Irony as a Mastered Moment")

[2] *CI*, pp. 246ff; *S.V.*, XIII, 303ff.

10   IRONY

returns to the idea of irony, but once again with polemical reference to modern figures.

A careful look at the structure then reveals that both Parts I and II begin with Socrates but pass on to modern material, viz. Hegel and the Romantics: to the Hegel who has a faulty conception of Socrates and to the Romantics who have a faulty conception of irony.

But what is really happening in the work in terms of developing the concept of irony? The concept is actualized in Socrates. After the discussion establishes this thesis, and even during the course of it, Kierkegaard indicates the essence of irony. This, as Michel Cornu has noted,[3] is never done clearly, but nonetheless two aspects of irony are established: irony as a mode of discourse and irony as an existence-stance.

The content of each of these aspects is sufficiently defined, but never systematically. Both positive and negative aspects are indicated apropos of irony as an existence-stance, and if there is profundity in this work, here undoubtedly is its source (the positive and negative aspects of this idea will later be presented more concretely, "clothed in the flesh" of the young aesthete of *Either/Or*). But when one takes pen in hand and lists the positive and negative aspects of the existence-stance one notices that the positive aspects are all rather arbitrarily described in the sections which have direct reference to Socrates and the negative in the sections on the Romantics. The structure of the argument itself thus represents a thinly disguised polemic! For as qualities and possibilities, both positive and negative aspects might refer to any ironic figure. And indeed certain of them are equally applicable to Socrates and the Romantics. But "applicable" does not mean "applied," and so one finds the positive and negative divided up and given their respective symbolic representatives.[4]

[3] *Kierkegaard et la Communication de l'Existence* (Lausanne: L'Age d'Homme, 1972), pp. 161–176.

[4] For the most part, Kierkegaard views the Romantic Ironists as a negative development in that their existence is misdirected, i.e. in movement away from spirit and away from enhanced subjectivity. However, their appearance in staid, bourgeois Europe of the late 18th Century does contain some positive aspects, which at least in justice to them must be pointed out. In addition, these positive aspects define a bit further the ironist in the more contemporary world (i.e. in our age in contrast to that of Socrates). The theory of the epochs of spirit underlies the discussion. Socrates, who lived before the epoch of spirit, existed in the direction of spirit; the Romantics, who live in the epoch of spirit, generally exist in a direction away from spirit.

Kierkegaard views the Romantics as a "breath of fresh air" in the stale, settled and ordered state of affairs prevailing at the time. One fell in love at 20 years old, one lived for domesticity and a posthumous reputation. Into such a world, Romanticism sent a chilling wind, a refreshing breeze. It represented a rejuvenation, away from a bourgeois mentality. However, according to Kierkegaard, the enthusiasm for rejuvenation went too far and Romanticism rendered the world a child again. (*CI*, p. 319; *S.V.*, XIII, 372-3.) Whereas before the bourgeois rational man lived in a world in which nature went to sleep (out of boredom), "so now everything awakens but *he* sleeps." (*CI*, p. 319; *S.V.*, XIII, 373.) In effect, and to continue the metaphor, he lives in a dream world, at best in a cycle of waking and sleeping. His fault is that he seeks content for his existence in the dreams which are his only actuality; he is never satisfied, and cannot be.

IRONY 11

Kierkegaard's dissertation on *The Concept of Irony with Continual Reference to Socrates* has always been considered a difficult work, first by the dissertation committee and since then by critics and scholars. Its first Danish readers criticized its pedantic style and apparently would have liked to ask the young academician to rewrite sections of it, had they not found his personality even more difficult. No one missed the thinly disguised polemic against Professor Martensen, least of all Professor Martensen who disqualified himself as a degree-committee judge of the work; nor did anyone miss the more substantive polemic against the Romantics. The criticism and treatment of Hegel in *The Concept of Irony* have been the subject of much discussion among scholars. There are those who find here evidence that Kierkegaard was once himself an Hegelian of sorts. Certainly much of the terminology rings Hegelian, and the division of the dissertation into the concept of irony made (I) possible, (II) actual, and (III) necessary evidences clear Hegelian imitation. However, style and terminology are hardly sure proof that one is a disciple, and this is the argument of those who point to the criticism of Hegel, as well as the satire upon Hegel and speculation, as showing that even as early as 1841 when the dissertation was submitted Kierkegaard was already in revolt against the Hegelians.

Kierkegaard goes along with Hegel's criticism of Schlegel and the Romantics, but he is critical of Hegel's overlooking an essential form of irony in Socrates, viz. mastered irony.[5] Professor Gregor Malantschuk notes a subtle combination of form and thought: Kierkegaard makes use of the Hegelian categories of possibility, actuality and necessity only to shift in Part II of the dissertation to positing the unity of actuality and the concept in existence, thus positing a paradox – and discarding Hegel. Thus Malantschuk views the dissertation on irony as irony upon Hegel.[6]

Despite any Hegelian or even Socratic influences upon the young thinker, there is no question but that the concept of irony which emerges is Kierkegaard's own. There are two sets of distinctions made in the work which are not always quite clear as one is reading the text itself, however, and these should be noted in order finally to glean Kierkegaard's concept. The first distinction is that between irony as an existence-stance and irony as a tool, or mode, of discourse. The second is the essential difference between the existence-stance of Socrates and that of the Romantics (an analysis which will concern us below in the study of the aesthete).

The essential difference between the Socratic and the Romantic is further heightened by Kierkegaard's theory of the history of spirit. This theory is not explicitly stated in this work, but it functions here as elsewhere in the writings. The theory is articulated in the writings of the

[5] Michel Cornu, *Kierkegaard*, pp. 165–168.
[6] *Kierkegaard's Thought* (Princeton, 1971), pp. 189–190.

12

IRONY

pseudonym Johannes Climacus (*Fragments* and *Postscript*) in which he points out the essential difference made in history by the Christ-event (the Eternal enters time, the Absolute takes on human finitude) and the consequences of this event for human possibility. Kierkegaard views the paganism of Socrates (religiousness A) as the highest natural development open to man before Christianity which is the result of God's super-natural act in entering time. The history of irony must also be viewed under this interpretation and theory of man's religious history, if Kierkegaard is to be clearly understood on this point. With this theory in mind one understands better Kierkegaard's distinction in the dissertation between the two different forms of irony, which are found in two different epochs of history. Socratic irony appeared *before* Christ, but appeared as a development of subjectivity and as a development in the direction of spirit (even though it was *before* spirit).[7] The Romantics and romantic irony, on the other hand, exist in that period of history which is *after* the appearance of spirit, but represent a development away from spirit. Thus Kierkegaard judges romantic irony (considered as an existence-stance) as a regression, as a "devolution" away from the subjectivity which made its appearance in Socrates and which was given the possibility of fulfillment due to the Christ event.

Considered as an existence-stance, irony would seem to offer two possibilities: that of Socrates and that of the Romantics. Are we not then in an either-or situation even as early as 1841? That is to say, after two historically actualized possibilities are described, where is the reader? The position of the Romantics is so undermined that it is untenable. However, the possibility of an existence-stance of irony such as that of Socrates is not recoverable. For, we recall, Socrates lived *before* spirit made its appearance in time. This means, quite simply, that the reader is living in a different epoch of spiritual history, with quite changed options open to him (should he decide on the life of irony). What then, for the contemporary reader would be the modern form of Socratic irony, which would be an irony properly directed toward spirit in the time *after* the appearance of spirit? Has the dialectician failed to give us a third possibility – a "Christian irony"? Indeed, he has not. Such a Christian irony would be an irony transformed by sin-consciousness and permeated with the Christian category of humor. It is an irony within the Christian sphere and as such also outside the formal scope of our study here. However, it is a new and Christian form of irony already clearly implied as early as the 1841 dissertation, when the underlying history of spirit is understood.

But let us recover more carefully our ground before going further forward. Let us examine the pure state of irony as found in Socrates – a state which cannot be recovered (although Kierkegaard never states this explicitly, it is a metaphysical sequitur of his presuppositions), and then let us turn to the deformed state of irony in the Romantics, who live in

[7] Cf. Jean Wahl, *Études Kierkegaardiennes* (Paris, 1967), 3rd ed., p. 61.

IRONY 13

the epoch of spirit but who try to ignore the significance of spirit's appearance in time.

IRONY AS TOOL

Having noted the polemic and style of the dissertation, we turn now more directly to its content. We have observed the somewhat arbitrary attribution of qualities when the discussion turns concrete (i.e., when the discussion turns from the idea of irony to ironic representatives) and we now set for ourselves the task of introducing some clarity into the abstract. We are more concerned with irony in the present age and less with Socrates. Thus emphasis will be upon aspects of the ironic which have more contemporary reference – to those who exist in the epoch of spirit.

Although the discussion will center below upon the essence of irony, we proceed at this point to that aspect of irony which is perhaps more familiar: irony as a tool and a mode of discourse. Here too of course (and as will be elaborated below) the perception of the at-least-possible disparity between essence and phenomenon is at work, and it is precisely upon this disparity that irony plays. In the case of irony as a mode of discourse, the disparity will naturally lie in the difference between the "word" and the "essential reality" of a situation. This basic disparity may then be played upon, consciously, in several ways and for several possible ends. In Kierkegaard's discussion, the Socrates of the dialogues is always the model: he who says seriously what is not intended seriously, he who says something not seriously which is intended seriously.[8]

EXPOSING IGNORANCE. As a tool, irony may be used to point up the ignorance of others. In the case of Socrates, this was a veritable mission as he went about in his celebrated "Socratic ignorance" challenging, and seeking knowledge from, those who "knew." Kierkegaard cites particularly on this point the dialogue *Protagoras* in which Socrates, in a discussion of virtue and of whether it can be taught, tricks Protagoras through a give-and-take of sophistries out of every concrete virtue which is mentioned. All virtues are reduced by degrees to the unity of Virtue – which is then dissolved because

this unity of Virtue becomes so abstract, so egotistically terminated in itself, that it becomes the very crag upon which all the individual virtues are stranded and torn asunder like heavily laden vessels.[9]

Socrates then makes Virtue something "so prudish and narrow that for this reason it never became experience,"[10] and since the argument had

[8] *CI*, p. 265; *S.V.*, XIII, 323.

[9] *CI*, p. 95. Danish text reads: "denne Dydens Eenhed bliver saa abstract, saa egoistisk afsluttet i sig selv, at den kun bliver den Klippe, paa hvilken de enkelte Dyder som velbefragtede Seilere strande og sønderslaaes." *S.V.*, XIII, 153.

[10] *CI*, p. 97. Danish text reads: "saa snerpet og knibsk, at den af den Grund aldrig kom til at gjøre Erfaring." *S.V.*, XIII, 155.

14 IRONY

previously established that only experience can be taught, it becomes clear that Virtue cannot be. Protagoras is refuted on both his points of affirmation regarding Virtue, and the man who "knew" is left in ignorance.

But irony may also push its victim a few steps in a positive direction, although it itself posits nothing. For irony may be used as a goad for thought, "quickening it when drowsy, disciplining it when dissipated."[11] This can be joined to a form of dialectic

which, in constant movement, is always watching to see that the problem does not become ensnared in an accidental conception; a dialectic which, never fatigued, is always ready to set the problem afloat should it ever go aground; in short, a dialectic which always knows how to keep the problem hovering, and precisely in and through this seeks to solve it.[12]

This combination is, for Kierkegaard, characteristic of Socrates' standpoint, which represents "irony in its total striving, and dialectic in its negative, emancipating activity."[13]

LEADING TO A HEIGHTENED AWARENESS OF FINITUDE. In the *Phaedo*, which takes place shortly before Socrates' death, Kierkegaard sees him using irony to drive men out of all safe corners, into a heightened sense of finitude. The dialogue proper concerns the subject of death and immortality. In the end, Socrates subtly robs men of all comfort about death, for man is ignorant about it. Death may represent annihilation, or it may be a transition. According to Kierkegaard's interpretation, Socrates' position does indeed remove some of the fear of death. For fear is groundless in a case where it is a "nothing" which one fears (and it is a "nothing" in the sense that one knows nothing about it). On the other hand, Socrates does not leave men in the comfort of speculative possibilities regarding an after-life, be it painless annihilation or a "heaven" of some kind. Rather, he leaves them with "the anxious representation of an inevitable something of which one knows nothing."[14] Thus, because of the irony which once again has pointed up the groundlessness of men's words and attitudes and the limits of knowledge, one is borne along towards the boundary of finitude by the same force which initially stirred one. Socrates' irony leaves one in the precarious situation which is one's own anyway – aroused from lethargy but entirely dependent upon one's own resources to extricate oneself, if indeed that is possible.

---

[11] *CI*, p. 151. Danish text reads: "fremskynder den, naar den bliver døsig, tugter den, naar den bliver udsvævende." *S.V.*, XIII, 207.

[12] *CI*, p. 151. Danish text reads: "der i idelig Bevægelse stedse vaager over, at Spørsmaalet ikke besnæres i en tilfældig Opfattelse, der aldrig trættet altid er rede til at gjøre Problemet flot, naar det er sat paa Grund, kort sagt, der altid veed at holde Problemet svævende, og netop heri og herved vil løse det" *S.V.*, XIII, 207.

[13] *CI*, p. 152. Danish text reads: "Ironien i sin *totale Stræben*, *Dialectiken* in sin *negativt frigjørende* Virksomhed." *S.V.*, XIII, 208.

[14] *CI*, p. 118. Danish text reads: "den ængstende Forestille om et uundgaaeligt Noget, man slet Intet veed om." *S.V.*, XIII, 174.

IRONY

FREES, BUT BRINGS UNDER POWER. However, the same ironist who frees others may also bind them to himself. And it is irony which Kierkegaard considers responsible for the binding love incited in Alcibiades for Socrates and also responsible for his seductive power over the youth of Athens.

Kierkegaard notes that the turmoil in the soul of Alcibiades for Socrates was not produced by any concrete out-pouring of sentiment. Indeed, expressions of sentiment could not awaken such passions. In the relationship between Socrates and Alcibiades, there was no third, common element in which they might have grounded a mutual love. Rather, irony was at the base of the relationship – an elusive, intangible, masked base which not only never unmasks itself but is Protean in its changing masks.[15]

The essential function of the ironist is to raise one out of immediate existence (spoken of in later works as "immediacy") and to leave one in mid-air.[16] But in the versatility involved (a versatility which is really a negativity), irony may bring another under its power. Irony itself is "nothing": it only hints at the Idea, but never expresses it;[17] it is the negative in love, the incitement to love, but never the third element which may join two people.[18]

Kierkegaard speaks of irony's power as follows:

The disguise and mysteriousness which it entails, the telegraphic communication which it initiates, inasmuch as the ironist must always be understood at a distance, the infinite sympathy which it assumes, the elusive and ineffable moment (flash) of understanding immediately displaced by the anxiety of misunderstanding – all this captivates with indissoluble bonds.[19]

Kierkegaard sees this same power as lying at the base of the charge against Socrates, at his trial, that he had seduced the youth.

...For he deceived the youth and awakened longings which he never satisfied, allowed them to become inflamed by the subtle pleasure of anticipation yet never gave them solid and nourishing food.[20]

Moreover, it is the same power of irony which did both: awakened them from their slumbering ignorance in the world of phenomena and then

---

[15] *CI*, p. 85; *S.V.*, XIII, 143.

[16] *Ibid.*

[17] *CI*, p. 86; *S.V.*, XIII, 144.

[18] *CI*, p. 88; *S.V.*, XIII, 146.

[19] *CI*, p. 85. Danish text reads: "Det Formummede og Hemmelighedsfulde, den had ved sig, den telegraphiske Communication, den aabner, fordi en Ironiker altid maa forstaaes langtfra, den uendelige Sympathi, den forudsætter, Forstaaelsens flygtige men ubeskrivelige Nu, der fortrænges øieblikkelig af Misforstaaelsens Angst, – alt dette fængsler med uopløselige Baand." *S.V.*, XIII, 143.

[20] *CI*, p. 213. Danish text reads: "...han bedaarede Ungdommen, *vakte Længsler* hos den, men *tilfreds-stillede* dem *ikke*, lod dem opblusse in Berøringens yppige Nydelse, men stærk og nærende Føde gav han dem ikke," *S.V.*, XIII, 270.

16 IRONY

left them, since irony proved incapable of delivering that at which it hinted, viz. the essential for a human existence.

IRONIST TAKES ON A FALSE APPEARANCE. The disparity upon which the ironist plays can be extended beyond words to existence itself. Here is one of irony's subtlest and most difficult usages. For what indeed is the result? The ironist takes upon himself an appearance which is not his essence. In effect, he plays a role which does not at all reflect his essence. He gives out that he is other than he is, deceives all and then experiences great satisfaction in this disparity.

As a result, no one knows his true essence. All one knows is the false phenomenon. But, should one afterwards get a clue to what the ironist has been doing, will one not have learned something negatively true from this display of irony: that one's existence never expresses one's essence?

Such irony is enjoyed in solitude, in which the ironist contrives that his deception not be noticed.[21] And in this he makes a fool of others without their realizing it. They believe that the phenomenon – which in this case is deliberately false – expresses the essence. The ironist laughs to himself.[22] Such a private, solitary irony has no ostensible outer purpose. It is in no way directed toward teaching others, even negatively, so long as it keeps entirely closed up within itself. Nor should this form be confused with "indirect communication" which is still communication, directed beyond the speaker no matter how strange its form. This private irony has no purpose other than the expression of one's ironic existence-stance for oneself as ironist, to confirm the discovered essence of irony (that the phenomenon is not the essence) for oneself alone. However strange a mode of expression (totally subjective and expressing one's non-self to others for the purpose of heightening one's sense of true self), it figures in the discussion here as a possible use and a potential danger of irony. For ultimately the ironist runs the risk of being seduced by his own irony and thus never moving beyond it.

MASTERED IRONY. Irony is most effective as a tool when it proceeds from the state of "mastered irony," i.e. when irony proceeds from philosophic depth in one's existence. In this case, irony emerges as a guide and counsellor.[23] serving as a check upon one's personal life. The result is a balanced attitude toward actuality, which properly values it, neither spurning it completely nor over-valuing it as reflection of the Idea. In achieving a balanced view and serving as a constant check upon one's personal life, the real significance of irony emerges.[24] Irony serves

[21] CI, p. 267; S.V., XIII, 235.

[22] Such was the irony of Kierkegaard himself when he appeared nightly at the theatre in Copenhagen so that he would be thought a scoundrel and a dissolute fellow, when in fact he was busy turning out several then-forthcoming large works.

[23] CI, p. 339; S.V., XIII, 391.

[24] CI, p. 338; S.V., XIII, 390.

IRONY 17

as a disciplinarian, still negative, still positing nothing, but coaxing one in the right direction. (Is this not the same negative function which Socrates' Voice performed for him?)

Irony now limits, renders finite, defines, and thereby yields truth, actuality, and content; it chastens and punishes and thereby imparts stability, character and consistence.[25]

It is indeed a disciplinarian, but one loved by those who know it.[26]

"Mastered irony" reflects an existence which has personally appropriated, and thus mastered, the "essence" of irony. Irony usually serves to drive one to a sense of finitude, to leave one in mid-air. Mastered irony, however, functioning within a deepened perspective on existence, serves as a check. This difference will be seen more clearly when the essence of irony as an existence-stance is discussed.

IRONY AS A STAGE OF DEVELOPMENT. THE IRONIC CONSCIOUSNESS.

Irony is an existential determination, and nothing is more ridiculous than to suppose that it consists in the use of certain phraseology . . . Whoever has essential irony has it all day long, not bound to any specific form, because it is the infinite within him.

– Johannes Climacus, *CUP*, p. 450 (*S.V.*, VII, 438)

The irony of any subject is perceived, to be sure, in its most common form, viz. as a tool of discourse. But the tool, the mode of discourse, proceeds from a "certain type of subject." Clearly not everyone merits the label "ironic." Irony is surely a quality little understood and a word often misused. One tends to label as ironic any sharp comment with a negative twist; and when real irony appears, one as often as not labels it sarcasm, due to the negativity sensed, which is an aspect of the ironic existence-stance.

Kierkegaard makes specific claims about the type of personality from which irony naturally proceeds: it is a personality that is already a little apart from the mass mentality, a personality that has sensed something which the non-ironic majority have not (yet) sensed, a personality that is already a little "other," although the specific nature of this otherness remains vague both to the ironist and to those around him. He explores this otherness as he makes several psychological observations about the nature of the ironist.

IRONIST IS ESTRANGED FROM EXISTENCE. The presence of irony in the personality indicates that there has been a rift in the everydayness in which men are usually caught up. Within the otherwise uninterrupted

---

[25] *Ibid.* Danish text reads: "*Ironien limiterer, endeliggjør, begrændser* og giver derved *Sandhed, Virkelighed, Indhold*; den *tugter* og *straffer* og giver derved *Holdning* og *Consistents.*" *S.V.*, XIII, 390.

[26] *CI*, p. 339; *S.V.*, XIII, 390.

18 IRONY

flow of existence among others, something has happened which breaks the flow and, as a result, a new consciousness emerges. For Kierkegaard this "something" is the stirring of the eternal within the depths of a person, a stirring which is still unconscious. The emerging ironist senses something has happened but does not know what. He begins to view the phenomenal world in a different light, almost as if his eyes had been closed before. And although the new sight is still blurred, others' descriptions no longer correspond to what he sees. And behold, he begins to emerge an ironist.

His new stance is first described negatively:

The whole of existence [Tilværelse] has become alien to the ironic subject,... he in turn has become estranged from existence [Tilværelse], and ... because actuality has lost its validity for him, so he, too, is to a certain extent no longer actual.[27]

Actuality, i.e. the actuality of the present historical moment, has lost its validity because he sees it now as it was: no more than a moment, and even though it is the actuality of the Idea in this moment, it is not the Idea itself. He has sensed the pretension of the present actuality in ascribing to itself more validity than it has. More negatively stated, and thus perhaps more accurately here, what has happened is that the ironist has had a glimpse, a perhaps-unconscious intuition, of the Idea which transcends any one historical actuality. But once he has had this glimpse, actuality can never look the same again: it has been rendered relative in the light of the Absolute. He rebels against the pretensions of the present actuality and against the assent which the majority of men so willingly give to it.

To some degree, the ironist thus takes on the role of prophet, but not exactly such. For, while the prophet has broken with the present, speaks against it and intimates the future (without possessing it), he remains a part of his age.[28] The ironic subject, on the other hand, has broken with his age. He points toward a vague future and denies absolutely the present age which does not correspond to the ideal. Irony rages against the present with a divine madness which leaves not a stone standing.[29] The ironist is, in effect, carried along by a passion that is stronger than he is, a force over which he has not yet become master.

Having had a vague intuition of the Idea, the ironist distains all reality and demands ideality.[30] He will be satisfied henceforth with nothing less, so he thinks (and it is clearly an impossible demand). Thus he rages, much like the mythological Hero in his adolescent phase. He directs his

[27] CI, p. 276. Danish text reads: "men at hele Tilværelsen er bleven fremmed for det ironiske Subjekt, og dette igjen fremmed for Tilværelsen, at idet Virkeligheden har tabt sin Gyldighed for det, det selv til en vis Grad er blevet uvirkeligt." S.V., XIII, 333.

[28] CI, pp. 277–278; S.V., XIII, 333–334.

[29] CI, p. 278; S.V., XIII, 334

[30] CI, p. 236; S.V., XIII, 293.

IRONY   19

rage, and extends it, to all actuality, not just a particular existence. For even the entirety of any present actuality will never add up to the ideal. He is equally negative both in relationship to the past and to the future. For neither will any future actuality ever fulfill his ideal demand.

For Kierkegaard, Socrates' standpoint is largely thus. All of existence is taken "sub specie ironiæ" in an Infinite Absolute Negativity: negative because it only negates; absolute, because it negates by virtue of a higher which is not; and infinite, because it negates all phenomena and not just any particular one.[31]

The ironist's existence is henceforth condemned to be without meaning – at least until the point when some way out of this existential impasse is found. For, he has broken with the false meaning given his existence by the present actuality and confirmed by the silent assent of his contemporaries. Since the present actuality is not the ideal, it has no content and hence confers no meaning. However, no future actuality will ever be the ideal, and thus his existence can never have content, never have meaning, it would seem. He is free from the deception of the present actuality, but he is left empty. And albeit he has reached a higher stage of consciousness, it provides him no support to bear the terrible realization of the absence of content and meaning in his existence.

As for his contemporaries, their existence is also contentless. But they do not know it, and so they are at least spared the heightened experience which a higher consciousness brings. What wonder then that this realization leads him to taunt his contemporaries. What wonder that he makes a show of his negative freedom by pretending, even exaggerating, the validity of the existent and that, under this guise, he tries to lead it to dissolution[32] in the consciousness of others as well. The passion which his own realization excites in him may lead others toward the same realization, may put them in movement, if possible, upon the same uncertain road, toward a goal which, according to his present understanding, is theoretically impossible to achieve, viz. the ideal.

IRONY AS DETERMINATION OF SUBJECTIVITY. Because of a new insight into actuality, a significant and irrevocable change has taken place in the personality of the emerged ironic individual. He has begun to become more defined as a human being, strange as that may at first sound and even though that definition rests for the moment wholly negative. He is free, in a negative sense, in that he is freed from the illusion that actuality has validity. As a consequence, he has broken with his age which continues under illusion. But, quite significantly, his is a break with no abstract age, but rather with the society of men with whom, up until now, he has been constituting the age (since the whole of mankind constitutes the age). He becomes isolated, estranged not only from the ideas of his time, but from all his contemporaries as well. He

[31] *CI*, p. 278; *S.V.*, XIII, 335.
[32] *CI*, p. 281; *S.V.*, XIII, 338.

20   IRONY

ceases to be mass-man and emerges an individual, negatively defined.[33] He is no longer "one" – the subject of an impersonal sentence (German: *Das Man*; French *On*).[34] Although he is but negatively defined, he nonetheless exists within a self-consciousness sufficiently defined to merit the appellation "subjectivity." True subjectivity first emerges in the history of the personality with the emergence of irony (just as it has emerged in the history of the race, according to the argument of Kierkegaard's dissertation, with the appearance of Socrates).[35]

The ironist's passion is a quality especially to be noted. It is not necessarily a conscious energy, but this does not diminish its power or, as will be seen, its directionality. The ironist is fundamentally he who has emerged skeptical, even cynical, about the moment: he who has experienced aesthetic ecstasy, but has also experienced deeply the period of emptiness afterwards. Beyond this, he has advanced sufficiently to discern the pattern of moments, the "ups" and "downs," and has begun to tire of the pattern's repetition. For every moment, even those of high ecstasy, endures but a moment, has no continuity with the moment which follows. Nor can this repetition of fragmented moments answer the vague and yet-unconscious need in the soul of the aesthete for a resolution to the endless cycle.[36] The ironist, to be sure, has not yet broken out of the cycle; the repetition has not ceased, nor has a resolution been found, until higher moods have been passed through and higher crises of the personality. At this point, the ironist has merely discerned the inability of the moment to answer the deeper yearnings of the human spirit, has emerged cynical about the seductive recurrence of vivid moments which are only followed by anguished emptiness.

The ironist then turns his passion against the deceiving moment in a

[33] His individuality at this point remains negative because he has as yet no positive content, and no apparent source of finding positive content either.

[34] German and French Existentialism have greatly employed this term. Cf. especially Martin Heidegger, *Sein und Zeit* and Jean-Paul Sartre, *L'Être et Le Néant.*

[35] For Kierkegaard, Socrates represents the appearance of both subjectivity and of irony. (*CI*, p. 281; *S.V.*, XIII, 337.) Socrates exemplified the ironist within his age: he had broken with it when it lost its validity for him, and he then employed irony in destroying it (the age being what Kierkegaard calls Hellenism).

"His behaviour towards [Hellenism] was always ironical; he was ignorant and knew nothing, constantly seeking enlightenment from others. But in thus allowing the established [Bestaaende] to endure [bestaae], it therefore perished. This tactic he maintained to the last, a fact which was especially apparent when he stood accused."

Danish text reads:

"...hans Adfærd mod den var bestandig ironisk; han var uvidende og vidste Intet, men søgte bestandig Oplysning hos Andre, men idet han saaledes lod det Bestaaende bestaae, gik det under. Denne Taktik vedligeholdt han til det Yderste, hvilket især viste sig, da han var bleven anklaget" *S.V.*, XIII, 338.

Socrates as the first ironic subject constitutes a model of ironic subjectivity: he broke with his age, broke with the heavy weight of actuality, and freed himself to the airy sensation of infinite possibility. Irony became Socrates' gift to Hellas and to every subsequent age, "preventing subjectivity from being taken in vain." (*CI*, p. 236; *S.V.*, XIII, 293.)

[36] This is one of the key problems which Constantine Constantius confronts in the *Repetition.*

IRONY

cold, biting scorn. Moreover, he extends his scorn to all his contemporaries: his mirror-images also deceived but in addition not having yet recognized the universal predicament which they collectively share and individually endure. He scorns them for what is also true of himself: unfreedom. And, paradoxically, he then soars above them in a negative freedom. For he is privy, by whatever chance-occurrence or grace which may have stirred the infinity within him, to the basic contradiction of his existence: that the phenomenon is not the essence to which he feels summoned, that his present existence does not reflect the deeper human reality toward which an inner dynamism impels him. Subjective truth emerges here with passion, and for the first time: in the first moments of subjectivity he discovers an essential truth about subjectivity imprisoned in phenomentality.

His passion is henceforward an effort to extricate himself from entanglements in which he is continuously finding himself, no matter how much he may not wish them.[37] He is constantly finding himself ensnared when he would run freely, weighed down when he would soar. And so his passion serves to propel him, from time to time, away from the contemporaries and from the weight of his existence which pulls him down and back. When his passion comes to the fore, he is thrust forward and away in infinite negative freedom. But precisely because it is only negative and contentless, it does not endure and so he falls again. He is the ironic Icarus who soars, but not high enough.

What Johannes Climacus says of the subjective existing thinker is applicable to the ironist who is indeed the appearance of subjectivity and the beginning of reflection. He is always in process, he is never satisfied with results. And thus he always remains negative. His negativity is the striving away from the finite and the moment, after the infinite and the eternal – a goal which, as it has already been pointed out, no moment can ever realize. On the other hand, his positivity (his only content) consists in the development of the inwardness which correspondingly heightens his negativity at this point. For his inwardness intensifies the experience of the disparity in the world and more importantly in himself between phenomenon and essence. Johannes Climacus writes:

The subjective existing thinker who has the infinite in his soul has it always, and for this reason his form is always negative. When it is the case that he actually reflects existentially the structure of existence in his own existence, he will always be precisely as negative as he is positive; for his positiveness consists in the continuous realization of the inwardness through which he becomes conscious of the negative.[38]

[37] Cf. *CI*, p. 321; *S.V.*, XIII, 374.
[38] *CUP*, p. 68. Danish text reads:
"Den subjektive existerende Tænker, der har Uendeligheden i sin Sjæl, har den altid, og derfor er hans Form bestandig negativ. Naar saa er, naar han virkeligen existerende gjengiver Tilværelsens Form i sin Existents, saa er han existerende bestandig lige saa negativ som positiv, thi hans Positivitet bestaaer i den fortsatte Inderliggjørelse, i hvilken han er vidende om det Negative." *S.V.*, VII, 65–66.
Note the two Danish words: *Tilværelse* (coming into existence), *Existents* (existing).

22 IRONY

IRONY AS PROPHECY OF COMPLETED PERSONALITY. The ironist is already (i.e. in the point of development reached in the above sketch) the singular one, the one who has broken with the crowd. He is, to be sure, still an incomplete personality (considered from the point of his destiny). But he is a subject, and he does exist in the direction of a higher subjectivity, even if its form is vague and unknown to him. There is no assurance, either in terms of the dynamism which impels him or on the basis of the effects of his ironic stance upon himself, that he will reach this destiny. However, insofar as he has begun and is moving in the proper direction and traces the outline of a higher subjectivity, one may say that "...the ironist is a prophecy of or abbreviation for a complete personality."[39] He has already broken out of the mass desperation which characterizes his contemporaries, the sophists and philodoxers of his time. "Whereas the Sophist runs about like a harassed merchant, the ironist moves proudly as one [secure] in himself – enjoying."[40] To be sure, the serenity of the ironist is relative. We see only too well how precarious his position is, how aggravated his pains are, because he has taken the first steps toward the authentic subjectivity at which his ironic development hints. He remains a prophecy and a prophetic figure, one who does not possess the future but merely intimates it and its possibility of realization.[41] By no means does his development indicate *how* the future and the possible can or will be realized. And so he remains in the sphere of the non-religious, even as he exists in the direction of the ethical (and the ethico-religious).

NEGATIVE ASPECTS OF IRONY

One cannot easily separate, even in the abstract, the positive and the negative aspects of irony, least of all when irony is spoken about as an existence-stance. Was it not precisely the purpose of Kierkegaard to prove that one could not carve existence up into tidy paragraphs, systematically ordered (if not subsumed into the System itself)?

On the negative side, indeed Kierkegaard has much to say. For irony is a stage which one must supercede and advance beyond. No one lives the ironic state purely, and thus some of the aspects which are spoken

---

[39] *CI*, p. 177. Danish text reads: "*Ironikeren* ... er en Propheti om eller en *Abbreviatur af en fuldstændig Personlighed.*" *S.V.*, XIII, 233.

[40] *CI*, p. 176. Danish text reads: "Medens derfor Sophisten løber omkring som en travl Forretningsmand, gaaer Ironikeren stolt og *indesluttet* i sig selv – nydende." *S.V.*, XIII, 232. (My emphasis.)

Note here the adjective *indesluttet* which the translator Capel translates as "terminated" and which we, in this instance, translate as "secure." The idea here is the contrast of the harassed and the serene; however the Danish word is the same which is the root of what various translators have rendered in English "reserve," "morbid reserve," "shutupness" – *Indesluttethed*. We shall render the noun as "closed-in-ness" and the adjective as "closed-in" hereafter, since they are better terms and allow consistency of terminology. But here the sense is "secure."

[41] *CI*, p. 277; *S.V.*, XIII, 334.

IRONY

about as "negative" should be considered negative possibilities within the ironic stance.

We have already alluded to the negative criticism of the ironic which is based on Kierkegaard's understanding of the ironic position of the Romantics. To be sure, the Romantics represent one possibility of ironic existence. Certainly Socrates' stance is viewed differently, although termed essential irony. In short, no pure model of irony exists, even as an idea. In a man's existence, irony is even less pure – even when it takes, in the pseudonymous characters, the form of "ideas clothed in the flesh." Johannes Climacus makes the following remarks, in *The Concluding Unscientific Postscript*, concerning pure irony:

... total irony once for all, like a bargain-priced notion set down on paper, is, like all abstractions, illegitimate over against every sphere of existence.[42]

THE IRONIST LIVES IN POSSIBLES. HE LIVES POETICALLY. The ironist, to repeat what has been said above, has broken out of the heavy chain constituted by the illusory content of the present actuality. But what has he won for himself in its place? Possibility. He is cut loose from the binding post, free from all the cares of actuality – but free from the joys and blessings as well.[43] This aspect must not be overlooked, for as he who negates all content, the ironist remains empty himself.

When the given actuality loses its validity for the ironist, therefore, this is not because it is an outlived actuality which shall be displaced by a truer, but because the ironist is the eternal ego for whom no actuality is adequate.[44]

The ironist is left a spectator to the unfolding drama of existence. What then is he left with? Only his possibles.

In a sense, he is negatively freed from himself and thus free to create himself poetically. But the self thus created in imagination is imaginary.[45] He really becomes nothing (the Hegelian language states that he has no *An Sich* which he becomes) and even notices this in his poeticizing.[46] For he is so free, so overwhelmed with the breadth of his imaginary possibles, that he does not know which something to choose and so he chooses nothing.[47] He lives poetically, hypothetically and subjunctively. Devoid of content, he is also without stability, without any perspective in which to understand his passing moods.

---

[42] *CUP*, p. 464. Danish text reads: "... total Ironie eengang for alle, som et Godtkjøbs Indfald paa Papiret, er som al Abstraktion uberettiget i Forhold til enhver Existents-Sphære." *S.V.*, VII, 454.

[43] *CI*, p. 296; *S.V.*, XIII, 351.

[44] *CI*, p. 300. Danish text reads: "Men naar den givne virkelighed saa led es for Ironikeren taber sin Gyldighed, saa er det ikke fordi den er en overlevet Virkelighed, der skal afløses af en sandere, men fordi Ironikeren er det evige Jeg, for hvilket ingen Virkelighed er den adæqvate." *S.V.*, XIII, 354–355.

[45] *CI*, p. 298; *S.V.*, XIII, 353.

[46] *Ibid.*

[47] *CI*, p. 299; *S.V.*, XIII, 353.

24 IRONY

With this, he sinks down entirely under mood. His life is sheer moods.[48]

He lives in abruptly ending, discontinuous moments and, without any positive source of equilibrium, he falls under the sway of any passing, strong feeling. Moreover, in a self which is without continuity, even the most contrary feelings are able to displace each other in rapid succession.

The end result and the final unity for the intense dissonances of the various feelings in the ironist is the state of boredom (as in the "Rotation Method" of *Either/Or*).

Boredom is the only continuity which the ironist has. Yes, boredom: this eternity devoid of content, this bliss without enjoyment, this superficial profundity, this hungry sateity. But boredom is the negative unity into which opposites disappear.[49]

Here Kierkegaard deals a blow to the "superficial profundity" of the Romantic poets who were profound enough to despise all actuality, including their own poetic productions (e.g., Heinrich Heine), but in the end superficial. Kierkegaard singles out Schlegel's *Lucinde* (the particular symbol of Romanticism against which Kierkegaard continued his polemic in *Either/Or* for its lack of ethics).[50] He sums up the passive sensuality of Lisette as "aesthetic stupor."[51] And this is the phrase which would characterize for Kierkegaard the result of the aesthetic and poetic attempt to solve one's actuality. As early as the dissertation and without any pseudonym, Kierkegaard states that only the religious can solve the essential problem of existence coming to the fore in the ironist, since it is the one course which can render actuality infinite without casting it into the realms of fantasy.[52] He who lives religiously has an infinity *within*, and this is the alternative open to one who presently lives poetically and fantastically, with an infinity outside himself in the form of infinite (unrealizable) possibilities.[53]

The religious possibility to the problem of existence, clearly suggested in Kierkegaard's thought as early as the dissertation, will emerge increasingly in the examination of the other cardinal moods which shake

---

[48] *CI*, p. 301 (corrected). Danish text reads: "Herved synker han aldeles ind under Stemning. Hans Liv er *lutter* Stemninger." *S.V.*, XIII, 355.

[49] *CI*, p. 302. Danish text reads: "*Kjedsomhed*, er den *eneste Continuitet*, Ironikeren har. Kjedsomhed, denne indholdsløse Evighed, denne nydelsesløse Salighed, denne overfladiske Dybde, denne hungrige Overmæthed. Men Kjedsomhed er netop den i en personlig Bevidsthed optagne negative Eenhed, hvori Modsætningerne forsvinde." *S.V.*, XIII, 356.

[50] The polemic of *Either/Or* can be viewed as a continuation of the battle with Romanticism begun here in *Concept of Irony*.

[51] *CI*, p. 311; Danish term is "æsthetisk Bedøvelse," *S.V.*, XIII, 365.

[52] *CI*, p. 313; *S.V.*, XIII, 367.

[53] *Ibid.*

IRONY 25

the aesthetic life, and the religious will be ever more loudly proclaimed as the sole resolution which is concretely realizable.[54]

DESPERATION OF THE IRONIST. An underlying desperation characterizes the ironist. Kierkegaard speaks about it in a Journal entry of 1837, and it will later be the underlying tone of the "Diapsalmata" in *Either/Or*:

> The quiet and the security one has in reading a classic or in association with a fully matured person is not found in the romantic; there it is something like watching a man write with hands which tremble so much that one fears the pen will run away from him any moment into some grotesque stroke. (This is dormant irony.)[55]

This is an irony which is either not yet controlled or else let out of control, in which the passion which fuels irony turns upon the ironist himself. The ironist risks thus becoming marionette pulled and jerked by his own ironic power. In a subsequent journal entry, Kierkegaard will call it "an abnormal development which, like the abnormality of Strasburger geese, ends by killing the individual."[56]

IRONIST AS NON-MORAL. In his criticisms of irony, Kierkegaard finally viewed it as making it impossible for the ironist to be moral, based on the fact that the ironist lives too abstractly for the concretion which morality is. In this assertion, degree-candidate Kierkegaard may have been caught off guard, as will be the role of his philosophically acute pseudonym Johannes Climacus to point out. Certainly Kierkegaard views Socrates as ironist, but he also viewed him as moralist. His criticism of Hegel, it will be remembered, was for the fact that Hegel had seen Socrates as moralist but had not seen him as ironist. In like manner, Climacus rebukes Magister Kierkegaard for neglecting the ethical side of Socrates (which the Magister did not make explicit enough, although one can only suppose that he fully saw it), as well as the ethical passion of irony.[57]

In assessing the moral vs. non-moral stance of the ironist, it is important to note again the direction in which the ironist is moving in

---

[54] As early as the dissertation, Kierkegaard understands and states the problem in terms of possibility and infinity. The aesthete-poet has his infinity in terms of infinite possibles which are realized externally (in poetic creation). The religious man, on the other hand, has his infinity *within* himself, in the form of one specific possible, and the theme of later writings, viz. becoming a Christian.

[55] *Journals and Papers*, no. 1679. Danish text reads: "Den Ro den Tryghed man har ved at læse et classisk Værk, (eller) ved at omgaaes med et fuldstændigt udviklet (Menneske), finder ikke Sted ved det Romantiske, det gaaer næsten ligesom naar man seer en Mand skrive, der ryster paa Haanden man frygter hvert Øieblik for at Pennen skal løbe fra ham til et (eller) andet fratzenagtigt Træk. (Dette er den slumrende Ironie.)" *Papirer* II, A 37.

[56] *Journals and Papers*, no. 1717. Danish text reads: "Ironien er en abnorm Udvikling, der ligesom Leverens Abnormitæt hos de Strasburger-Gjæs ender med at slaae Individet ihjel." *Papirer* II, A 682.

[57] *CUP*, p. 449; *S.V.*, VIII, 437.

26 IRONY

terms of his spiritual development. To repeat, for Kierkegaard, the Romantics represented a movement away from spirit, a devolution. That is to say, they refused to heed the awakening of the infinite within them, refused to follow its natural course toward the ethico-religious at whose borderline they stood by virtue of an ironic consciousness. Instead, according to Kierkegaard, they preferred to wallow in their negation of all actuality, preferred to make life into an engrossing drama in which each Romantic is both actor and spectator. What is missing in this self-contained and solitary drama, to which no validity is conceded, is a sense of fellow actors. For a sense of others in the universal human drama would take the ironist into the ethical realm. But such would mean sharing the stage, and this the ironist is still too egoistic to do. Instead the Romantic ironist swoons alone in the realm of possibilities, his sole consolation for the actuality which his irony has negated.

There is another ironist who is indeed moral, for whom irony is but an incognito. And this is Johannes Climacus' view of Socrates as ironist. Climacus concedes that an ironist may be an ethicist, but not necessarily one, since he views irony as the boundary between the aesthetic and the ethical. The infinite movement which the ethicist has made is not externally perceptible, while the immediacy of the aesthete (and aesthetic ironist) is.[58] Irony can reflect, provided it is not simply an aping of the ironic, the fact that one has exercised the infinite movement, and that one has moved on to the ethical, that the ironist is beyond the immediacy of the aesthete. But it does not *per se* indicate anything more than this.[59]

Kierkegaard links irony and ethical passion in at least two places in his writings, and they should be noted for the link is not casual. In a Journal entry of 1845, Kierkegaard defines irony thus:

Irony is the unity of ethical passion, which in inwardness infinitely accentuates the private self, and of development, which in outwardness (in association with people) infinitely abstracts from the private self. The effect of the second is that no one notices the first; therein lies the art, and the true infinitizing of the first is conditioned thereby.[60]

In *The Concluding Unscientific Postscript*, Johannes Climacus modifies the definition somewhat:

Irony is a synthesis of ethical passion which infinitely accentuates inwardly the personal ego in relation to the ethical requirement – and of culture, which

---

[58] *CUP*, p. 448; *S.V.*, VIII, 436.

[59] *Ibid.* If the true inner nature of the ironist is not perceptible, how much less so the nature and movements of the religious person. Cf. *Fear and Trembling* and the infinite movements of the Knight of Faith.

[60] *Journals and Papers*, no. 1745. Danish text reads: "Ironi er Eenheden af ethisk Lidenskab, der i Inderlighed uendelig accentuerer det egne Jeg – og af Dannelse der i Udvorteshed (i Omgang med Msk.) uendeligt abstraherer fra det egne Jeg. (det Sidste gjør, at Ingen mærker det Første, og deri ligger kunsten og derved betinges det Første sande Uendeliggjørelse.)" *Papirer* VI A 38.

IRONY 27

infinitely abstracts externally from the personal ego, as one finitude among all other finitudes and particularities.[61]

But such links between irony and ethical passion are beyond the stance of the Romantics, and are rather in the direction of a contemporary Socratic, "mastered irony."

MASTERED IRONY

The highest form of irony takes one beyond the formal scope of the present study and consists of the ironist's mastery of his own irony. When this is achieved, the ironist has crossed the dividing line, passed through the transition phase which irony represents among the stages of existence, or existence spheres. He who has mastered irony has passed beyond the aesthetic into the mature realm of the ethico-religious. Kierkegaard writes in his Journal in 1837 (even before the dissertation study on irony) that "The self-overcoming of irony is the crisis of the higher spiritual life."[62] Since mastered irony lies beyond the aesthetic, it also lies beyond the formal limits set for the present discussion. However, since here as elsewhere the aesthetic part can only be properly understood in relation to the ethico-religious whole, mastered irony is discussed in order to present the complete scope and perspective of irony in which the ironic stance of the aesthete is to be viewed and the mood phase to be understood.

SELF-OVERCOMING NEGATIVITY. Irony is first overcome when the infinite negativity of irony is extended even to irony itself, when the negating power negates itself and thus escapes positing itself as a final state. Kierkegaard wrote on June 2, 1837:

... for irony is first surmounted when the individual, elevated above everything and looking down from this position, is finally elevated beyond himself and from this dizzy height sees himself in his nothingness, and thereby he finds his true elevation.[63]

"Seeing himself in his nothingness" takes him far beyond irony. It takes him beyond the dangerous self-assertion of the ironic personality in its negative freedom. Ultimately, it takes him further and further toward the religious, toward the will to despair in which a person recognizes his nothingness in sin before God and his own helplessness to rise above it.

THE INFINITY WHICH STIRS. It has already been pointed out above that the emergence of the ironic in the personality results from the

[61] CUP, p. 449. Danish text reads: "Ironie er Eenheden af ethisk Lidenskab, der i Inderlighed uendeligt accentuerer det egne Jeg i Forhold til den ethiske Fordring – og af Dannelse, der i Udvorteshed uendeligt abstraherer fra det egne Jeg, som en Endelighed med blandt alle de andre Endeligheder af Enkeltheder." S.V., VII, 437.

[62] Journals and Papers, no. 1688. Danish text reads: "Denne sig-selv-Overviden af Ironien er det høiere aandelige Livs Krise..." Papirer II A 627.

[63] Ibid. Danish text reads: "...thi Ironien er først overlevet naar Individet, hævet op over Alt, skuende ned derpaa tilsidst er hævet op over sig selv og har seet sig selv i sin Intethed fra hiin svimlede Høide og derved fundet sin sande Høide." Papirer II A 627.

28 IRONY

effects of the first stirrings of the infinite upon consciousness. However, one can still remain unconscious of, but not unaffected by, the infinite itself (as is witnessed in the ironist of non-mastered irony), even after the hold of the everyday world has been shattered in the first emergence of irony. But he who becomes conscious of the infinite, becomes acquainted with it, does not remain subject to it, but moves rather toward mastery of the self and of irony.[64] Thus there is a distinction between the aesthetic ironist whose consciousness is affected but who remains unconscious of the source, on the one hand, and the man of mastered irony who has risen to consciousness of the infinity which stirs, on the other hand.

MASTERING WILD INFINITY. But the infinity which stirs is initially a wildness in the soul, and mastered irony requires mastery of this "wild infinity" which threatens to storm forth. Mastery comes about when the ironic individual is able to give direction to his passions, even to his passion of irony, by becoming a philosopher, i.e. by developing a life-view (*Livsanskuelse, Lebensanschauung*).

In this way the problem of the literary ironist and poet's relation to his creation is also resolved. The first discussion of the proper relationship of the artist to the work of art is first taken up in Kierkegaard's very first published work, *From the Papers of One Still Living* (1838), in which he polemically asserts that Hans Christian Andersen cannot write epic because this elevated form of poetry requires a philosophy of life, which he believed Andersen lacked. When a poet and literary man has a life-view, then he has an internal relationship to his poetic work. The poetic work is then an external representation, or articulation, of something internal and is thus in relation to the poet's own existence. In this case, an ironic work does not merely have an external relation to the poet, but rather he will see in a poem or other piece a moment in his own development.[65]

OTHER ASPECTS OF MASTERED IRONY. Irony is also mastered when one's longings are properly directed towards a worthy end. Kierkegaard criticizes the Romantics for the unworthy attempt to sneak out of the world, for trying to make actuality hollow and reject it.[66] The sole worthy end which incorporates man's passions and longings will be the self. But the understanding of the self which will provide the perspective and direction for a mastered irony comes only after one has passed through subsequent moods of transition. Hence mastered irony emerges only after subsequent crises have been resolved.

Mastered irony preserves the negating function of irony in ascribing validity to actuality and cuts short the all-too-human tendency to absolutize the relative and the immediate. But mastered irony is inspired negativity existing within a larger perspective: within a life-view and world-view

---

[64] *CI*, p. 339; *S.V.*, XIII, 390f.

[65] *CI*, p. 337; *S.V.*, XIII, 389.

[66] *CI*, p. 341; *S.V.*, XIII, 392.

IRONY   29

which assigns proper validity to actuality, while holding all excess in check. In no way does irony's self-overcoming annihilate itself. It remains and elevates the self by placing it within a larger developmental process which is then allowed to function according to an inner dynamism of growth (the role of the will is crucial here, as will be seen below). In this sense, Kierkegaard goes so far as to say that "... no authentic human life is possible without irony."[67]

When irony is mastered, it serves as a check upon the ironist's personal life, much as doubt functions as a check in philosophy.[68] Mastered irony no longer emphasizes the ideality behind phenomenal reality to such an extent that the phenomenon is reduced to illusion, yet at the same time it prevents any idolatry of phenomena (which of course non-mastered irony also achieves). Mastered irony thus places proper emphasis upon reality – neither too little as the Romantics do nor too much as do most men. Mastered irony finds and actualizes the elusive "golden mean" which was so much the ideal of another age. Yet, amidst the paeans to mastered irony, let one not be distracted from a decisive and existential question which is here left unanswered: does the ironic personality have within itself the power to reach mastered irony of its own power? Indeed something greater will be needed for that, something which launches well beyond the sphere of the aesthetic. For mastered irony requires a series of developments in the personality, through and beyond anxiety and despair, to the point where one requires the grace of God.[69]

THE ESSENCE OF IRONY AS EXISTENCE-STANCE

The essence of irony is negativity. In the consciousness which irony represents, one sees through the illusions of the actual world which implies itself to be all-fulfilling. But in arriving at the ironic consciousness and mood of negativity, one has not only seen through but first *lived through* the unfulfillment which uncovers the illusory nature of the promise of the phenomenal world. As a result, one adopts an attitude of negativity toward the phenomenal world, and demands the essential which alone one has begun to realize can satisfy one's yearnings. Dissatisfaction with the phenomenal world, and the enthusiasm of the discovery of illusion, works itself into an initial passion of infinite

---

[67] *CI*. p. 338. This is also Thesis XV of the dissertation. Cf. motto for this chapter, where the Latin version is quoted. Danish text reads: "... at intet ægte humant Liv er muligt uden Ironi." *S.V.*, XIII, 390.

[68] *Ibid.*

[69] Socrates mastered irony in *his epoch* if any man did, Socrates who reached the summit of pagan religiousness. But since he lived in the pre-Christian epoch, he could not have mastered irony within the enhanced scope of spiritual possibility open to man in the Christian epoch. Mastered irony, as does the entire spiritual evolutionary process, depends on the metaphysics of history. That, however, is a moot point in terms of the evolution of man in the Christian epoch. For him all is open. It is now but a matter of willing such spiritual evolution.

30 IRONY

negativity, of sweeping rejection, in which one refuses the actual moment and every actual moment which does not contain the essential or ideal (which we have seen is an impossible requirement).

As a consciousness thoroughly pervading one's being, irony is a mood in which one regards oneself, the individual elements of the actual world, the entirety of the actual, and all future possible actuals in an attitude of passionate rejection because they do not comprise the ideal.

But, having broken with illusion, irony may prepare the groundwork for an authentic subjectivity whose content may thus be derived from some source other than the illusory actual. However, Kierkegaard wishes to emphasize that new content cannot be derived from the products of imagination, of fantasy, in the manner of the Romantics. Irony points to spirit for higher movement and new content. For in irony, it is the stirring of spirit which produces the yearning for the infinite and the ideal which actuality cannot satisfy. The individual, having risen from immersion in the actual and having broken with the age and his fellows, is "deprived" of inauthentic content and henceforth estranged, but because of this stands in sharp relief as an individual subject. Subjectivity is heightened both by the estrangement, which renders him individual and alone, and by the developing inwardness reflecting greater surgings of spirit in the individual.

Irony emphasizes the individual's yearning for the infinite, while at the same time eliminates false – and all apparent – human avenues to the infinite and ideal. In order finally to reach the infinite, one must break through human limitation, not in fantasy but through Spirit itself which takes the individual through the growth process we will continue to trace in subsequent chapters and finally acts decisively and supernaturally in grace. The irony which passes through this transformation process is mastered irony: irony which sees through the limits of the purely negative stance. But irony "sees" beyond itself in mastered irony only by *experiencing* what is beyond itself, beginning with the ambiguous and shaking discernment of positivity in the experience of anxiety. In mastered irony, infinite negativity fades as one comes to re-acceptance of an actuality in which one contacts the infinite, by grace.

B. IRONY AS A MEASUREMENT AND TOOL IN THE ANALYSIS OF THE AESTHETIC LIFE-VIEW

In the section above, we have emphasized particularly two aspects of irony: irony as a tool of discourse and irony as an existence-stance with various possible phases and degrees, and thus a measurement for the development of personality. We have found it important to discuss the tool of discourse not only because it is the aspect most often understood by the term, but also because it functions so prominently in Kierkegaard's aesthetic characters. Johannes, the author of *Either/Or* Pt. I, is an ironic individual whose irony we will have occasion to examine

IRONY 31

below; Constantine Constantius, author of the *Repetition*, is called an ironist; and other aesthetic characters are not wanting in ironic skills; nor of course is Kierkegaard, either as puppeteer in this aesthetic theatre or as author in his own name.

However, our particular concern here is the role of irony as a measurement of personality development in the direction of the religious, and as a tool in the analysis of the aesthetic life. In order to re-emphasize this dimension of the ironic and to make it perhaps a little clearer, certain aspects merit further attention before leaving this mood and passing on to the discussion of the mood of anxiety.

The presence of irony is the indication of an existence-stance. Irony bespeaks a life-view, at least negatively. It is most often negative and indicates a breaking away from the empty life-view shared by mass-man. Irony indicates an awareness of the limits of the phenomenal world, a pained and passionate consciousness of finitude, with a corresponding desire to soar beyond constraints. It speaks of a passion which has grown to significant force within the personality and now seeks to carry the personality forward to a new stage of development. The existence-stance of irony is a rejection of the past and the recognized need to move beyond it. Irony is an affirmation of the future, or at least a theoretical openness to the future. But not until irony has negated and mastered itself does it begin to bespeak the positive and the beginning of a positive life-view.

Irony is the result of the same sensitivity which initially renders the personality melancholy (*melankolsk*). And while melancholy and irony go hand-in-hand, irony indicates a higher consciousness than the initial *Melancholi* phase within *Tungsindighed*. (See Chapter Three below, especially section D.) Irony indicates a crisis in the personality which is not yet resolved, but it is higher than *Melancholi* in that it indicates an awareness of the bankruptcy of the melancholic yearning for the ideal in the moment. One might say that the ironist has seen through the view which the melancholic still suffers through. However, the ironist too remains within the essential problem of melancholy, even though he is one step closer to the threshold of the exit door. Thus Kierkegaard views irony as a transitional stage to the ethical, but not yet quite ethical. The self has not yet been chosen in a positive act of the will, nor have the ethical and the universal human. The ironist has merely broken with mass-man. He has not yet taken up a new higher ethical relationship to men.

But irony is the prophecy of a completed personality, one which is close to making the necessary self-affirming, self-saving movement. Not every prophecy is fulfilled, and so there is no guarantee of a higher development, a higher consciousness, despite the appearance of hopeful signs. And this non-guarantee will be seen in the analysis of the Young Aesthete below. For he is an ironic personality who, for the moment, is blocked in his development. The ethicist Judge William prophesies an eventual remedy of sorts (a monastery, as for the mythological Don

32   IRONY

Juan), but there is no evidence given in the presentation that the
character Johannes will ever reach a genuine solution.

While irony indicates that one is still far from the pristine reintegration of the personality represented by a true "repetition,"
nonetheless irony attests to purification from the hold of finitude by
means of the cleansing baptism of irony.[70] Irony indicates the possibility,
and gives ground for the hope, that a higher development of the
personality is coming. It is well beyond the long-ailing melancholic who
suffers such dispersion that all sense of possibility is lost. A "healthy
irony" indicates the proper advance beyond the initial crisis of melancholy. Indeed one must go through the heavy dark depths of melancholy
before the lightness of irony comes, and the one tends to come in the
train of the other, as the alternating melancholic yearnings and soaring
ironic comments of the Young Aesthete will indicate.

[70] *CI*, p. 339; *S. V.* XIII, 390.

CHAPTER II

ANXIETY[1]

In anxiety the state out of which a man longs to be delivered announces itself, and it announces itself because longing alone is not enough to save the man.

– Vigilius Haufniensis, *Concept of Anxiety*, 52.

Anxiety is the first reflex of possibility, a glimpse, and yet a terrible sorcery.

– *Papirer*, X^2 A 22.

With the mood of anxiety, we enter a level of greater seriousness and greater crisis within the aesthetic life. The stirring which will be shown to have led to *Melancholi* and to the infinite negativity of irony leads further to the threshold of new positivity for which the experience of anxiety serves as a passageway. However, anxiety exists as well, and quite importantly, as an enduring structure in the human person both before and after the anxiety experience proper which will principally occupy our attention in the analysis of the aesthetic life.

In the case of anxiety and each of the other cardinal moods, it will be important to describe the scope of the mood as it applies to all of existence and its structures, to sketch the presentation of the concept of each mood in Kierkegaard's writings, and then finally to re-situate the discussion in terms of the critique of aesthetic existence and the emergence of religious subjectivity.

As is the case with the three existence-spheres (viz. the aesthetic, the ethical, and the religious), the mood of anxiety cannot be treated in isolation from other aspects of psychic life. It forms and indicates a stage attained within the evolution of the psyche, but is also closely tied with moods which can only be very loosely spoken of as "preceding" and "succeeding" it. We prefer here also the image of existence "spheres," whereby the possibility of an over-lapping is more readily seen. For anxiety and the other moods do overlap, as Kierkegaard does not hesitate to remind his readers.

Although there are clear differences and distinctions between them, absolutely no clear line of demarcation exists between the four cardinal moods which are the focus of our discussion. Each mood and structure continues throughout the life of the individual. There is a crisis point or period within each mood, which we isolate for discussion in each chapter to show its relation to the upheaval of the psyche in aesthetic existence.

[1] The title of Lowrie's translation of *Begrebet Angest* is well known as *The Concept of Dread*. Since "anxiety" is both less misleading and is consistent with the normal translation of *Angest/Angst* from Danish and German respectively, the work will be hereafter referred to as *The Concept of Anxiety*, despite the limitations of this word as well. This title will also be adopted for the forthcoming revised translation in English.

34   ANXIETY

But even after a successful resolution of the crisis period, the structure endures and is experienced, although in a markedly different manner.

For purposes of philosophical contemplation, abstraction is capable of a type of separation of the moods. However, it would be grossly unfaithful to Kierkegaard's thought and the thrust of his writings not to emphasize that within existence the cardinal moods so overlap each other that as a result separation cannot be enforced, even abstractly, without perceptible strain. Thus, for example, the essential structure of anxiety precedes all other moods and mood structures. Kierkegaard speaks at length of a primal anxiety – an anxiety before the first sin – which is posited by the fact of the synthesis which man is as body, mind, and spirit. This primal anxiety exists while spirit still dreams, before the stirring which leads to *Melancholi*. In relation to despair (which will be the subject of Chapter Four) anxiety can justly be viewed as a degree of the one same state which in its heightened form is despair. In fact, in *The Sickness Unto Death*, the pseudonym Anti-Climacus links anxiety and despair in several places.[2] One can thus speak of despair as the heightened form of anxiety. The point here is to acknowledge an overlapping of the moods in existence and of their structures throughout the psychic development of the individual, despite the perhaps overly clear distinctions which abstraction may suggest. Clarity is only possible from a certain stance, and our own standpoint for artificial clarity in the course of this study is the upheaval in the aesthetic life which seeks to go beyond itself.

That the danger of artificial clarity was a concern of Kierkegaard's, and that he affirmed the impossibility of reaching full clarity about anxiety precisely because its ambiguous structure finally defies systematization, can be readily seen in Vigilius Haufniensis' Preface and Introduction to *The Concept of Anxiety* and in the continued jibes at the System and at systematizers which run throughout the work. It may perhaps seem self-defeating to devote so much space to affirming the essential vagueness and ambiguity in a mood for which we ourselves will attempt to formulate a clear and distinct idea below. However, to do anything less than affirm essential obscurities and limits would be to fall into the error of the systematizers whom Kierkegaard so roundly criticized. And while at many points this study has to deal with the "ghost of Kierkegaard," the anti-systematizer, as it proceeds in attempting to present clearly and systematically Kierkegaard's analysis of aesthetic existence and description of the birth of subjectivity, it proceeds with the conviction that abstraction and systematization have a value, so long as limits are acknowledged and so long as ideas are neither absolutized nor mistaken for existence. In holding to this conviction, we can find good precedent in Kierkegaard's pseudonyms. For such works as *The Concept of Anxiety* and *The Sickness Unto Death* are, one may dare to say, systematically organized treatises whose value and

---

[2] *SUD*, p. 155, p. 158, *et al.*, *S.V.*, XI, 136, 139.

ANXIETY

significance depend not only upon their wealth of insights but also upon their manner of presentation.

In the treatise on anxiety, Kierkegaard quite unmistakably enters the province of psychology. He, first and foremost, is aware of this, as the subtitle of *The Concept of Anxiety* indicates, in which a "psychological deliberation" is spoken of. The avowed method of procedure is psychological observation and, although this claim may be doubted in places where metaphysics seems to underly the discussion and marshall observation, the work is indeed psychological, even by the standards of contemporary psychology. Its evident metaphysical underpinnings and *a priori*'s will not be to the taste of the positivist psychologist. Nonetheless such writers on the subject of anxiety as Rollo May (*The Meaning of Anxiety*)[3] in the United States, Juliette Favez-Boutonier (*L'Angoisse*)[4] in France, and Martin Heidegger (*Sein und Zeit*) in Germany, among others, have depended heavily upon the insights of psychologist Kierkegaard.[5]

While Kierkegaard, in Danish and in translation, shares with the later generations a common psychological vocabulary, it must be borne in mind that neither in Danish nor in translation does "anxiety" have its more usual meaning. In *L'Angoisse*, Favez-Boutonier makes the useful distinction between *inquiétude, anxiété*, and *angoisse* as three ascending degrees of the same state. It is the highest level, *angoisse* in her schematization, which she identifies as the subject of Kierkegaard's discussion. For while *inquiétude* is about forthcoming destiny, and *anxiété* is about more ultimate questions of destiny as they apply to the exterior world, in *angoisse* the totally unknown, a nothing, is in question and the self is *en cause*.[6]

Kierkegaard himself proceeds immediately to the highest form. He does, however, make the important distinction between anxiety and fear, before taking up the analysis. Fear is always *about something*; in fear, a clear object can be localized. In anxiety, on the other hand, there is no clear object, no object at all, and this gives rise to speaking of the "nothing" of anxiety – a topic to be engaged more fully below. One must be aware in proceeding with his text that here, as elsewhere, Kierkegaard begins with a not uncommon term soon to be given a

---

[3] (New York, 1950).

[4] (Paris, 1863).

[5] Favez-Boutonier has the greatest sympathy for Kierkegaard's approach and distorts his position the least. Rollo May, while his *Meaning of Anxiety* has proven merits, does not give Kierkegaard his due. That is to say, May takes Kierkegaard's insights out of context and to that extent distorts them. Heidegger formally acknowledges no debt to Kierkegaard, but it is obvious nonetheless. Cf. *Introduction to Metaphysics* and *Being and Time* on anxiety, especially p. 228ff. in the latter.

For discussion by another prominent recent philosopher, cf. Karl Jasper's *Psychologie der Weltanschauungen.*

[6] *L'Angoisse*, p. 37.

36 ANXIETY

special definition; and it is important to suspend one's normal definitions and associations until the eventual new definition is made.[7]

A. ANXIETY IN *THE CONCEPT OF ANXIETY*

It is in the work of Vigilius Haufniensis, which is only thinly pseudonymous,[8] that the treatise on anxiety is found. Other mentions of anxiety in the writings are quite abundant, but only in this work does Kierkegaard–Haufniensis give a developed treatment to the idea of anxiety.

STYLE AND FORMAT

As we have already suggested, hardly a work of Kierkegaard's can be fully taken account of without careful attention to the form of presentation. This applies certainly to *The Concept of Anxiety*. Walter Lowrie, in the Translator's Preface, quotes a letter from the translator Alexander Dru which says of Kierkegaard, "One of these days I am going to say what I think of his vile, slovenly style, his clumsy, unnecessary terminology."[9] With all due sympathy for the translator's difficulties and frustrations, we might say that it is not particularly this work and this translation which merits Dru's challenge. There are indeed limitations to *The Concept of Anxiety*, but the present writer is here at least inclined to be tolerant of Kierkegaard's efforts to deal with a subject which had been almost never before treated. But if the work is confusing, the cause lies perhaps in the format and chapter headings.

It is generally acknowledged that *The Concept of Anxiety* is Kierkegaard's most difficult work. The subject matter is extremely dense. However, what one might reproach Kierkegaard for is attempting once again to do too much at one time. For he takes up (1) the dogmatic problem of original sin, (2) the ultimately more important problem of sin itself and the individual's responsibility, (3) a psychological investigation of anxiety, and adds all along (4) a running polemic against the System, philosophers and theologians. In a work which is rather small in size, one thus finds a vast scope of problems treated and commented upon, and no reader can be overly faulted if he becomes entangled and understands less than clearly Kierkegaard–Haufniensis' various points on the several admittedly-not-unrelated topics.

The title page merits citation in full: *The Concept of Anxiety: a simple psychological-demonstrative Deliberation in the Direction of the dogmatic Problem of Original Sin*, by Vigilius Haufniensis.[10] Indeed, as the title suggests, anxiety does form the center of the discussion, but it is surrounded on all sides by sin. For the discussion commences with the

[7] The past English translators of Kierkegaard have, unfortunately, not been consistent in translating this key term (as others). Thus one reads "anxiety," "anguish," and "dread" where the Danish has but one term, *Angest [Angst]*.

[8] Kierkegaard apparently had considered publishing it under his own name, according to the *Papirer* drafts.

[9] Quoted *CA*, viii.

[10] *CA*, p. 1; *S.V.*, IV, 275.

ANXIETY

problem of original sin and launches an attempt to approach psychologically the state just prior to the qualitative leap to original sin. There is much here to provoke the theologians. Haufniensis attacks the mythologizers who would make the sin of Adam essentially different from the sin of his descendants and thus relegate Adam to the realm of the "fantastic," outside the universal human. As a psychologist, Haufniensis will not try to explain sin,[11] as he repeats continually, but rather he observes the leap which is made to sin, a leap for which every individual himself is responsible and a leap whose movements every individual makes for himself, as Adam did. Sin comes into the world by sin – a refrain in the work declaring each individual's responsibility. The Danish term is important here. *Arvesynden* literally means "the sin of inheritance" or "the inherited sin" (English: "original sin"). Haufniensis points out that, despite the name "inherited sin," it is we who are responsible for our first sin, and not Adam (who is only responsible for his own). Anxiety is the state which exists before sin, and this is as close as psychology can come to the leap. *Why* one leaps psychology cannot say; but *that* one leaps psychology can observe, along with theology.

However, while the anxiety before the first sin (of Adam and of every man) is indeed important, it is not the main point. The major portion of *The Concept of Anxiety* is devoted to anxiety *after* the first sin, as is announced in the heading of Chapter Two, "Anxiety as Original Sin Progressively." As will be seen, the essence of the anxiety after the first sin is not qualitatively different from anxiety pre-sin. However, man's state is significantly changed by sin, as are his possibilities – possibility being essentially at the root of anxiety.

The essential possibility, in which one can come to experience and be conscious of anxiety, is remaining in sin or else overcoming it. Thus the discussion, *de facto*, turns to a discussion of man in the state of sin and the ways of overcoming it (a discussion to be carried further in *The Sickness Unto Death*).

The reader is never told so by chapter headings, but he is moving back and forth between phases of anxiety and sin which, while not essentially qualitatively different, do have some important quantitative differences. The dogmatic problem of original sin, which launches the discussion, is fundamentally a theologian's problem. And while *The Concept of Anxiety* does take the form of a theological treatise, its major portions are concerned with what would nowadays be termed the "existential" problem of anxiety and sin. For what is said of anxiety and sin, after Adam's sin, has personal relevance for the individual reader. It is not the sort of treatise which would compel the attention of those pseudonyms lost in the false paradise of aesthetic existence but it will indeed serve those, aesthetes or not, who seek an analysis of that existence sphere.

In the discussion, anxiety and sin are intertwined. The problem of

[11] This is left for the Christian pseudonym Anti-Climacus. Cf. Discussion of despair in Chapter Four.

38   ANXIETY

original sin leads to the consideration of anxiety, where it is observed
that anxiety comes before and after all sin. In terms of the first sin, what is
significant is the first, pre-conscious anxiety. For, prior to the first sin,
spirit, the vehicle of consciousness, is in a dreaming state.

In proceeding through *The Concept of Anxiety*, the reader finds himself
confronted with a treatise which is theological in form, but which claims
to proceed with psychological deliberation. This claim is at times suspect
in a work which is full of highly abstract, metaphysical terminology. In
the sections of the work on objective anxiety one may well wonder if it
is the psychologist or dialectician who is operating. For the section
makes the claim that objective anxiety is anxiety in the world and that it
increases quantitatively by every sin. No psychological observation is
offered in support of this claim, and the discussion quickly turns to the
subjective problem. And when one reads the confident description of
the human synthesis (body, mind, spirit) and how it operates *before*
birth, one may well wonder at the locus in time and space for these
so-called psychological descriptions. If Vigilius is a psychologist, he is
supplementing his practice with a good bit of metaphysics.

The essence of anxiety occupies relatively little space within the
formal discussion, in no small way due to the ambiguity and nothingness
which is essential to anxiety. Much of the discussion is concerned with
secondary characteristics of anxiety and, more importantly, with the role
of anxiety in leading one toward sin-consciousness and faith. Anxiety is
thus a state which points beyond itself, and Haufniensis emphasizes this
as he discusses the alternative of going through anxiety (and thus
moving to a higher consciousness) or else attempting to flee it. (The
flight from anxiety, which is always *in* anxiety, contains the analysis
most pertinent to aesthetic existence, it will be seen). The final chapter
announces the end-point to which anxiety can lead: Faith.

THEORY AND HISTORY OF SPIRIT

In the preceding chapter, we make allusion to the theory of spirit
operative in the thought and writings of Kierkegaard, and shared by his
pseudonyms with consistency. This theory underlies *The Concept of
Anxiety* just as *The Concept of Irony* and *Either/Or* (particularly the
"Immediate States of the Musical Erotic"). Because it is especially significant for understanding anxiety and hence the treatise on anxiety, a sketch
of the theory as it applies here is in order.

There are two planes in the history of spirit: the race and the
individual, and Haufniensis remarks that it is the genius who lives out
the experience of the race in its fullness. As regards the individual, this
theory roughly parallels a theory of physical evolution which understands the human fetus to repeat certain basic stages which the race
itself went through in the process of developing the present human
form. A parallel theory applies to spirit, and the basic phases can be
pinpointed as the major phases of man's religious history. According to
this theory, the three great religious phases are paganism, Judaism, and
Christianity. These represent basic planes in the development of spirit.

ANXIETY 39

Paganism represents a basically dreaming state of spirit, Judaism a waking, and Christianity the fully awaked. Within Christianity however there are tendencies toward a "devolution," specifically symbolized by Romanticism and its intellectual offshoot Idealism, according to Kïerkegaard.

The three phases are also historical epochs. Contemporary man is within the Christian epoch and the highest phase of the race's spiritual development. However, the Christian epoch is not completed and even the genius who goes through the previous movements is still evolving.[12] Thus evolution continues to take place within the Christian epoch of spirit, on the individual level. And because the possibility of evolution is present, the possibility of devolution, as well as non-evolution, is present as well. The dynamism of evolution in the spirit ties in, in Kierkegaard's thought, with the theory of the body-mind-spirit synthesis. According to it, the genuine synthesis is not activated so long as the spirit is in a dreaming state. However, because spirit is present, even when dreaming, man is always a synthesis. But when spirit awakens, the synthesis becomes active and is in movement toward becoming an inter-acting whole. While anxiety's roots are in spirit confronting its own possibilities in freedom, its manifestations are on the mental-emotional plane, which is where psychology observes the symptoms. But the cause of the symptoms is supplied by metaphysics which here states that the eternal is present only potentially, that spirit is not yet integrated actively into the synthesis, and that the need for the integration of spirit is the essential revelation of this mood.

Initially anxiety appears in spirit in the dreaming state. Quite interestingly here, Kierkegaard–Haufniensis clearly suggests a causal relationship between the first sin of man and the awaking of spirit. Dreaming spirit precedes the state of sin and the manifestation of the nothingness of anxiety. Sin brings about the waking of spirit.

FELIX CULPA. More interesting still is the fact that Kierkegaard implies by this theory of the inter-action of spirit and sin that, indeed because of sin, a higher state in the evolution of the spirit has come about. For if Adam had not sinned, he would have remained in innocence and also in ignorance.[13]

[12] Given this understanding of individual spiritual evolution, it is small wonder that Kierkegaard strongly opposed infant baptism which claimed to produce a Christian merely by pouring water.

[13] The Eastern Church proclaims that Adam recovered his initial innocence in a higher state (a "repetition" in the Kierkegaard sense) in celebrating the feast of *St. Adam*. And in the Western Church, the notion that the fall of man ultimately brings about a higher destiny for the whole race is found quite explicitly. In the Latin Easter Liturgy, the "Exultet," which is chanted by the deacon at the Service of Light before the newly kindled Easter candle representing the Risen Christ, speaks of the *felix culpa*, the "blessed fault" of Adam. For it is said that the fall of Adam ultimately led to the Christ-event which not only brings God among men but allows a new relationship of sonship to the Father and of brotherhood with his Christ. Implicit, and fairly evident, despite the poetic expression of another age, is the idea that because of sin man can ultimately reach a higher state. Kierkegaard–Haufniensis' theory of spirit is entirely in accord with this idea and might even be said to be a more modern articulation of the same sense of higher possibility as a result of fall.

40 ANXIETY

Sin has reference to anxiety because in anxiety possibility – both to fall and rise – is agonizingly experienced. In anxiety one senses the dizziness of freedom in which Adam and every man swoons and from which he arises to discover himself in sin. And it is in the same essentially ambiguous dizziness that the sinner discovers his higher possibility. For the experience of anxiety can move him toward a higher state of spiritual evolution, if he does not attempt to escape but instead wills to go through it. This higher state consists first of all of a guilt-consciousness, the acknowledgement that one has fallen and is responsible for one's own fall, and next a sin-consciousness, the realization that one is a sinner without justification before the judgement of God. The final phase of the evolution of spirit takes place by an act of grace which one cannot merit or presume, which overcomes sin and effects the relationship of faith, in which the essential problems of the integration of the elements of the human synthesis are overcome. (The evolution of spirit is never complete, since it continues so long as the synthesis endures, which is to say so long as a man lives. Thus the evolution is one of degrees, but with critical stages reached at discernible points.)

TYPES OF, AND STANCES IN RELATION TO, ANXIETY

Subjective anxiety and the individual's relation to it are at the core of *The Concept of Anxiety* and the principal concern of its author, as witnessed by so many references to subjective anxiety and by the simple fact of space devoted to the topic. Although one notes a neat division between subjective and objective anxiety, one observes that but few pages are devoted to the objective. Much as in Climacus' *Postscript*, the objective problem is treated rather more for form's sake and only as prelude to the more important consideration of the subjective. (Compare, for example, the Table of Contents in the *Postscript* as regards space devoted to various topics. One notes that even in the few pages devoted to the Objective Problem, it is the Subjective Problem which is discussed. Anti-Hegelian polemic is at the root of this and the contrast of objective and subjective is in part satire upon the System.)

PRIMAL ANXIETY. In order to make a distinction between anxiety before and after sin – a distinction Haufniensis makes in theory, but not in terminology – we shall speak of anxiety before the first sin as "primal anxiety." As has been pointed out above, this anxiety arises in dreaming spirit. Primal anxiety is the dizziness of freedom before sin and the state out of which one emerges to discover that one has fallen into sin. It is a pre-conscious anxiety, in distinction from the later form of anxiety which is conscious. It is the anxiety experience which arises in ignorance and confronts the individual with the set of possibilities of either continuing in innocence and ignorance or else sinning.

ANXIETY AFTER THE FALL. Anxiety after sin consists of two types, objective and subjective. As regards the individual, anxiety is always subjective.

ANXIETY 41

(a) OBJECTIVE ANXIETY. Haufniensis claims that objective anxiety is the reflection of sinfulness in the whole world, after the quantitative entrance of sin into creation by the sin of Adam. However, the discussion is a bit forced, in the sense that Kierkegaard–Haufniensis seems compelled to find something through which he can give meaning to the expression "objective anxiety," because obviously "subjective" and "objective" only have meaning in reference to one another. This is perhaps the weakest part of *The Concept of Anxiety*, for it is a section which is seemingly taken up out of necessity, handled briefly and ended abruptly, as the author acknowledges.[14] (We have already alluded to the debatable term "psychological" to speak of an un-evidenced and non-described anxiety in the whole world.) In terms of the dogmatic considerations, objective anxiety becomes a way of making Adam at least responsible for something and giving him some historic-metaphysical role in the history of the race, while at the same time safeguarding his position within the race. (Adam, by the first sin, is responsible for objective anxiety in the world, which each individual increases by sin. For his own sin, Adam and everyman remains individually responsible.)

(b) SUBJECTIVE ANXIETY. With the focused and sustained discussion of subjective anxiety, we are led to the central concern of the work and to its treasury of insights. The anxiety before sin, which we have called primal anxiety, is subjective anxiety, as is all anxiety which has reference to individual existence. Anxiety is always essentially and qualitatively the same, before and after sin. It has one essence in both instances. However, since man's position in the universe is radically altered by sin, so are man's possibilities, and hence so is the role of anxiety in relation to the individual. For Adam the first anguished possibility was really the very simple alternative of remaining in innocence (and ignorance) or sinning. Since sin comes into the world by sin, as Haufniensis continually reaffirms, all men make the same choice as Adam did. But the first consciousness of this is always as a choice which *has been made*,[15] for everyman has already fallen into sin. Thus the essential possibility for every individual now concerns the relation to the state of sinfulness: to remain in it or seek to overcome it. And this is not merely a possibility which thus brings about further anxiety, but it is *the* possibility in which the experience of anxiety plays a crucial role. The accepting and willing passage through anxiety constitute a decisive step toward overcoming sinfulness.

Subjective anxiety is the confrontation with one's infinite possibilities as a being essentially qualified by spirit. And one specific possibility anxiously raised in the experience is development or evolution of the spiritual dimension. Faced with this infinite, ambiguous possibility – the nothing which one is compelled to experience and complete in order to

[14] *CA*, p. 54; *S.V.*, IV, 330.

[15] This notion has its parallel in the later philosophy of Heidegger, in the concept of *Verfallenheit*. Cf. *Being and Time*, section 38, p. 219ff.

42   ANXIETY

become oneself in a higher and fuller sense, one is in anxiety. For the infinite, undefined and virtually unknown[16] possibilities which one has as an evolving spiritually-qualified subject alarm and fascinate. Since it is one oneself who is *en cause*, and because one is always interesting to oneself, the experience of possibility is fascinating in the sense that it excites and rouses one's entire being and compels attention to oneself. On the other hand, as un-actualized possibility, one's destiny is undecided and sensed as a potentially perilous course, because unknowable in advance, and thus alarm equally permeates the person. Fascination and alarm correspond to the sympathy and antipathy, respectively, which are essential characteristics of the anxiety experience. Haufniensis does not want to run the risk here of false clarity, and so he describes the integral connection of sympathy and antipathy as "antipathetic sympathy" and "sympathetic antipathy."[17]

The possibility one now confronts hinges on two realities: one's being a spiritually qualified being and one's being a sinner. By the fact of sin one's spiritual possibilities have been modified and the essential possibility now revolves around one's status in sin. One's ownmost possibility consists in taking up a stance in regard to "becoming a sinner" (i.e., taking on the consciousness of being already a sinner before God.) Thus the alternatives are either overcoming sin or else continuing in sin.

The anxiety experience will, in its unimpeded movement, carry one beyond the guilt-consciousness assumed in anxiety (responsible to oneself) into sin-consciousness (responsibility before God) and finally into a position where one can receive grace. However, no movement takes place without the cooperation of the individual, for which an act of the will is required. In Kierkegaard's theory of the evolution of the personality and consciousness through the evolution of spirit, the will constantly plays a decisive role. Without an act of will, the dynamism of growth is effectively stopped, and this is the essential problem in the aesthetic life: that the aesthete refuses to will, refuses to allow the processes at work within him to move toward natural fruition.

Since anxiety is never annihilated even in the man who has reached the highest spiritual level (anxiety continues so long as possibility is experienced), the individual always remains in a state of anxiety even after the critical anxiety experience has been gone through. Thus Haufniensis characterizes the two possible stances which one can take in terms of moving toward sin-consciousness and the overcoming of anxiety as (1) anxiety for the evil and (2) anxiety for the good.

In a certain sense, anxiety for the evil refers to the individual who through false repentance shies away still from the characterization of himself as sinner. However, in another sense, it continues to apply to one who has submitted to this characterization. For repentance too is a

[16] Unknown, because knowledge here comes only in experience and only to the individual subject. Hence others' experience cannot be a sure guide. For no one else has knowledge of another's inner possibilities as a spiritually-qualified person.

[17] *CA*, p. 38; *S.V.*, IV, 313.

ANXIETY 43

matter of degrees, and sin-consciousness can always be greater than it is. Thus to whatever extent further heightening of this consciousness is possible (and it of course always is) one can be said to be in anxiety for the evil. However, Haufniensis' discussion has basically to do with the man who cooperates with the inner movement of evolution but who does not yet go through the anxiety experience which will characterize him as "sinner." It can be a momentary reluctance, or a tragic final point of progress in a movement which always maintains the hope, but never the guarantee, of being fulfilled, since at every step it depends upon the active cooperation of the individual.

Anxiety for the evil represents the attempt to avoid the assaults of the spirit. In effect, this form of anxiety, if not overcome, constitutes an abortion of the higher life which exists fetus-like in the spirit.[18] Here Kierkegaard–Haufniensis uses a clear metaphor of evolution regarding the life of the spirit and the threat posed to that life before higher birth in faith. For faith represents the overcoming of anxiety and, at the same time, puts an end to the sophistry of remorse to which the individual in anxiety for the evil is particularly prone. For this remorse represents ineffectual sorrowing which deroutes the individual from movement toward sin-consciousness in which a higher sorrowing in repentance leads to faith and forgiveness.

The second possible stance which may be taken up in relation to the spirit's evolution and the surfacing anxiety experience is anxiety for the good. The relative importance of this stance is reflected in the space it occupies within the treatise. It constitutes roughly one-fourth of the entire work, in contrast to the few pages devoted to anxiety for the evil. As was the case with subjective and objective anxiety, Vigilius Haufniensis indicates by time and space devoted to a topic its relative importance in the hierarchy of his concerns. And in this instance, he reveals himself as a critic of the aesthetic life. For anxiety for the good (the demonic) represents the stance taken up by those in the aesthetic modality. Their point in attempting flight occurs long before the characterization of sinner becomes imminent. Rather, they take to flight as soon as the eternal stirs with the movement of spirit; they seek escape into exteriority as soon as the movement of interiority begins; they seek immersion in the frivolous as soon as the serious becomes manifest.

As anxiety, anxiety for the good is qualitatively and essentially the same as other forms of anxiety. What allows speaking of a special form is the particular set of possibilities which it represents and the stance which it represents in relation to them.

In anxiety for the good, the *good* of which one is anxious signifies the reintegration of freedom, as well as redemption and salvation.[19] For one has been, and is, in a state of sin and hence unfreedom. The particular possibility which confronts one here is the possibility of freedom, of

[18] *CA*, p. 104; *S.V.*, IV, 384–385.
[19] *CA*, p. 106; *S.V.*, IV, 387.

44 ANXIETY

recovered freedom, and a new integration ("repetition"). The desperate flight from the call *back* and call *to* a higher state is characterized by the term "demoniacal."

The demoniacal is unfreedom which would avoid a confrontation with the possibility of freedom. But the avoidance of such an encounter is impossible, for even unfreedom maintains a relationship to freedom.[20] The demoniacal takes several forms of flight from confrontation with the good and each of these has particular bearing on the aesthetic life. The first form of flight is "closed-in-ness" (*Indesluttethed*), a word which has in other places also been translated as "reserve" and "morbid reserve" by Kierkegaard's past English translators. Here the image is particularly apt, for the demoniacal individual seeks to wrap himself up in himself by way of avoiding the good which calls him to self-revelation. But even in the attempt to close himself in, he unfreely reveals himself despite himself.[21]

The demoniacal is also the sudden, which is an expression for closed-in-ness applied to time. The closed-in-man seeks to cut himself off from the natural flow of time, to isolate himself in the moment and to break the natural connection with the past and future, for he is trying to avoid his own possibilities which naturally are oriented in a future direction. He seeks to avoid any continuity, and thus any communication or self-revealing. (For communication, which is the opposite of closed-in-ness, is the expression of continuity.)

The demoniacal is the vacuous, the tedious as "continuity in nothingness" to which flight from the good relegates one. This is reflected in the "Rotation Method" of *Either/Or* where the arbitrary cultivation of the momentarily interesting scarcely disguises the vacuous quality of the existence there unfreely revealed – an existence which self-admittedly seeks escape from the boring. Closed-in-ness becomes the form and vacuousness the content of this escape from self.[22]

In effect, the demoniacal is self-destructive flight from seriousness. For the natural movement in the spirit is the stirring of the eternal, which leads to inwardness and which in turn leads to seriousness.[23] The demoniacal is flight from inwardness into the external world, flight from the eternal in an attempt to absorb oneself in time. It is flight from taking oneself, one's destiny and one's possibility seriously. It declares the exterior to be the serious instead, thus negating the inward man. For

---

[20] *CA*, p. 110; *S.V.*, IV, 391.

Paul Tillich, influenced by both Schelling and Kierkegaard, develops the notion of the demonic in his *Courage To Be* (New Haven: Yale University Press, 1952) pp. 33–34, 58–60, 128–130 *et al.*, a work substantially paralleling Kierkegaard's *Concept of Anxiety*.

[21] *Ibid.* This is the case with the revealing-himself-despite-himself of the young aesthete of *Either/Or*. He is self-admittedly closed-in and yet he bursts unfreely out of himself revealing what he has made of himself in his desperate unfreedom and flight from the good.

[22] *CA*, p. 119; *S.V.*, IV, 400.

[23] *CA*, p. 130; *S.v.*, IV, 412.

ANXIETY 45

the truly inward individual is not he or she who is withdrawn, closed-in and shut-up against the world, but rather the individual who is in harmony with an inner spiritual dynamism and from that stance goes back to the world as a religiously qualified subject.

The connections here with the major categories of aesthetic existence are evident. All that the aesthetic life posits can be seen as flight from a higher calling. The desperation and the inability of this life to give equilibrium to the personality is depicted vividly in the characterization of *Either/Or,* and in the analysis of the anxiety for the good we are presented with the underlying reasons, as if they had not already been "unfreely revealed" in the earlier work. (See fuller discussion of *Either/Or* below in Chapter Three.)

Aesthetic existence is, in the main, anxiety for the good, while anxiety for the evil also applies. For aesthetic existence refuses to follow, and seeks to flee, the natural movement of spirit which calls it out of its fallen state and toward a higher reintegration which, while still ambiguous (because it is unrealized possibility), is nonetheless hinted at. Aesthetic existence is existence which attempts to be static, in the face of a natural dynamism within it. Since it cannot destroy this dynamic propulsion forward, it clashes with it time and again and never succeeds in dominating it – thus the constant eruptions in the soul of the aesthete mirrored in the "Diapsalmata" of *Either/Or.*

The scope of aesthetic existence is indeed large, including as it does every existence which has not fundamentally resolved its being in sin. The scope of anxiety within such an existence is also of grand dimensions. But there are moments of crisis when the spirit stirs with a particular force, when the eternal would break forth in the personality. In such moments anxiety for the good takes place, as seriousness, inwardness and a new freedom become the possibilities before which the individual stands in anxiety, as he shudders before specific possibilities and seeks to escape them. Here the "fascinating" element has momentarily lost out, and the "alarm" has won the day. The individual flees from himself, in reckless self-abandonment and self-destruction, in an attempt at spiritual suicide. Haufniensis devotes so much attention to this form of anxiety because, he feels, it has never been such a widespread phenomenon as in his own day, manifesting itself in both spiritual and intellectual spheres.[24] It is not going too far to connect Haufniensis' concern to the warnings made by other pseudonyms about the major trends of the day, viz. Romanticism (the philosophy of aesthetic existence, in theory and practice) and its intellectual form Idealism.

RESOLUTION AND SIGNIFICANCE OF ANXIETY. Anxiety as both a state and an experience points beyond itself, and this is an important aspect. Anxiety is the anguish of the spirit in the face of its unrealized, infinite possibilities as spirit, in the face of the "nothingness" which it as yet is.

---

[24] *CA*, p. 121; *S.V.*, IV, 402.

46 ANXIETY

On the other hand, while the possibilities are ambiguous and infinite, there is directionality, and it is vital for the overcoming of anxiety that the perceived direction be followed. Indeed, although anxiety arises from the fact of infinite possibilities, spirit has what may be called its specific and authentic possibility: a relationship in faith to God (although this can only be seen in retrospect and through Revelation). The title of Chapter V, "Anxiety as a Saving Experience by Means of Faith," clearly indicates where the discussion and, Haufniensis–Kierkegaard feels, anxiety lead – to a higher spiritual relationship.

The true significance of anxiety lies in the direction in which the experience leads – the evolution of spirit, the growth of the personality into a relationship with Absolute Spirit, for which the anxiety experience serves as a passageway. In the end, for Haufniensis, the attainment of faith represents the goal of spiritual evolution and the sole solution to overcoming the state of anxiety. Haufniensis distinguishes on several occasions between "overcoming" and "annihilating" anxiety and asserts that anxiety is never annihilated. It remains part of the structure within the incompleted synthesis which is human being. However, depending upon the stance one takes up, anxiety may be ineffectually suffered through time and again (if one does not utterly deaden one's sensitivity) or it may be gone through willingly as a transforming experience.

Such willingness to be transferred can only be actualized by an act of the will, an act which in turn can only come about after one has moved to the higher consciousness of human destiny by moving with the stirring of spirit through preceding stages.

Anxiety is thus the measure of a man,[25] nor merely in the sense of where he is going to in his evolution, but also where he is coming from. The anxiety primarily of concern in Haufniensis' work is the anxiety which constitutes an assault upon the infinite. Bondage to finitude was the result of a fall after the first confrontation with possibility in primal anxiety. But the state of anxiety endures, and a new anxiety experience arises in the condition of altered possibilities. By the stirring of spirit, a sensitivity and finally a revulsion against finitude develops, in *Melancholi* and irony respectively. When the anxiety experience comes the second time (i.e. after the fall), it is a thrust toward the infinite. For, as Haufniensis notes, "He then who does not wish to sink in the wretchedness of the finite is constrained, in the deepest sense, to assault the infinite."[26] In accepting and undergoing the anxiety experience this second time, a man finally cleanses himself from the finite and the petty[27] and begins the long assault upon the infinite. Thus, negatively speaking, the anxiety experience completes the break with finitude begun in the negative passion of irony, through the tormenting experience of the

[25] *CA*, p. 139, *S.V.*, IV, 421.

[26] *CA*, p. 144. Danish text reads: "Den, der da ikke ønsker at synke i Endelighedens Elendighed, han nødsages til den dybeste Forstand at gaae løs paa Uendeligheden." *S.V.*, IV, 426.

[27] *CA*, p. 142; *S.V.*, IV, 425.

ANXIETY

47

nothingness of one's unrealized possibilities. And from purification one moves to new possibility.

Anxiety is only the beginning of the assault; it constitutes but the initial movement in the direction of a God-relationship, in the consciousness of oneself as a being qualified by spirit. Anxiety indeed serves as the measure of a man: of his rising to higher consciousness, to a higher relationship to himself and to God – i.e. anxiety rightly understood and accepted. For what is crucial is learning *rightly* to be in anxiety.[28] In this case, anxiety serves as a saving experience, delivering one from the finitude, from which one was already in flight, over to the portals of the infinite. Haufniensis perceives that anxiety is only a stage, and that it too is left behind eventually as the development of spirit continues.[29] Accepting the cleansing anxiety experience can never serve as the solution to the full problem of oneself as a spiritually qualified being. But the higher spiritual realm and fuller resolution are left for the higher pseudonym Anti-Climacus to sketch, in the treatise on despair.

B. THE CONCEPT OF ANXIETY IN KIERKEGAARD'S OTHER WRITINGS

While anxiety as a crucial mood figures in very many of the published writings of Kierkegaard, and is mentioned in the Journals quite frequently as well, none of these other writings adds significantly to the understanding of the mood. As was the case with irony, the formal treatise sets out the subject in all its major aspects. Other writings present minor additional facets, or else explanations of what has already been written and published. Among the pseudonymous writings, those which can be singled out with regard to anxiety are *Either/Or, Fear and Trembling*, and *Sickness Unto Death*. Each of the three speaks of anxiety from a slightly different angle and with a different concern.

Anxiety figures in *Either/Or* as the root energy of the aesthete, as he attempts to flee from finitude with a demonic energy (anxiety for the good). But he is also fueled with the negativity of irony, as he tries to escape the world as well as his spiritual possibility. We will consider this more fully below in the analysis of the aesthete in Chapter Five.

In *Fear and Trembling*, we are presented with a higher anxiety, after the essential choice of life-direction has already been made. The anxiety of Abraham is anxiety within the religious and its higher calling. It is not anxiety before faith, but anxiety before the demands of faith. In Abraham's anxiety, the conflict is between the ethical and the religious,

---

[28] *CA*, p. 139; *S.V.*, IV, 421.

[29] Here perhaps the meaning of the two different metaphors which Kierkegaard applies to the three divisions of existence possibilities (the aesthetic, the ethical, and the religious), and which we apply to the moods as well, can be seen. *States* are spoken of, in so far as there are definite aspects of an existence possibility left behind; *spheres* in so far as there are underlying and overlapping aspects and structures which continue.

48   ANXIETY

unlike the aesthete who remains entirely under aesthetic categories as
he desperately flees evolution toward the ethico-religious.

Sickness Unto Death posits the important links between anxiety,
melancholy and despair. And the existential despair of which Anti-
Climacus speaks represents a movement further toward the discernment
of specific, authentic possibilities. *Sickness Unto Death* sees the dangers
of anxiety, as of despair, and warns against the possibility of being
misled by anxiety and perishing in possibility. By no means is arrival at
one's spiritual destiny ever assured – that destiny and demand expressed
by anxiety: that man be spirit.[30] *Sickness Unto Death* represents the
treatise on the highest mood in the spiritual evolution (before the
consolidating movement in the mood of resignation), and it maintains
the same psychological perspective and metaphysical theory of spirit
which we find in *Either/Or* and *The Concept of Anxiety*, as the implicit
theory of spirit becomes ever more explicit.

C. THE IDEA OF ANXIETY. THE EXPERIENCE AND STRUCTURE OF ANXIETY

In speaking of the "idea" of anxiety, and in seeking to outline it, we use
a term from phenomenology which speaks of essence. In using the term,
we remain, it is hoped, faithful to Kierkegaard, by not pretending that
the "idea" is the reality, that the intellectual apprehension of the mood
is the mood itself. Kierkegaard-Haufniensis distinguished, although
perhaps not always clearly enough, between the state of anxiety and the
anxiety experience. Since he always uses but the single term "anxiety,"
he sometimes causes confusion, since he may mean the one or the other
aspect, depending upon the context. Clearly, what is crucial with reference to the transformation of the personality beyond the aesthetic is the
anxiety experience, when consciousness confronts the possibility of
freedom. There are moments when such an experience comes to the
surface, but always proceeding from an underlying state or structure. It
is this essential structure with which we are here concerned. Whatever
pertains to the essential structure is also true of its manifestation in the
anxiety experience. However, the anxiety experience, since it is concrete, includes variables which do not pertain to the essence of the state.
Thus, for example, both primal anxiety and anxiety before the good are
manifestations in experience of the underlying state of anxiety in which
a man lives so long as he has possibility and freedom, i.e. so long as he
lives. But primal anxiety and anxiety before the good relate to different
sets of possibilities, because of the different state man is in in each
period, viz. innocence and sinfulness respectively.

Although the title of Haufniensis' work is *The Concept of Anxiety*, a
quick glance at the chapter headings reveals that much more is being

---

[30] *SUD*, p. 155; *S.V.*, XI, 136.

ANXIETY   49

considered. For example, the discussion of anxiety is constantly interwoven with that of sin. Here we attempt to pause and consider what Haufniensis' treatise never engages directly: the essence of the structure of anxiety.

OBJECTLESS. Haufniensis' points out that anxiety is an objectless fear, without relation to anything concrete and specific. It has no exterior reference and throws the subject back upon himself in his fear. Because there is no exterior object, the resolution of this fear is clearly not outside in the world of objects and things. Juliette Favez-Boutonier, in *L'Angoisse*, writes of a "something which anxiety may seem to be related to, but that even in such a case it is something which cannot justify the anxiety, and thus there is talk of a 'nothing'."[31]

THE NOTHING OF ANXIETY. It is clearly the nothing of anxiety which poses the greatest difficulty in understanding the mood. Later philosophers, particularly those of European Existentialism, have been highly influenced by Haufniensis–Kierkegaard's treatise. If Kierkegaard stretches language by speaking of a nothing which functions as a something, it is little by comparison to the "Das Nichts nichtet" of Heidegger (*Einführung in die Metaphysik*) and the "anéantir" of Sartre (*L' Être et Le Néant*). However, this is hardly a defense before critics of baffling neologisms. What Kierkegaard seems to be trying to say is that there is a "something" functioning which causes the shudder of anxiety and which potentiates its repetition. But this something is entirely vague and contentless, such that it can best be spoken of as "nothing." Later writers, à la Heidegger, begin to take the word apart by way of explaining and thus say that this "something" is no-thing: that it is man himself in his possibility for freedom which confronts man as he is, that an intuition of the potential self is at the base. This potential self is contentless and entirely in the realm of possibility until the real self moves toward actualizing it.

AMBIGUITY. In the anguished confrontation with one's possibility for freedom, there is a liking-fearing which renders the experience the more jarring because there is no emotional stability in the face of an inner quaking. Haufniensis speaks of a sympathy and antipathy, and emphasizes their overlapping by speaking of antipathetic sympathy and sympathetic antipathy. One fears what one likes, and likes what one fears. The liking has fear within it, as the fear has a certain liking within it also.[32]

---

[31] P. 47.

[32] This is much the same language in which Ruldolph Otto, in his celebrated work *The Idea of the Holy* (New York: Oxford University Press, 1950), speaks of the higher levels of religious experience: a "mysterium tremendum" which is *fascinans et tremendum*, which fascinates and entices at the same time as it terrifies and incites to flight. Since it is the religious self, grounded in the God-relationship and the God who is the Constituting Power of the synthesis, about which Kierkegaard speaks and toward which anxiety leads, one may not be going too far in linking the sympathy-antipathy to a vague intuition of the holy, religious dimension of the potential self.

50 ANXIETY

INTENTIONALITY. While anxiety is objectless and is characterized by ambiguity, there is nonetheless an intentionality in the experience. Anxiety is the possibility of freedom, but not an abstract or subjectless possibility. It is precisely the subject of anxiety which is never in doubt, for it is oneself as human being, as being qualified by spirit. The subject's possibility lies at the root of the anxiety experience. More specifically it is the subject's possibility of freedom in a higher subjectivity. Thus the anxiety experience points toward recovery of freedom, recovery of authentic possibility which is evolution as spirit.

In anxiety, the subject himself, the self, is *en cause*, not only as he is but as he can be. Anxiety is the wrenching away from a would-be static, unfree self and a thrust in the exciting-terrifying direction of one possibility: return to authentic ever-evolving selfhood. This higher self, precisely because it is who the subject shall be, is no "object" and, so long and in so far as it remains undefined and unrealized, is "nothing."

In the midst of the obscurity of the anxiety experience, here breaks forth revelation and clarity: that it is the self which is in question, not just as it is, but as it can be; that one is in an inescapable relationship to oneself; that one has the authentic possibility of recovering oneself and that it is to this task that one is called.

But this is a terrifying call from which one may well wish to flee. And since possibility is infinite, one may indeed flee into inauthentic possibilities, refusing to pass into freedom by the refusal to choose or else by the despairing choice of unfreedom. It is such flight which aesthetic life represents by its very nature; and to the degree that it is conscious of this, it is demonic in its flight.

D. ATTITUDES TOWARD ANXIETY

FLIGHT, OR THE ATTEMPT. Because people by nature always have possibility for change and development so long as they live, they always have anxiety. And because the structure of anxiety exists in the depths of their being (since they are always in relationship to possibility), the anxiety experience may at any time come to the surface. When the experience does come, the attitude which one takes up in relation to it is crucial. For the most part, people flee, and thereby they refuse to harness this storehouse of energy for spiritual transformation. But even the flight from anxiety is useless and represents defeat. For anxiety will come again, with equal force and equal terror, so long as it is not overcome. The battle with anxiety is a battle with oneself, the flight from it is flight from oneself – an effort that can never totally succeed, for one remains oneself no matter how externalized. Flight from the anxiety experience, in what Kierkegaard has called "anxiety for the evil" and "anxiety for the good," is the attempt to deny that one is qualified by spirit. More than any verbal denial, it is an attempt to ignore on an existential level the presence and movement of spirit. But because one cannot extinguish spirit, despite the metaphors of spiritual

ANXIETY

suicide, anxiety continues and the experience returns, with its attendant storms. Thus the flight from anxiety is not escape but rather surrendering oneself to the cyclone's wrath. Anxiety for the evil refuses to follow the movement through, seeks to cut it short and go no further, essaying as it does to substitute remorse for the true movement of repentance. Anxiety for the good refuses the movement altogether, from its very inception.

The result of such flight is no existential *status quo*, for anxiety is an energy, a force which will be spent, as is reflected in the agonized outcries of the aesthete, in the "Diapsalmata" of *Either/Or*. For here Kierkegaard presents a sensitive existence in whom the stirrings of spirit are coming to the surface, an existence which refuses to acknowledge their presence but cannot ignore the harrowing result.

TRANSFORMING ANXIETY. Just as anxiety cannot be annihilated by seeking to flee or ignore it, so can it not be annihilated even if one chooses to pass through it. As structure it remains, and as experience it returns. It is overcome when it is gone through and the personality is thus transformed.

In passing through anxiety, an essential choice is made by the self in an act of the will, which thus brings about an inner cohesion. Both an act of will and an act of choice are inwardly directed, for it is in an inner direction that anxiety points. All flight is the attempt to resolve it in an external direction. In pointing inward, anxiety confronts the individual with his own self as both the essential problem and the destiny (the higher self) in the struggle which compels him and in which he is thrust *in medias res*. In terms of the schematization of existence-spheres, the choice to pass through anxiety immediately moves one beyond aesthetic existence and into the ethico-religious; it is the movement of the individual's struggle from the external to the internal where its sole resolution is possible.

This choice results in the seriousness and the inwardness to which the unimpeded stirring of the eternal naturally leads. The anxiety experience brings the individual to the threshold of a new positivity. Above we observed how irony constituted a movement away from finitude, a negative movement of rejection and repulsion which as yet posited nothing new to replace what was thus negated. Anxiety constitutes the first assault upon the infinite which is to be the source of authentic positivity. Specifically, and in terms of Kierkegaard's religious psychology, this means that anxiety takes one toward the seriousness and inwardness of a God-relationship. But what is important here, and what Kierkegaard has guarded by his images, is that movement toward the God-relationship is the *natural* growth process within the person. Stopping-short, refusing to proceed is the unnatural process which would express the view that man is a static being who can find meaning within the existential bounds (the finite) which he himself delimits, arbitrarily, by refusing to acknowledge the existence of that which lies beyond.

52 ANXIETY

Anxiety is the energy arising from the movement of the spirit which feels the constraint of this boundary and seeks to burst beyond it, seeks to destroy the false boundary and restore the person to the realm of possibility into which his being's structure defines him and into which the dynamism essential to his being propels him.

E. ANXIETY AND THE AESTHETIC LIFE-VIEW

The essential crisis of the anxiety experience arises in aesthetic existence, precisely because aesthetic existence is the antithesis of all that one is called to as a spiritually qualified being. Aesthetic existence posits frivolity, fragmentation, and exteriority in place of the seriousness, wholeness and inwardness which the anxiety experience leads towards. Aesthetic existence is a static life-view which attempts to ignore the movement of spirit and seeks to flee in the face of its unmistakable revelation. It is basically defined as anxiety for the good, as the frivolous, the sudden, the moment fleeing before the possibility of seriousness and continuity.

Ironically, aesthetic existence is under the category of necessity even when it boasts of its freedom. It flees inner freedom and directs itself to manipulation of the exterior world and deceives itself into thinking this real freedom. But in the midst of arbitrary denial of the nature of human being as qualified by spirit and having an inner relation to himself, the anxiety experience summons a person back to himself, forces him to confront the possibility of inner freedom, the "nothingness" within. From the revelation of the possibility of an inner directedness to which a person would devote himself, one may finally flee. But one cannot flee the anxiety experience itself, nor the underlying state. Only by the choice of the self can its terror be overcome, in the modification of one's possibilities to re-establish the possibility of an on-going and developing God-relationship.

Anxiety continues in the religious life, as is evidenced in the anxiety of Abraham in *Fear and Trembling*. But since Abraham made the essential choices, anxiety for him had been overcome already, even if not extinguished. The overcoming lies within the aesthetic sphere, as one experiences the thrust and energy which would carry one toward spiritual transformation.

Anxiety then is not in itself a measure of subjectivity. For all subjects experience anxiety. What increases the measure of subjectivity, and transforms anxiety into a creative mood, is willing acceptance of the crisis phase and its attendant self-consciousness which allows one to profit from and pass through the experience, rather than merely enduring it. "Willing acceptance" means the courage to face a nothingness within and internalizing consciousness of it, in order to discover the possibility of authentic subjectivity.

CHAPTER III

MELANCHOLY

> Ich fühls, vergebens hab ich alle Schätze
> Des menschengeists auf nich herbeigerafft,
> Und wenn ich mich am End niedersetze,
> Quillt innerlich doch keine neue Kraft;
> Ich bin nicht um ein Haar breit höher,
> Bis dem Unendlichen nicht näher.
>
> – Goethe, *Faust*, 1. 1810–1815

Of the four cardinal moods in the analysis of aesthetic life, melancholy is the sole without a treatise formally and explicitly devoted to itself. Irony is the dissertation subject; anxiety and despair each are the subject of a treatise. Or, might it be that melancholy is the subject of a work after all?

The pseudonym Johannes Climacus, in the *Postscript's* review of the pseudonymous authorship, says of the two-part *Either/Or*:

The *first* part represents an existential possibility which cannot win through to existence, a melancholy *[Tungsind]* that needs to be ethically worked up. Melancholy *[Tungsind]* is its essential character ...[1]

In addition, Vigilius Haufniensis, in a footnote to *The Concept of Anxiety*, says that *Either/Or* Part I represents melancholy "in its anguished sympathy and egotism" which Part II then explains.[2]

If one accepts the claim-interpretation of Johannes Climacus (who among the pseudonyms so often speaks for Søren Kierkegaard) as well as the testimony of Haufniensis (who, as was remarked above, is a very thin pseudonym), then an attempt may be made to see how Part I of *Either/Or* can be understood as a work depicting melancholy, as the "missing treatise" on melancholy in Kierkegaard's authorship. This will become our task in these pages (in section B), as well as an attempt to discern a functioning "concept of melancholy" (the task of section D).

However, while melancholy functions prominently in *Either/Or* and other works, in no place does Kierkegaard explicitly formulate a concept of melancholy. In the course of this essay, one must ask why and attempt to answer.

In Kierkegaard scholarship to date, there have been two lamentable extremes in the treatment of this mood. The first presumes that the meaning of this opaque term of medieval medicine is clear and then passes over it quickly, alluding to its presence but never engaging it for

---

[1] *CUP*, p, 226. Danish text reads: "*Første Deel* er en Existents-Mulighed der ikke kan vinde Existents, et Tungsind, der ethisk skal arbeides op. Den er væsentlig Tungsind ..." *S.V.*, VIII, 213.

[2] *CA*, p. 39; *S.V.*, IV, 314.

54 MELANCHOLY

reflection. References to it are so obscure and so vague that the term has easily become a rival to the aesthete's favorite term "*Schnur*" in the "Diapsalmata" which, the aesthete notes, is used to mean so many things that it means nothing.[3] The second extreme contents itself with the observation that Kierkegaard was throughout his life melancholy, victim of an inherited melancholy, even pathologically melancholy. Since this is the more frequent form of treating melancholy in Kierkegaard, it deserves fuller comment.

While one can readily concede the prominence of melancholy in Kierkegaard's autobiographical statements, one must be wary of those who have succumbed to biographical distraction and thus no longer seem to recognize the term as playing a role in his thoughts on the aesthetic life. It seems to suffice to find an author melancholy and thereby justify the total disregard of any attempt to understand the term and its role in his thought.[4]

To be sure, the analyses and reflections on melancholy are anything but systematized in Kierkegaard's authorship or even collected in any one central place. They are scattered about in pseudonymous works where the life-views of the characters do not represent the real author's stance, but where reflections and insights into the moods often do.[5] Gathering these statements together may advance the understanding of this neglected mood and its functioning in the thoughts of Kierkegaard about the aesthetic life.

A. THE TERM "MELANCHOLY"

Before we can seek out the meaning of melancholy in the various pseudonymous works and then in the thought of Kierkegaard itself, we must first attend to language, which Kierkegaard loved so well. Without turning pedant, we should point out that there is far more going on in the Danish text than meets the eye of the English-language reader. One must of course guard against the foreigner's penchant for discovering

---

[3] *EO* 1, p. 35; *S.V.*, I, 20.

[4] In *La Mélancholie de Kierkegaard* of Marguerite Grimault (Paris, 1965) the author gives only a biographical account of Kierkegaard's melancholy, and succumbs to a frequent form of reductionism in Kierkegaard scholarship. The second part of Grimault's work contains a history of the psychoanalytic studies of Kierkegaard which, in their vast array of contradictory analyses, contribute far more to discrediting psychobiography and psychoanalysis' grasp of melancholy than to understanding Kierkegaard's personal situation.

With reference to psychoanalysis, it should be noted that Kierkegaard's own analysis of melancholy as a spiritual malady represents a challenge which psychoanalysis is yet to take up.

Had the author and psychoanalysts had Kierkegaard's appreciation of grammar and written in the subjunctive, *La Mélancholie de Kierkegaard* might have been an interesting hypothesis. Instead, the sole value of Grimault's work is to underline the abuses and neglect to which Kierkegaard's comments on melancholy have been subjected.

[5] This is confirmed by the Journals which often contain insights later placed into the mouth of a pseudonym.

MELANCHOLY 55

more in a language (in this case, Danish) than strikes even the linguistically sensitive native speaker. At the same time, one must remember the limitations and almost unavoidable mistakes in the enterprise of translating, especially in the case of so difficult and self-conscious an author as Kierkegaard. With these words of sympathy and warning, we try to take a new look at the terms used.

Precisely because Kierkegaard was so self-conscious a stylist, one must scrutinize terms. All the English translations render by the word "melancholy" a series of words in Danish, including nouns, adjectival substantives and adjectives. What is more noteworthy, and ultimately quite important, is that the Danish text evidences two different root words: *Melancholi* being the same Greek word from medieval medicine as we have in English and meaning literally "black bile," and *Tungsindighed* being a Danish-root word meaning literally "heavy-spiritedness." (German has corresponding terms, viz. *Melancholie* and *Schwermut*, which the German translators have been able to employ.) The two roots present two different images: blackness and heaviness.

The Danish terms which Kierkegaard uses are as follows:

(noun)	*Melancholi*	*Tungsindighed*
(adject.)	*melancholsk*	*tungsindig*
(subst.)	*den Melancholske*	*det Tungsind* (for person, *den Tungsindige*)

In our study, when reference is made to the two different roots, we will follow Kierkegaard's own usage of *Melancholi* and *Tungsind* to indicate the two degrees of the mood.

Walter Lowrie, the major English-language translator up to the present time, has made no mention of this difference, and he has rendered the various Danish terms uniformly by the English "melancholy," except for a place or two where he gives a variation such as "gloomy" for *tungsindig*.[6] There is one place in Part I of *Either/Or* where the pitfalls of translation can be seen. Both Danish terms occur in the same phrase – *der er eiendommelig for Melancholi og Tungsindighed* – rendered into the unfortunate English "which is characteristic of melancholy and heaviness."[7] In this instance, the translator has been forced to acknowledge two distinct words, but even then the fact that they both occur together does not lead him to suspect a difference of nuance or meaning. Let it be added that throughout this section, and within three pages of the essay on "The Immediate Stages of the Erotic," the Danish gives all these terms, while Lowrie always gives us "melancholy," except for the above noted exceptions. What Lowrie's often commendable translations lack, on this point and others

[6] *EO* 1, p. 74 line 20; *S.V.*, I, 57.
[7] English: *EO* 1, p. 75 line 28.
Danish: *S. V.*, I, 58.

56 MELANCHOLY

as well, is consistency of terminology, especially in key terms in Kierkegaard's thought. We have not found a satisfactory solution for the two Danish words, except to leave them here in the Danish, thus *Melancholi* and *Tungsind*. At points, Kierkegaard does use substantives, but our maintaining the most commonly employed forms of each root word is a step, it is hoped, in the direction of clarity and precision.

The use of so many terms by a writer might possibly be a stylistic attempt to avoid repetition of one word. And this does seem to account for some of the variations of each root word. A study of the text, and of the immediate context of each occurrence, suggests this. In addition, however, it reveals that there is a difference of meaning between the two distinct root words, a difference which corresponds to the not-always-strictly-adhered-to difference in common Danish usage. Indeed, the words correspond to and indicate two degrees of the same essential mood: *Melancholi* being lighter, having a certain sweetness and the associations of passivity which the word also has in English; *Tungsind* being deeper, heavier, more intense, closer to brooding, and with an element of reflection present in it.[8]

This distinction corresponds to Judge William's usage in *Either/Or* Part II where he makes only a few passing references to *Melancholi* in contrast to the serious mood *Tungsind* which he so forcefully analyzes and critiques. We will pursue the meaning of each term further below. Suffice it here to establish a difference of words and senses which, while they should not be unduly exaggerated, are important in understanding this mood.

B. MELANCHOLY IN *EITHER/OR*

MELANCHOLY AS REFLECTED IN THE STRUCTURE OF PART I

As contemporary reviews and Kierkegaard's own annoyance indicate, the effect of *Either/Or* upon the Danish readers of 1843 was overwhelming rather than thought-provoking as Kierkegaard had hoped. In our own day, the effect upon the uninitiated reader is much the same. The Danish literary public was bewildered by its size and format, and even further distracted from the content by the seemingly endless series of "Chinese puzzles" in which the author enclosed the work. The identity of the real author engaged much attention, and Kierkegaard must be considered responsible for encouraging this first, by writing a letter in his own name against the rumor that he was the true author and then by writing letters in the name of Victor Eremita, the pseudonymous editor

---

[8] It is generally accepted that, in Kierkegaard's use of words, when there is a parallel foreign-loan word in Danish, as there is in *Melancholi-Tungsind*, the corresponding Danish root word often has a special Kierkegaardian meaning. In this regard, compare also *Existents* and *Tilværelse*, "existence."

MELANCHOLY 57

of *Either/Or*. In all this, the content of the work receded while the structure and the mysterious author commanded attention.

We propose now to pursue Climacus' assertion that *Either/Or* was concerned with melancholy. Simply stated, how can we understand the work as a study of melancholy? In addition to the direct statements made about melancholy in the work, can we not take the work itself as mirroring the mood, in the concrete? Do the style and structure of the work not contribute, at least in part, to the analysis and depiction of melancholy?

A careful study of the structure of *Either/Or* goes far toward unravelling the meaning of the diverse papers which constitute *Either/Or*. Johannes Climacus has perhaps given us a key, if we require one, by telling us what to look for. A structural study may reveal how it was "hidden."

INTERNAL RELATIONSHIPS IN THE CHINESE PUZZLE. Part I numbers eight essays of varying lengths and styles. All have been collected and published in the happenstance order in which they were found, according to the pseudonymous editor Victor Eremita. There are subdivisions which can be made within the work, however, by way of re-grouping the essays. The "Diapsalmata" are a series of lyrical effusions and aphorisms. There follows an essay in abstract musical criticism, "The Immediate Stages of the Erotic." Next comes a triad of addresses to the "Symparanekromenoi" (loosely translated by Lowrie as "the fellowship of buried lives"): "The Ancient Tragical Motif," "Shadowgraphs," and "The Unhappiest Man." All three are psychological in tone. Next follows "The First Love," an appreciation of the play of that name, an essay in which the literary critic is carried away in his enthusiasm. The penultimate essay is the witty, biting, ironic "Rotation Method." The "ultimate" entry is the culmination of the aesthetic life, the celebrated "Diary of the Seducer."

There is no obvious coherence among the essays, although there are internal cross-references to suggest that all have the same author, even if Victor Eremita as editor had not already suggested this. The styles and tones have the following sequence: personal, musical criticism, psychological, literary criticism, ironic-witty, personal. Victor Eremita emphasizes that the ordering of publication simply corresponds to the order in which he found the papers in his desk. He does not add what is only obvious: that there is no logical progression in his presentation of the papers, although a more programmatic presentation would find "Rotation Method" toward the beginning, the "Diary" as penultimate, and "Diapsalmata" as the final entry. But, as they are, the very jumbled order of the papers is indicative of the life style of the young aesthete expressed in the sub-title of the work: "A fragment of life."

With regard to the "personal" papers in the collection, some additional observations are in order. The work begins with the highly personal, tortured outcries of a young man who has been living the sort of life abstractly embodied in the papers to follow. Thus we have the

58 MELANCHOLY

"result" of a life-view before we are even aware of the view itself. The title of the piece is itself striking, chosen by the editor Victor Eremita from among the loose scraps which comprise the "Diapsalmata." The ninety un-numbered diapsalmata (the word evokes "psalm") or "refrains" are *ad se ipsum*, "to him himself." The Latin phrase here is the intensive reflexive form of the personal pronoun, emphasizing the self-enclosed character, or closed-in-ness, of the writer – a characteristic to figure in his stormy, unquiet effusions. The work opens, after the pseudonymous editor's romantic story of how he found the papers, with an element of *fascinans et tremendum*. One is both attracted and repelled by the revelations of this closed-in-ness.

The essays which follow indicate in part why the young aesthete is in this desperate state. For they articulate, in moments when he is in intellectual good form and when mood has relaxed its hold, the attitudes which contribute to forming the life-view he has been living out. But the philosophy of life is carried to its climax in the "Diary of the Seducer." This last entry is the only one, besides the "Diapsalmata," which is personal and direct. All the other essays are concerned with aesthetic topics; and while the "Rotation Method" comes close to indicating a philosophy of life, it is the "Diary" which gives a record of it. What is significant about the publication of the "Diary" is a preface by the young aesthete who admits the "Diary" into the company of his papers but in which he denies that he is the author. There is enough internal evidence within the "Diary" to demonstrate the author of the "Diary's" awareness of the other essays and their content: the Don Juan legend, the stages of the erotic, the ancient tragical motif, shadowgraphs, the arbitrariness and experimentation are all echoed in the "Diary." Within this elaborate Chinese puzzle, the pseudonymous editor Victor Eremita indicates that he believes the young aesthete to be the same "Johannes" who is the author of the "Diary" but that Johannes is now afraid of his creation.[9] Victor Eremita is generally a good detective whose conclusions are to be followed. What is significant then is the aesthete's attempt to deny his authorship (within a work in which everyone denies authorship: the aesthete, Victor, and of course Kierkegaard as well). The anonymous pseudonym "A" claims that he is merely the editor of the "Diary" and adds that it is written in the subjunctive (Danish: *conjuntivisk*).[10] The closed-in-ness and refusal to reveal himself, which Judge William later analyzes as one of the major characteristics in the life-view of the aesthete, are simply mirrored in his attempts to hide his authorship. Moreover, we never directly learn the real identity of the aesthete, while "B," the author of Part II, indicates his own name in passing and tells us much about himself, in ethical contrast to the contrived reserve of "A."

STRUCTURE AND THE AESTHETIC LIFE. Before we even turn our attention to the content then, the "Papers of A" will have already told

[9] *EO* 1, p. 9; *S.V.*, I, xi.
[10] *EO* 1, p. 300; *S.V.*, I, 276.

MELANCHOLY 59

us much, not only about the aesthete himself, but about the way of life he follows.

THE FRAGMENTARY. The first emphasis in the work is upon the fragmentary. The title page proclaims the collection *Either/Or* "A Fragment of Life" ("*Livs-Fragment*") The papers themselves are "fragments" put together to make a whole by the pseudonymous editor. Within these fragments are others: the "Diapsalmata" are found on scraps of paper. Within the scraps themselves, there is no order, no whole, no continuity. The subtitle of the essay "The Ancient Tragical Motif" is "An essay in the Fragmentary." This first of three essays delivered at meetings of the Symparanekromenoi is itself a fragment within an evident unit. But the three are left as fragments, rather than gathered into a unit and made into a sub-division of the papers. There are several possible ways to order the papers, but, to repeat, the editor has left them in the happenstance, arbitrary, fragmentary order in which they were pulled from the writing-table.

The last reflection of the fragmentary is perhaps the term "melancholy" itself. The reader finds four different forms, two different root-words, in referring to the state of melancholy. Furthermore, within the essay "The Immediate Stages of the Erotic" where all occur within three pages (English: pp. 174–177; *S.V.* I, 154–156), they are found with what at first appears as no more reason than the whim of displaying the richness of the Danish language in expressing this mood. While there is a subtle difference between the root-words, there is no apparent reason to have used so many forms of each root.

CLOSED-IN-NESS. The second stylistic emphasis within the work is upon closed-in-ness. The "Diapsalmata" are written *ad se ipsum* and exhibit a morbid reserve torturing itself. The author of the papers never indicates his identity, and in that section which comes closest to revealing himself and his identity, viz. the "Diary," he attempts to insert a pseudonymous author "Johannes." According to Victor's romantic tale, of course, the papers were not published by their author but were hidden in a writing-table and only by chance did they come out of concealment into print. Thus whatever "revelation" does occur in the work does so "unconsciously" both in the sense that the "anonymous author" is not aware of the papers being published and also in the sense that he is not aware of how much he reveals about himself, in spite of himself and sometimes in his very attempts to conceal himself.

ALTERNATION OF MOODS. The sequence of themes in the essays represents an erratic alternation of moods. The first essay opens in Jobian style, with the victim lamenting his fate (except that he has no "Job's friends"). There follow essays which seek the heights of the abstract (in the case of the erotic, music being the highest form), psychological pastimes (subtitle of "Shadowgraphs"), a display of intellectual prowess and then of cynical wit ("Rotation Method"), followed by the cold and calculating "Diary."

INTELLECTUALIZING. The essays following the "Diapsalmata" intellectualize existence, revealing an author attempting to think his way

60 MELANCHOLY

through existence. The "Diary" is the record of action, of the philosophy of life as it has been carried out, after its theoretic development by the reflective aesthete in preceding papers.

The fragmentary, the closed-in-ness, the gamesmanship, the intellectual prowess of one minute vs. the desperation of the next, the lack of coherence – all in general have mirrored in the style and structure of Part I what will be confirmed and further defined in the reflective comments of the aesthete upon melancholy and then in William's analysis of it in Part II.

MELANCHOLY AS DESCRIBED IN PART I

Within *Either/Or* as a whole, there are two distinct sets of comments and reflections upon melancholy. First are the internal remarks of the melancholy aesthete himself. Although the aesthete is still prisoner of this mood, and suffering in this malady, he is a reflective melancholic and as such his observations, as well as outcries, merit careful attention. If an understanding from within the mood risks being overly subjective, it will be a contribution toward understanding nonetheless and can be better evaluated only after it is gathered together from its disjointed presentation. Part II of *Either/Or* presents the analysis and counsel of Judge William, a 32 year old ethicist who is more of a match for the young aesthete than he is usually given credit for. Despite his inability to edit his interminable and sometimes soporific letters, he brings flashes of insight which show in a penetrating way that the much-heralded, colorful aesthete is only attractive at first sight, that he is really a cacophony of moods which initially compel attention but cannot sustain it.

THE "DIAPSALMATA." The "Diapsalmata" represent a series of outcries and aphorisms. The ninety may be grouped into three general categories: 1) outcries of pain and suffering, 2) general reflections and cynical remarks born of sufferings and 3) small gems of self-analysis. In them all, the aesthete tells us much about how he feels about himself and about his world. At no time does he see a connection between his attitudes and his suffering – a connection which cannot but strike his reader. The theme of world-weariness runs throughout; existence has become stale. The aesthete is in fact tired of pleasure and desperately wishing for potentiality, and so he cries:

My soul has lost its potentiality. If I were to wish for anything, I should not wish for wealth and power, but for the passionate sense of the potential, for the eye which, ever young and ardent sees the possible. Pleasure disappoints, possibility never.[11]

He seeks power over himself and his external world. His defeat is

[11] *EO* 1, p. 40. Danish text reads: "Min Sjæl har tabt Muligheden. Skulde jeg ønske mig Noget, da vilde jeg ikke ønske mig Rigdom eller Magt, men Mulighedens Lidenskab, det Øie, der overalt evigt ungt, evigt brændende seer Muligheden. Nydelsen skuffer, Muligheden ikke." *S.V.*, I, 25.

MELANCHOLY   61

revealed in his being prisoner of his moods, anxieties, and thoughts – and so he cries:

And thus I, too, am bound in a chain formed of dark imaginings, of unquiet dreams, of restless thoughts, of dread presentiments, of inexplicable anxieties.[12]

His passionate frustration is reflected in his death-wish at an imaginary grave:

Why do we not finish it at once, why do we not stay and step down into the grave with him, and draw lots to see who shall happen to be the last unhappy living being to throw the last three spadefulls of earth over the last of the dead?[13]

His self-analysis revolves around the themes of 1) seeking self-mastery, 2) frustration and emptiness in barren existence, 3) passivity and indifference now to himself and the world, 4) an awareness of being closed-in, locked up in himself and isolated from others, 5) being a victim of moods and a mystery to himself, and 6) loving his melancholy and sorrow. He is here in an implicit and not-too-subtle crisis of the will: he is destroying himself, and yet he *will* do nothing about it. For that which he has willed to do cannot solve his problem. The life of pleasure has left him barren, yet he has willed only pleasure, thus ignoring his own insight: "How absurd men are. They never use the liberties they have, they demand those they do not have."[14]

We will not be "stealing the fire" of Judge William if we posit here a connection between mood and life-view. For Johannes himself in one of his lucid self-observations notes, "The result of my life is simply nothing, a mood, a single color."[15] The basic mood in which and against which the aesthete is so ineffectually struggling is melancholy. The mood leaves him passive, apathetic.

I do not care for anything. I do not care to ride, for the exercise is too violent. I do not care to walk, walking is too strenuous. I do not care to lie down, for I should either have to remain lying, and I do not care to do that, or I should have to get up again, and I do not care to do that either. *Summa summarum*: I do not care at all.[16]

[12] *EO* 1, p. 33. Danish text reads: "Saaledes er ogsaa jeg bunden i en Lænke, der er dannet af mørke Indbildninger, af ængstende Drømme, af urolige Tanker, af bange Anelser, af uforklarede Angester." *S.V.*, I, 18.

[13] *EO* 1, p. 29. Danish text reads: "Hvorfor gjør man det ikke af paa eengang, hvorfor bliver man ikke derude, og gaaer ned med i Graven, og trækker Lod om, hvem den Ulykke skal times, at være den sidst Levende, der Kaster de sidste tre Spader Jord paa den Sidste Døde?" *S.V.*, I, 13–14.

[14] *EO* 1, p. 19. Danish text reads: "Menneskene ere dog urimelige. De bruge aldrig de Friheder, de har, men fordre dem, de ikke har..." *S.V.*, I, 4.

[15] *EO* 1, p. 28. Danish text reads: "Mit Livs-Resultat bliver slet Intet, en Stemning, en enkelt Farve." *S.V.*, I, 12.

[16] *EO* 1, pp. 19–20. Danish text reads: "Jeg gider slet ikke. Jeg gider ikke ride, det er for stærk en Bevægelse; jeg gider ikke gaae, det er for andstængende; jeg gider ikke lægge mig ned, thi enten skulde jeg blive liggende, og det gider jeg ikke, eller jeg skulde reise mig op igjen, og det gider jeg heller ikke. *Summa Summarum:* jeg gider slet ikke." *S. V.*, I, 4.

62 MELANCHOLY

In terms of his relation to himself, he feels not only prisoner of the moods which issue from himself but entirely closed-in, locked in upon himself.

Cornelius Nepos tells of a certain commander, who was closed-in in a fortress with a considerable force of cavalry, and who ordered the horses to be whipped every day...so I live these days like one besieged...[17]

I am as shrunken as a Hebrew *shewa*, weak and silent as a *daghesh lene*; I feel like a letter printed backwards in the line, and yet as ungovernable as a three-tailed Pasha, as jealous for myself and my thoughts as a bank for its notes, and as generally introverted as any *pronomen reflexivum*.[18]

These diapsalmata indicate an important dimension of this psychological situation: a great force at work within the spirit or psyche of the young man. The very fact of being closed makes the force so violent, drives him to tiring himself out with tears in the first instance and leaves him victim of an ungovernable energy in the second. "Over my inmost being there broods a depression, an anxiety, that presages an earthquake."[19] Here is the source of the anguish and pain of his poet's existence: he is locked up inside himself with an energy which he can neither understand nor control. And even if he reaches the poetic, where moans and cries are transformed into ravishing music,[20] essentially, he never achieves more than pleasing an audience. After the energy is spent, after some of its force is reduced (the earthquake imagery is quite rich here), he stumbles about exhausted, awaiting always another bout with this non-directed, and hence demonic, energy from within.

The type of melancholy here is *Tungsind*. The images of heaviness, seriousness and gloom have recurred throughout. The passion and frustration of the aesthete, as well as his reflection, take him well beyond the sweet, passive *Melancholi* of youth and romances. The energy which causes such havoc within him, because he has not found the way to release it properly, is already evidence of a stirring of spirit about which Judge William will speak in Part II. However, spirit's stirring is countered by passivity of the will and this remains an essential problem, as William will point out.

"THE IMMEDIATE STAGES OF THE EROTIC." In this highly abstract essay upon the erotic, including an appreciation of Mozart, the anonym-

---

[17] *EO* 1, p. 21. Danish text reads: "Cornelius Nepos fortæller om en Feltherre, der blev holdt indesluttet med et betydeligt Cavelleri i en Fæstning, at han hver Dag lod Hestene Pidske...saaledes lever jeg i deene Tid, som en Beleiret...." *S.V.*, I, 5–6.

[18] *EO* 1, p. 22. Danish text reads: "Forknyttet er jeg som et *Scheva*, svag og overhørt et *Dagesch lene*, tilmode som et Bogstav, der er trykket bagvendt i Linien, og dog umaneerlig som en Pascha af tre Hestehaler, iversyg paa mig selv og mine Tanker som Banken paa sine Seddel-Skriverier, overhovedet saa reflekteret i mig selv som noget *pronomen reflexivum*." *S.V.*, I, 6.

[19] *EO* 1, p. 28. Danish text reads: "Over mit indre Væsen ruger en Beklemmelse, en Angst, der ahner et Jordskjælv." *S. V.*, I, 13.

[20] *EO* 1, p. 19; *S.V.*, I, 3.

MELANCHOLY

63

ous aesthete gives us the most sustained treatment of his understanding
of melancholy. To be sure, melancholy is not the primary concern in this
essay; it enters in as a phenomenon within the erotic.

The author, for all his superior insight and critical ability, reminds the
reader from the outset that he himself is lost in the phenomenon he is
about to describe. For despite the brilliance of the essay, mastery of
thought has not carried over to mastery of existence. In fact, it is the
contrary: thought has left him more victim than ever and he confesses
this:

...I shall beg Mozart to forgive me, because his music did not inspire me to
great deeds, but turned me into a fool, who lost through him the little reason I
had, and spent most of my time in quiet sadness humming what I do not
understand, haunting like a specter day and night what I am not permitted to
enter.[21]

The aesthete analyzes the three stages of the musical erotic, among
which melancholy is treated in only the first stage, viz. the Page in
"Figaro." But first he posits an understanding of spiritual history. Thus,
the discussion of this mood also can only be understood in the context of
spiritual history and spiritual evolution. The author sees Christianity as
positing sensuousness in the world. For Christianity brought spirit into
the world. making something that was already there stand out in relief
as the "sensuous."[22] All comments about the sensuous relate to the
epoch of spirit, in which the conflict and tension between spirit and
sensuousness is posited.

The author finds the awakening of the sensuous symbolically expressed in Mozart's "Figaro," in the character of the Page.

The sensuous awakens, not yet to movement, but to a hushed tranquility; not
to joy and gladness, but to a deep melancholy [Melancholi].[23]

Awakening without movement occurs in the mood of *Melancholi*. Desire is not yet awake, although the object of desire is present and
possessed in an ambiguous way. This is a form of *non-desiring possession
of the object of desire, prior to the desiring*. Sleeping desire and its object
are understood and described in primal unity before any movement
occurs.[24]

---

[21] *EO* 1, pp. 46–47. Danish text reads: "...og Mozart vil jeg bede at tilgive mig, at
hans Musik ikke begeistrede mig til store Bedrifter, men gjorde mig til en Nar, der over
han tabte den Smule Forstand, jeg havde, og nu som oftest i stille Veemod fordriver Tiden
med at nynne hvad jeg ikke forstaaer, som et Spøgelse Dag og Nat lister mig omkring
hvad jeg ikke kan komme ind i." *S.V.*, I, 32–33.

[22] *EO* 1, p. 74; *S.V.*, I, 57.

[23] *EO* 1, p. 74. Danish text reads: "Det Sandselige vaagner, dog ikke til Bevægelse, men
til stille Qviescents, ikke til Fryd og Glæde, men til dyb Melancholi." *S.V.*, I, 57.

[24] This section is highly evocative of Creation Mythologies where a primal unity is
spoken of prior to the action of some separating agent, usually a Cosmic Hero, who
breaks the primal unity and thus potentiates a new, higher unity. It is not going too far to
speculate that the young Kierkegaard, having read widely in mythology and folk-tales,
might have been influenced here by this notion.

64 MELANCHOLY

In another sense, the object of desire is *not* possessed because it is not desired, and the result is sadness and melancholy. Unawakened desire is charmed and frightened by its object and becomes melancholy because it cannot come to the point of desiring. Awakened desire would bring about and experience a gap between the desire itself and the object of desire, if it could find the way to desire, to come to movement.

However, active desire is not really possible, since the "object" cannot become an object of desire in an active sense. For the true object of desire is infinity which cannot become an *object*.[25] Were there a concrete object which could be desired but not attained, the result would be pain and sorrow rather than melancholy which revolves around an impossible object.

Behold then the contradiction within desire. In one sense there is an object, even for unawakened desire, and this object is somehow already contained within the androgynous, unproductive union with desire. In a deeper sense, there is no object, since infinity cannot truly be an object which one can possess. Thus one is in a situation in which one cannot be freed from the hold over oneself of an object-which-is-no-object. Because of this contradiction, and the intensity produced by the unattainability of the object of desire, the result is *Melancholi* and *Tungsind*. *Melancholi* is the innocent, passive and unawakened desire for the impossible object; *Tungsind* is also desire for the impossible object, but already with some awareness and intensity present. The ambiguity of the object-which-is-no-object constitutes the sweetness associated with *Melancholi*,[26] while it later constitutes the gloom and heaviness of the reflective form *Tungsind*.

The sensuous is linked exclusively to *Melancholi* because of its non-reflective quality. *Melancholi* is the expression of, and is caused by, the profound inner contradiction of desiring an impossible object which in another sense one is already united to and thus possesses. *Tungsind* is the heavy, gloomy and critical phase which sets in as unawakened desire is prolonged and then intensified and frustrated as it moves toward reflection upon and awareness of non-possession. *Tungsind* is thus reflective, pained non-possession of the impossible object of desire: infinity.

The above sketch of a highly complex and obscure passage in "The Immediate Stages of the Erotic" might well represent a riddle, did the aesthete not indicate in the following essay that this first stage is really desire for the One ideally (with obvious Plotinian echoes).[27] The riddle might even be formulated thus: What is it that one possesses and desires dreamingly, yet because it is not desired will-fully is not possessed? Were it not for the qualification that the object is an impossible one, one might answer "the Self." But this is the answer to a higher riddle, in

[25] *EO* 1, p. 75; *S.V.*, I, 58.

[26] *Ibid.*

[27] *EO* 1, p. 83; *S.V.*, I, 67. Also Cf. Plotinus' *Enneads*.

MELANCHOLY 65

which melancholy is but one aspect. For the riddle of the Self is solved by all the moods, in a dialectic of moods.

It is in the second of the three stages of the erotic that desire awakens. With this, the state of dreaming desire is ended and a state of seeking commences. Object is separated from desire and disperses itself in the manifold (in which the aesthete will pursue it). In the third stage, desire truly desires: amidst the manifold, it chooses one particular and makes it absolute. It thus desires a particular absolutely and concretely in contrast to the first stage which dreamily desires the one (or absolute) ideally and abstractly. In the latter stages, melancholy does not figure in the discussion. It is restricted to the first stage, according to the aesthete's thinking, where one experiences the *Melancholi* and *Tungsind* of desiring the one (The One) ideally. In the sensuous desiring of Don Juan, the phase of desiring the one is left behind, and his object becomes the particular – any particular – elevated to absolute significance.

SYMPARANEKROMENOI ADDRESSES. In the three addresses delivered to the "Fellowship of Buried Lives," the aesthete provides further insight into the significance of reflection for the basically melancholy nature. We recall that the form of reflective melancholy is *Tungsind*, the more serious and critical form. In this essay, the image of the transparent term *Tungsind* is explained: the movement of reflection within the melancholy personality accentuates or brings about a heavy (*tung*) quality within the spirit.

In "The Ancient Tragical Motif as Reflected in the Modern," the aesthete, in contrasting our age to that of the Greeks, associates *Tungsind* with responsibility,[28] which stems from the movement of reflection within the melancholy man. The essay also associates reflection with heightened suffering.[29] What becomes clear here is that the movement of reflection brings one first to a sense of responsibility and then in suffering to a sense of pain and guilt. Reflectively, one comes to the awareness that one personally has some responsibility for one's suffering, that one does not suffer innocently (as was the first impression in *Melancholi*).

In "Shadowgraphs," the aesthete speaks of a person in whom blood flows backwards. He is the reflective man who still remains under aesthetic categories, who in his sorrow becomes more silent and withdrawn into himself. He tends to turn grief into "reflective grief." The reflective man's silent grief has little or no outward manifestation, but its power wreaks an inner vengeance upon the reflective man himself, driving him ever deeper into himself. The aesthete speaks thus of it:

... outwardly everything is quiet and calm, and far within, in its little secret recess, grief dwells like a prisoner strictly guarded in a subterranean dungeon,

---

[28] *EO* 1, p. 140; *S.V.*, I, 119–120.
[29] *EO* 1, pp. 145–146; *S.V.*, I, 126.

66 MELANCHOLY

who spends year after year in monotonously moving back and forth within his little enclosure, never weary of traversing sorrow's longer or shorter path.[30]

The aesthete acknowledges this as a morbid condition, likely to come about in an overly reflective nature. A reflective nature within the aesthetic, as we have noted, leads to *Tungsind* and, as the gloom of *Tungsind* deepens, the eventuality of succumbing to this self-destructive, silent grief seems the natural result of a nature already locked in upon itself, devouring itself in reflection upon its sufferings.

The third address, "The Unhappiest Man," also speaks, although not explicitly, of the reflective man. It speculates upon the unhappiest man, but the description implies an already reflective nature. The unhappiest man might be described in the terms of the much later Heidegger as someone suffering acutely from conflicting temporal ecstases. That is, man within time has a relation to the past and the future; he stands out in such a temporal relation, or ecstasis. The healthy relation to the future is hope, and to the past is memory. In both directions, he finds an aspect of himself: the self that was, the self that will be. However, the unhappiest man suffers a disorientation in time, and is in a sense without time. Because of a conflict between hope and memory, memory prevents him from finding himself in hope, and hope prevents him from finding himself in memory.[31] In both cases, the reason is that he does not stand in proper relation to the *present*. The consequences are a misrelation to past and memory on the one hand and to future and hope on the other.

The unhappiest man combines silent grief and pain with the reflection stressed in the immediately preceding essays:

For there he stands, the ambassador from the kingdom of sighs, the chosen favorite of the realm of suffering, the apostle of grief, the silent friend of pain, the unhappy lover of memory, in his memories confounded by the light of hope, in his hope deceived by the shadows of memory.[32]

JUDGE WILLIAM ON THE SUBJECT OF MELANCHOLY (*EITHER/OR*, PART II)

Part II of *Either/Or* contains three letters to the aesthete by an older man (called "B" in order to parallel the designation of the anonymous aesthete as "A"). "B" reveals in passing that his name is William. In so doing he immediately sets up a contrast between himself and the studiously concealed aesthete. Self-revelation stems from and charac-

---

[30] *EO* 1, p. 169. Danish text reads: "... det Udvortes er stille og roligt, og inderst inde i sin lille Afkrog level Sorgen som en velforvaret Fange i et underjordisk Fangsel, der henlever den det ene Aar efter det andet i sin eensformige Bevægelse, gaaer frem og tilbage i sit Aflukke, aldrig traet af at tilbagelægge Sorgens lange eller korte Vei." *S.V.*, I, 149.

[31] *EO* p. 223; *S.V.*, I, 198–199.

[32] *EO* 1, p. 227. Danish text reads: "Thi der staaer han, Udsendingen fra Sukkenes Rige, Lidelsernes udkaarne Yndling, Sorgens Apostel, Smertens tause Ven, Erindringens ulykkelige Elsker, in sin Erindren forvirret af Haabets Lys, i sin Haaben skuffet af Erindringens Skygger." *S.V.*, I, 202.

MELANCHOLY 67

terizes the ethical life which William proposes as an alternative to the desperate ways of the aesthete. Part II consists of two major letters of equal size, followed by a smaller letter which contains a sermon by a Jutland pastor introduced by William. The letters' piercing analyses of the bankruptcy of aesthetic existence go into many areas beyond the scope of this section. Here we will consider only the analysis of melancholy. Other aspects of William's larger analysis will figure below in the section on despair.

Part II opens with a quote from Chateaubriand, the meaning of which is the thrust of William's critique, viz. that to deal with the passions in one's solitude is to give them complete sway over oneself: "Les grandes passions sont solitaires, et les transporter au désert, c'est les rendre à leur empire."[33]

FIRST LETTER: "THE AESTHETIC VALIDITY OF MARRIAGE." The theme of the first letter is the preservation of the best of the aesthetical in the higher, ethical state of marriage. Here William contrasts marriage and first love: on the one hand existence which has duration because of commitment and recognition of the presence of the eternal in oneself and in the relationship and on the other hand existence which consists of endless beginnings, of momentary bursts of enthusiasm never carrying over beyond the moment which breeds them.

William sees a connection between the young aesthete's style, which in his own view represents so many of the unfortunately glamorized tendencies of the times, and the melancholy from which he believes the aesthete is suffering. (The aesthete has already admitted melancholy as his problem.) In the second letter, William says that he believes he is in a position to understand melancholy, because he himself is beyond it. Having reached a higher plane, he has a certain objectivity about the problem. He is no longer victim of the seductive power of melancholy which saps the will and leaves one passive.[34]

Melancholy, according to William, is the aesthete's stumbling-block and principal problem. It is the problem of the age as well:

People have now been talking about the frivolity of this age; I believe it is now high time to talk a little about its melancholy [Tungsind]...Or is not melancholy the defect of our age? Is it not this which echoes with frivolous laughter, is it not melancholy which has deprived us of courage to command, of courage to obey, of power to act, of the confidence necessary to hope?[35]

[33] EO 2, p. 1; S.V., II, 1.

[34] EO 2, pp. 183–184; S.V., II, 162–163.

[35] EO 2, p. 24 Note here a play on words, which has some bearing on the full appreciation of the passage. The contrast between frivolity and melancholy is better seen in the Danish in the two words Letsind (literally: light-mindedness) and Tungsind (heavy-mindedness). Danish text reads: "Man har nu talt længe nok om Tidens Letsind, jet troer, et er paa den høie Tid at tale lidt om dens Tungsind...Eller er Tungsind ikke Tidens Brøst, er det ikke den, der gjenlyder endog i letsindige Latter, er det ikke Tungsind, der har berøvet os Mod til at befale, Mod til at lyde, Kraft til at handle, Tillid til at haabe?" S.V., II, 22. Note too that in Part II, except for a few occasional references to Melancholi, William talks exclusively of Tungsind as the problem to be analyzed.

68 MELANCHOLY

William considers A's fragmented life-view of moments as the probable result of a combination of a "melancholy which is partly egoistic, partly sympathetic."[36] He defines the difference between the two forms thus: egoistic melancholy fears for itself and is self-indulgent, like all melancholy. It is self-consciously defiant. It cannot give itself or commit itself to anything because it is always awaiting the sudden arrival of the ideal.[37] (This corresponds to A's own analysis of melancholy as the desire for the one ideally.) Sympathetic melancholy, on the other hand, is more painful, nobler and is further distinguished from the egoistic form by the fact that it is fearful of itself for the sake of the other.[38]

William's attitude throughout this letter is highly critical of the mood. He constantly remarks that it is essentially involved with the closed-inness of the aesthete, to which he contrasts the openness of the married man, and with the outwardness of the aesthete, to which he contrasts the inwardness of the married man.[39]

William gives no sustained treatment to melancholy. Although he considers it an essential problem, his references to it are episodic, and perhaps even digressions from the main argument of the letters. Still, the references and comments are frequent. And in the second letter, he gives his passionate and penetrating judgement of melancholy.

SECOND LETTER: "EQUILIBRIUM BETWEEN THE AESTHETICAL AND THE ETHICAL IN THE COMPOSITION OF THE PERSONALITY." In this letter, William elaborates more completely his ideas about melancholy. He considers it an essential problem within the aesthete's life and a direct result of the aesthete's maintained life-view (for even the refusal to choose or to reform a life-view is still a life-view).

After alluding to the melancholy of Nero, William proceeds to the attack and says, "I attach myself to an earlier church doctrine which reckoned melancholy among the cardinal sins," and this in strong opposition to a tendency of the age to consider melancholy as a sign of greatness.[40] Melancholy (in the form of *Tungsind*) is sin, *instar omnium*, because it is the refusal to will.[41]

The above remarks are perhaps clearer within the larger context of William's thought. William too subscribes to a theory of the evolution of spirit, against which melancholy works. On the individual level, the evolution of spirit becomes visible in a marked way precisely around the age of the aesthete, a youth of 25 years.

... There comes a moment in a man's life when his immediacy is, as it were, ripened and the spirit demands a higher form in which it will apprehend itself as

[36] *EO* 2, p. 25; *S.V.*, II, 23.
[37] *EO* 2, p. 25; *S.V.*, II, 23.
[38] *EO* 2, p. 26; *S.V.*, II, 24.
[39] *EO* 2, p. 155; *S.V.*, II, 138.
[40] *EO* 2, p. 190; *S.V.*, II, 168.
[41] *EO* 2, p. 193; *S.V.*, II, 171.

MELANCHOLY

69

spirit. Man, so long as he is immediate spirit, coheres with the whole earthly life, and now the spirit would collect itself, as it were, out of this dispersion and become in itself transformed, the personality would be conscious of itself in its eternal validity.[42]

Thus William believes in an evolution of consciousness, in which the eternal element, man's spiritual dimension (his eternal validity) comes to the fore. "If this does not come to pass, if the movement is checked, if it is forced back, melancholy *[Tungsind]* ensues."[43] The movement is checked precisely by the refusal to will, the refusal to affirm the stirring of the spiritual dimension. Spirit moves to collect itself out of the dispersion in which it finds itself.[44] Any check of this produces a reverse effect in which dispersion is accentuated, in which concentric movement halts and the eccentric increases.

Implicit here then are two stages: the initial stage of dispersion at the moment when spirit begins to stir, and a later stage of further dispersion because of the refusal to will. The first stage corresponds to the usage elsewhere of *Melancholi.* The latter stage is *Tungsind,* is sin and guilt. Here is refusal to will. Thus William can say that a man becomes melancholy (*tungsindig*) only by his own fault.[45]

"What then is melancholy *[Tungsind]*? It is hysteria of the spirit."[46] It is the refusal of spirit to come unto itself in a higher form, to become transformed. (Cf. the theme of transformation apropos of melancholy in the *Repetition* as well.) The result is spirit's wild flight away from itself, the *de facto* attempt at spiritual suicide.

The attempt to flee self-creation is self-enfeeblement. The initial passive *Melancholi* becomes heavier, gloomy (*tungsindig*) as the will weakens itself in refusing to will. William rebukes the aesthete and says that one must deplore the fact that *Tungsind* (heavy-mindedness) or *Letsind* (light-mindedness) has enfeebled his spirit.[47] From William's vantage point, the aesthete weakens himself and gives himself over to *Tungsind* insofar as he will not reverse dispersion and affirm himself, and this can only appear as light-mindedness or madness to one who understands both the process at work within spirit and the only possible

---

[42] *EO* 2, p. 193. Danish text reads: "Der kommer et Øieblik i et Menneskes Liv, hvor Umiddelbarheden ligesom er modnet og hvor Aanden fordrer en høiere Form, hvor den vil gribe sig selv som Aand. Som umiddelbar Aand hænger Mennesket sammen med det hele jordiske Liv, og nu vil Aanden ligesom samle sig ud af denne Adspredthed, og forklare sig i sig selv; Personligheden vil blive sig bevidst i sin evige Gyldighed." *S.V.,* II, 170.

[43] *Ibid.* Danish text reads: "Skeer dette ikke, standes Bevægelsen, trykkes den tilbage, saa indtrær Tungsind." *S.V.,* II, 171.

[44] Cf. Heidegger on *Befindlichkeit* and *Verfallenheit* in *Being and Time,* section 29, p. 172ff. and section 38, p. 219ff. respectively.

[45] *EO* 2, p. 190; *S.V.,* II, 168.

[46] *EO* 2, p. 193. Danish text reads: "Hvad er Tungsind? Det er Aandens Hysteri." *S.V.,* II, 170.

[47] *EO* 2, p. 163; *S.V.,* II, 145.

70   MELANCHOLY

solution. "...The spirit will not let itself be mocked, it revenges itself upon you, it binds you with the chain of melancholy."[48]

Yet melancholy has a positive side. Judge William states this explicitly and adds that only the most sensitive natures are subject to it.[49] That is, only those natures with a great potential for spiritual transformation find themselves victims of melancholy. Those of less sensitive nature never reach the critical state of *Tungsind*. There may be occasional moodiness, a *Melancholi* which surfaces from time to time. It is, however, with the sensitive spiritual nature that Judge William, and Kierkegaard, concern themselves throughout. Without melancholy, there simply is no metamorphosis.[50] If one asks why Judge William addresses the problem of the more highly sensitive nature, one might reply that this is the case concretely before him in his friend the aesthete. If one asks the question of Kierkegaard, one might imagine that he had somewhat the same purpose as Plato in the *Republic* when Socrates seeks Justice writ-large so as to see it more easily. When he will later seek it on a smaller scale, he will then know the clear outlines. For Kierkegaard, the problems of the spiritual life – of potentialities and pitfalls – are more clearly visible in a more sensitive nature.

William's advice to the sensitive and suffering aesthete is to master melancholy in the actualization of spiritual potentiality.[51]

In order to live, you must acquire mastery over your innate melancholy...This melancholy has been your misfortune, but you will see the day when you yourself will admit that it has been your good fortune.[52]

This good fortune consists of the potentiality for self-realization evidenced in the sensitive nature of the melancholy aesthete.

William does not ask the aesthete to try to penetrate to the ground of his melancholy. He has already judged the aesthete's psychological observations, even if valuable, as nothing more than the result of a "hypochondriac curiosity"[53] which will lead the aesthete nowhere. William views A's intellectuality as only so many attempts to distract himself from melancholy, without facing up to the central problem. The judge tells him that he will never understand melancholy until he has transcended it,[54] and therefore that he should move on toward the

---

[48] *EO* 2, p. 208. Danish text reads: "...Aanden lader sig ikke spotte, den hævner sig paa Dig, den binder Dig i Tungsinds Lænke." *S.V.*, II, 184.

[49] *EO* 2, pp. 193–194; *S.V.*, II, 171.

[50] *EO* 2, p. 194; *S.V.*, II, 171. While the authorship is concerned with the analysis of special cases, it must be emphasized that, in setting out both the ethical and the religious, Kierkegaard pointed out over and over that they were open to everyman and not reserved to the especially gifted.

[51] *EO* 2, p. 194; *S.V.*, II, 171–172.

[52] *EO* 2, p. 293. Danish text reads: "For at Du skal kunne leve, maa Du see at blive Herre over Dit medfødte Tungsind...dette Tungsind har været Din Ulykke, men Du skal see, der kommer en Tid, Du selv vil tilstaae, at det har været Din Lykke." *S.V.*, II, 259.

[53] *EO* 2, p. 8; *S.V.*, II, 8.

[54] *EO* 2, p. 193; *S.V.*, II, 170–171

MELANCHOLY 71

transcending immediately. Such transcending can only come about, for reasons we will see more clearly below, through the movement of despair, and so William repeats again and again his call: "Despair!"

So, then, despair with all your soul and with all your mind; the longer you put it off, the harder the conditions become, and the demand remains the same.[55]

The despair spoken of here is the first movement of choice, and the discovery of the "eternal man"[56] in passing from current ailment to spiritual destiny.

... This self of which I despair is a finite thing like every other finitude, whereas the self I choose is the absolute self, or myself according to its absolute validity.[57]

(Despair will be treated extensively in the following chapter.)

William says, "Despair, and never more will your spirit sigh in melancholy [Tungsind]..."[58] However, this remark is modified in two places. William's meaning here is that melancholy (as Tungsind) is essentially overcome by despair as an act of will affirming, even in helplessness and remoteness, one's spiritual destiny. However, the fulfilling of one's spiritual potentiality is always relative fulfillment. No one is fully transparent to himself, no one totally overcomes original sin (we have already seen the links between sin and melancholy in the chapter on Anxiety). Thus Judge William admits that even the man who makes spiritual movements will always retain a little melancholy (lidt Tungsind).[59] He says that this is occasionally the case with himself when something melancholy (noget melancholsk) in his temperament gains the ascendency. (Note here, that it is not the brooding, desperate Tungsind of which he speaks, for this has been overcome, although above he has spoken of retaining a little melancholy: lidt Tungsind.) He adds that it is his wife who helps him with this "something melancholy" and thus brings the discussion full circle back to marriage as the symbol of a life in which choices have been made, in which self-revelation takes place, in which one moves beyond closed-in-ness and selfishness.

William's analysis is not fundamentally different from that given, in part unconsciously, by the aesthete himself in Part I. It is a more essential analysis which the good judge gives us, however. A's was descriptive and intellectual; B's is practical as well as positing the deeper

---

[55] EO 2, p. 213. Danish text reads: "Saa fortvivl da, af Din ganske Sjæl og af al Din Tanke, jo længere Du udsætter det, jo haardere blive Vilkaarene, og Fordringen den samme." S.V., II, 187.

[56] EO 2, p. 214; S.V., II, 188.

[57] EO 2, p. 223. Danish text reads: ".,, det Selv, jeg fortvivler over, er en Endelighed, ligesom enhver anden Endelighed, det Selv, jeg vælger, er det absolute Selv, eller mit Selv efter sin absolute Gyldighed." S.V., II, 196.

[58] EO 2, p. 223. Danish text reads: "...Fortvivl, og Din Aand skal aldrig mere sukke i Tungsind." S.V., II, 196.

[59] EO 2, p. 194; S.V., II, 171.

72 MELANCHOLY

ground, man's spiritual calling, which is the ground of melancholy never fathomed by the aesthete so long as he remains the observing intellectual who never acts. The aesthete speaks of "Grundens til dens Melancholi"[60] as a profound inner contradiction. William, as one beyond the essential problem, goes to the root of both *Melancholi*, which he associates with spiritual movement, and *Tungsind*, which he associates with the desperate attempt to refuse this movement. In the process, the inner contradiction of which the aesthete speaks is placed in broader perspective. As the aesthete seeks the awakening of desire, William sees the awakening of spirit.

C. MELANCHOLY IN *REPETITION* AND *STAGES*

THE *REPETITION*.

The *Repetition* is the sort of puzzle which Kierkegaard delighted in. As usual, it is pseudonymous, the purported author being the ironist Constantine Constantius. In the *Papirer*, Volume IV, Kierkegaard writes that "like Clement Alexandrinus I have tried to write in such a way that the heretics could not understand it."[61] He has probably had more success than he wished here, for the work is not only devilishly entangled but speaks of a new category whose reality is obscured by its puzzling name, viz. repetition.

The work provides the opportunity for commentators to succumb once again to biographical fascination because of so many thinly veiled autobiographical references here. The story parallels in great part Kierkegaard's own unfortunate romance with Regine Olsen and her reaction to his attempts to break the engagement. Kierkegaard, like Constantine, went to Berlin, where he wrote most of the book and hoped, as did Constantine, for an external form of repetition.[62]

Repetition is essentially concerned with an inner repetition, and the importance of this is stressed by repeating the title at the beginning of Part II of the work. The inner repetition is a transformation of the spirit which happens only in a movement toward the future, but it has an aspect of recovery about it and thus its nominal relation to the past. For what is transformed is that which is recovered, viz. the self. The eternal dimension of the person is uncovered only to be termed "recovery." In distinction from the Platonic category of recollection (which is movement backwards, as Constantine notes), the forward movement must be stressed, as well as the fact that repetition is a deed, whereas recollection is intellectual.

[60] *EO* 1, p. 77; *S.V.*, I, 60.

[61] *Side* 280; quoted by Lowrie in *Repetition*, p. 11.

[62] Kierkegaard hoped for the restoration of his relationship with Regina by virtue of the absurd. Cf. also *Fear and Trembling*, published the same day. Constantine seeks repetition in the theatre, in Berlin life. The use of so many German phrases is undoubtedly the result of tourist Kierkegaard-Constantine's stay in Berlin as well.

MELANCHOLY 73

Within *Repetition*, melancholy plays a significant role. The use of melancholy is consistent with the usage of the other pseudonyms. What is stressed in this work is the sensitivity and potentiality for spiritual development indicated by melancholy and, in part, brought about through its agency.

The slim poetic novel relates the story of a young man in a crisis of melancholy and of an engagement. Constantine points out that the very presence of enduring melancholy in a man in love significantly discredits the usual superficial analysis of melancholy as merely the need to fall in love.[63] Constantine acknowledges that the story of the young man's engagement is one simple enough, but the fact that it is elevated to such significance by him tells us something about him and his sensitivity. We are dealing with a poet—

... if for no other [reason], that an occurrence which, if it had happened to a commonplace man would quietly have come to nothing, assumed in his case the proportions of a cosmic event.[64]

It is to the ground of this sensitivity that Constantine seeks to penetrate – but Constantine himself, our observant psychologist, is an ironist and thus not himself essentially beyond the problem of melancholy where he might have the perspective of a Judge William.

The melancholy of the young man attracts the attention of Constantine who observes that the young man is beginning to give signs of reaching maturity of spirit.[65] His sensitivity, which is related to melancholy, has the soul of the young man in turmoil, and not only about the love affair. In a letter to Constantine, he writes:

Every morning I lay aside all the impatience and infinite striving of my soul – to no avail, the next instant it is there again.[66]

The melancholy and its attendant sensitivity represents a double snare. On the one hand, it is a seductive power. The very sensitivity, which is not yet beyond the girl renders her more attached to him. "Nothing is more seductive to a young girl," notes the psychologist Constantine, "than to be loved by a poetically melancholy nature."[67] On the other hand the initial sensitivity of the young man makes it difficult for him to go through the seemingly insensitive action of breaking the relationship, and Constantine suspects that the young girl is trying to make a captive of the young man by his *Melancholi*.

[63] *R*, p. 38; *SV.*, III, 177–178.

[64] *R*, p. 137. Danish text reads: "... om ikke paa andet saa derpaa, at en Begivenhed, der hvis den var hændt et trivielt Menneske, var bleven i god Ro og Mag til ingen Ting, for ham svulmede ot til en Verdensbegivenhed." *S.V.*, III, 264.

[65] *R*, p. 36; *S.V.*, III, 175.

[66] *R*, p. 120. Danish text reads: "Hver Morgen aflægger jeg al min Sjæls Utaalmodighed og uendelige Stræben, det hjælper ikke, i næste Øieblik, er den der igjen." *S. V.*, III, 248.

[67] *R*, p. 41; *S.V.*, III, 180; "poetisk-tungsindig."

74 MELANCHOLY

Observing the young man in his relationship, Constantine notes that a melancholy (*tungsindig*) longing is actually leading the young man by degrees to forsake the beloved.[68] For what is happening is that a *melancholsk* young man has fallen in love and by degrees feels the need to get out of the relationship because of a deeper and still unconscious crisis developing, viz. *Tungsind*. As he moves into *Tungsind*, he moves beyond her and begins to recognize that she was not his love but instead only "the occasion of awakening the primitive poetic talent within him and making him a poet."[69] She is only the visible semblance of something higher which he is seeking.[70]

The young man has simply moved beyond the young girl. She has acted as a catalyst in turning him in his sensitivity into a poet, in moving him from an initial *Melancholi* to *Tungsind* which demands a higher solution. Constantine notes that now, even if the young girl were to die, it would not matter much.

So again the girl is not a reality but a reflection of the movements within him and their exciting cause ... what gives her importance is not herself but her relation to him. She is as it were the boundary of his being.[71]

This is as far as Constantine takes his analysis with its roots in his "ideal" interest in people, an interest which he pursues in all those in whom the idea is in motion.[72] What this pseudonymous commentary stresses about melancholy is its role as agent in moving a man toward inner transformation. In Constantine's tale, the young girl suddenly marries, the young man is free and comes back to himself – and this Constantine recognizes as a repetition. Constantine has learned that a higher and true repetition is inward (in contrast to his Berlin experiences). In its completed movement, sensitivity set into motion by the stirring of the eternal takes one through the two degrees of *Melancholi* and *Tungsind* to the demand for resolution in a higher transformation. (It should be noted that the young man of *Repetition* never moves into *Tungsind* within the work, although Constantine sees its coming.) In the chapter on Despair, the need for transformation will be pursued further.

[68] *R*, pp. 89–90; *S.V.*, III, 220–221.

[69] *R*, p. 40. Danish text reads: "... der vakte det Poetiske i ham og gjorde ham til Digter." *S.V.*, III, 179.

[70] *R*, p. 44; *S.V.*, III, 182. This recalls the "Anima" in Jung's religious theories of the Unconscious. According to the Jungian analysis, what would have happened in this story is that, after an initial anima-captivation through falling in love with the anima-bearer, the young man wins through to a consciousness of this and will now be satisfied with nothing less than the Anima itself. Here again the problem of the aesthete of *Either/Or* enters in – the desire for something ideally. Constantine does not tell us how the young man might find this "something higher" concretely, whereas Jung would talk of uncovering the feminine aspects of the masculine psyche.

[71] *R*, p. 89. Danish text reads: "Pigen er da igjen ingen Virkelighed, men en Reflex af Bevægelserne i ham og Incitament for disse ... det, hvorved hun har Betydning, er ikke sig selv, men ved Forholdet til ham. Hun er ligesom Grændsen for hans Væsen ..." *S. V.*, III, 220.

[72] *R*, p. 83; *S.V.*, III, 215.

MELANCHOLY

STAGES ON LIFE'S WAY Stages on Life's Way, insofar as it addresses itself to the problem of melancholy, is concerned with *Tungsind*. And, excepting one brief mention in "Various Observations About Marriage,"[73] the discussion of melancholy is reserved to "Guilty?/Not Guilty?." Published in 1845, *Stages* is a reiteration of aesthetic and ethical positions, with the addition of the religious as the third stage or existence-sphere. The pseudonymous characters who make a reappearance are changed: Johannes the Seducer is older and more cynical, Judge William is ten years older and develops a somewhat different argument in defense of marriage, other characters are more completely drawn in "In Vino Veritas." What particularly concerns our discussion is the third part of *Stages*, Frater Taciturnus' psychological experiment and passion narrative entitled "Guilty?/Not Guilty?." This "novel" is embellished by the tale of the diary being found in a lake – a tale subsequently denied in Frater Taciturnus' Epistle to any readers who manage to finish the book. Here Taciturnus admits that he conjured up and fashioned the character Quidam (as well as the absent presence "Quædam," or young girl).

"Guilty?/Not Guilty?" consists of morning and evening diary entries which for the most part are from the same dates over the course of seven months. The morning entries trace the crisis in the engagement of a melancholy man, in each instance "a year ago" from the date of the entry. The midnight entries trace the crisis which has developed in trying to break free of the broken engagement. In addition to constantly pondering the question of guilt expressed in the title, the author of the diary, who is termed Quidam (Latin: "someone") reveals a spiritual problem as the basis of the rupture – a spiritual problem which is reflected in his melancholy (*Tungsind*).

In the morning entries (which refer to one year previous) the writer gradually comes to realize the impossibility of his marrying. This impossibility is directly connected with a melancholy whose deeper roots he also comes to understand by degrees. He realizes at first that melancholy (*Tungsind*) is his very nature[74] and that he does not want to bring another into it and inflict its miseries upon her. But he begins to perceive at the same time that the young girl has no "spiritual nature" and that his own agitated spiritual nature is at the base of his melancholy. By degrees, he moves beyond her and beyond the relationship – at the same time seeing that the familiar saying that marriage is the cure for a young man's melancholy is simply not true for him. After exploring the relationship and discovering its limits, he writes:

This ideal figure which I embraced with the anxious responsibility of an eternal obligation became in fact something less, something so inconspicuous that I

---

[73] Page 171; *S.V.*, VI, 166–167.

[74] *SLW*, P. 189; *S.V.*, VI, 186: "Mit Væsen er Tungsind."

76   MELANCHOLY

could hardly descry her. My *[Tungsind]* was as if wafted away by the wind, I beheld what I had before me – heaven and earth! a saucy little miss![75]

The realization does not really take away his melancholy, but it moves him beyond the young girl. There is an element of ambiguity in his statements. For he refers on several occasions to the morbid reserve (*Indesluttethed*; closed-in-ness) which is connected with his melancholy and which means that he cannot fulfill a marriage's ethical obligation of self-revelation to the beloved. When he sees the necessity of breaking the engagement, he writes, "My melancholy has triumphed after all."[76]

The problem of guilt with which his conscience wrestles throughout the diary entries moves him by degrees towards a crisis, beyond what he terms the lethargy of melancholy.[77] He becomes aware of the melancholy whose weight consists in seeking ideality;[78] and the spiritual roots of his love crisis and of his melancholy become clear to him. He becomes aware that the religious is the sole solution for his melancholy:

My *[Tungsind]* searches in every direction for the dreadful. Then it grips me with its terror. I cannot and will not flee from it. I must endure the thought; then I find a religious composure, and only then am I free and happy as spirit.[79]

Even as he regrets that melancholy makes a confidant impossible, he notes the religious basis for melancholy:

A confidant will not think my melancholy idea so passionately as I do, and so will not understand that for me it is a religious starting-point.[80]

He sees more and more clearly that melancholy, something which a confidant might urge him to remedy by a marriage, is a pull to a higher plane:

But the strange ideas of melancholy I do not give up; for these, which perhaps a third person would call crotchets, which she perhaps would sympathetically call distressing fancies, I call pulls – if only I follow them and hold out, they lead me to the eternal certainty of the infinite.[81]

---

[75] *SLW*, p. 251. Danish text reads: "Denne ideale Skikkelse, som jeg omfavnede med en evig Forpligtelses bekymrede Ansvar, hun blev jo rigtignok noget mindre, saa uanseelig, at jeg knap kunde opdage hende. Mit Tungsind er som blæst bort, jeg seer hvad jeg har for mig: Død und Pestilence saadan en lille Jomfru!" *S. V.*, VI, 252.

[76] *SLW*, p. 295; *S.V.*, VI, 298: "Mit Tungsind har dog seiret."

[77] *SLW*, p. 246; *S.V.*, VI, 246.

[78] *SLW*, p. 322; *S.V.*, VI, 327.

[79] *SLW*, p. 342. Danish text reads: "I enhver Retning opsøger mit Tungsind det Forfærdelige. Nu griber det mig med hele sin Rædsel. Undflye det kan og vil jeg ikke, jeg maa holde Tanken ud; da finder jeg en religieus Beroligelse, og da først er jeg fri og lykkelig som Aand." *S.V.*, VI, 349.

[80] *SLW*, p. 343. Danish text reads: "En Fortrolig vil ikke tænke min **tungsindige** Idee med den Lidenskab, som jeg, og altsaa heller ikke forstaae, at den bliver mig et religieust Udgangspunkt." *S. V.*, VI, 350.

[81] *SLW*, p. 345. Danish text reads: "Men Tungsindets sære Ideer opgive jeg ikke, thi disse, hvad maaske en Trediemand vilde kalde Nykker, disse, hvad hun deeltagende maaske vilde kalde sørgelige Indfald, kalder jeg Rykkere: naar jeg blot følger dem og holder ud, da føre de mig til Uendelighedens evige Vished." *S.V.*, VI, 353.

MELANCHOLY 77

In terms of the scheme of the existence-spheres, Quidam is a character who is wrestling with ethical categories but who, while standing within a mood which most would regard as strictly limited to the aesthetic, sees and experiences a pull to a higher plane.

In his Epistle, Frater Taciturnus analyzes the character whom he has created. He sees Quidam's problem as essentially religious in nature; Quidam as not an aesthetic hero, i.e. one who has his opposition outside himself (and is thus by implication a potential religious hero, or one who has his opposition within himself).[82] His *Tungsind* is the "condensation of possibility."[83] Marriage is not the solution; rather, he needs to enter further into crisis before solution will come. The condensed possibility which confronts him is nothing less than the possibility of religious subjectivity[84] and this condensed possibility is linked directly with melancholy which "must be gone through with in the experience of a crisis if he is to become clear to himself in the experience of the religious."[85]

Frater Taciturnus makes a distinction between the melancholy of poets, artists and thinkers and that of the religious man, but in confusing terms. He says that there is a difference between *Tungsind* and *Tungsind*,[86] between "melancholy" and "melancholy." The melancholy of each individual is special, but there are also different types of melancholy. Taciturnus dismisses the melancholy of the artists as warmed-up sufferings, connected with self-doubts, whose religious dimension will only be evident at a much later point.[87] The melancholy of the religious man accompanies him as he moves through the stages between the immediacy of the aesthetic and that of the religious.

He must be aesthetically developed in imagination and must be able to conceive the ethical with primitive passion in order to be properly offended at it, so that the pristine possibility in the religious man may break its way out in this catastrophe.[88]

As has been pointed out, *Stages* represents in the main a restatement of themes of previous pseudonymous works. The theme of melancholy, which is so central to the aesthetic existence-sphere, is of course once again orchestrated. As is the case for other themes, one finds variations,

[82] *SLW*, p. 370; *S.V.*, VI, 379.

[83] *SLW*, p. 385; *S.V.*, VI, 396.

[84] *SLW*, p. 388; *S.V.*, VI, 399.

[85] *SLW*, p. 388. Danish text reads: "... der gjennem en Krise maa gaaes igjennem, for at han kan blive sig selv klar i det Religieuse." *S.V.*, VI, 399.

[86] Interesting here, and necessary to point out, is the fact that Taciturnus uses here the term *Tungsind* of both poets and the religious man. One might have expected *Melancholi* vs. *Tungsind*. Might it be that Taciturnus here is referring to a melancholy which is already advanced to a heavier state? *S.V.*, VI, 400.

[87] *SLW*, p. 390; *S.V.*, VI, 401.

[88] *SLW*, p. 390. Danish text reads: "... Han maa være aesthetisk udviklet i Phantasi, maa kunne fatte det Ethiske med primitiv Lidenskab, for rigtig at støde an, at det Religieuses oprindelige Mulighed i denne Katastrophe kan bryde frem." *S.V.*, VI, 401.

and the variation for melancholy consists essentially in making explicit the religious ground of melancholy and the necessity of passing through the crisis of melancholy and on to a religious resolution.

D. TOWARDS A CONCEPT OF MELANCHOLY

From the array of analyses of and comments upon melancholy by :psuedonymous aesthetes, by ironists and ethicists, can we finally arrive at a concept of melancholy? First, let us reassert that there are no contradictory analyses among the pseudonyms. Apparent differences represent only different degrees of understanding, from the melancholy aesthete of *Either/Or*, who is immersed in the problem, to Judge William, who claims to have surmounted it. A distinction between two essential degrees of the state of melancholy is maintained consistently, as textual observations above have established. It remains to be asked at least, if not answered, why Kierkegaard did not formulate a concept of melancholy explicitly. He recognizes melancholy as a problem in his pseudonymous characters, in his own family, and in the age itself, yet he never explicitly gives a sustained discussion of his *concept* of this mood. In saying this, of course, we imply that there is a concept of the mood functioning all the time in the writings. We may speculate that, had Kierkegaard given a concept of the mood, he might have been guilty of the aesthete's mistake: trying to come to grips intellectually with a problem for which intellectual analysis may say nothing. Certainly at the point when he penned *Either/Or* he was far more concerned with solutions. His own maieutic method, especially in its early uses, emphasized indirect communication to a high degree. If one accepts the statement of *The Point of View for my Work as an Author* that he needed to win people over before he could set them on the right path, one sees the advantage of an indirect, artful critique of melancholy over an abstract treatise which would have had much smaller appeal. (One need only compare the fate of *The Concept of Anxiety* and *The Sickness Unto Death*, treatises both, against *Either/Or* in terms both of sales and audience appeal in order to see that his point is well taken.) According to his plan, such a treatise never could have accomplished his purposes, however much it might have simplified for later ages the task of discerning his understanding of melancholy.

We then, of this later age, who here refuse to be led off by Kierkegaard to ethical choice and the task of becoming a Christian, are left with the task of attempting to discern that concept. This abstract enterprise will have its critics among those who already have their own interpretation of melancholy. And Kierkegaard's understanding of melancholy, as it is here interpreted, clearly presents a definite challenge to other interpretations. But the challenge and the debate cannot be taken up until the concept is itself articulated.

MELANCHOLY 79

Romano Guardini in *De la Mélancholie*[89] says that melancholy is the sorrow caused by the childbirth of the eternal in a man. This image can be viewed as the essence of the many diverse comments upon melancholy in the pseudonymous works.

MELANCHOLI AS A GIVEN. Within the analyses of melancholy, we are always confronted with a melancholy which is "given." It is there and to be accounted for: no state is entirely without melancholy, either before a crisis within the personality develops, or even after the essential problem is resolved. This aspect of *Melancholi* is the innocent throb of suffering within the sensitive nature, which is an indication of sensitivity and religious potentiality. *Melancholi* indicates a personality which has already been impregnated with the eternal, with a spiritual dimension, but still gestating. In the language which is so frequent in the authorship, spirit sleeps. However, it is present and will awaken. Awakening comes about as the result of a natural dynamism within the evolving personality. The beginning of the evolutionary movement has been called the stirring of spirit. The image here is important. For it speaks of an agitation, by the laws of inner necessity, in the depths of the personality. The agitation seeks a resolution, a calming – something which comes about only relatively and only through a transformation of personality.

As the stirring increases, a conflict begins to become apparent between one's way of life and the movement itself. For the given, posited way of life in which one finds oneself living is the "natural" state beyond which the dynamism of spirit calls one. The natural state is not to be entirely abandoned, but rather modified and transformed (*aufgehoben*).

DEMAND FOR THE ABSOLUTE. The stirring within the personality indicates that an encounter with the Absolute is sought, with the grounding and transforming Power. Longing for the Absolute may be termed a "metaphysical wound" within the personality. For it seeks its healing, and ultimately can only find it, in religious experience in which the Absolute is encountered – a wound which festers so long as it is not healed, yet in some sense permanent: it is never entirely healed. For even after the essential solution is discovered and transformation of the personality takes place, one finds an enduring melancholy indicating that the process of transformation is never entirely completed.

The demand for the Absolute, the Ideal, the One, which is sensed vaguely does not indicate of itself where such an encounter can take place. But the experience of searching for an external solution, in frantic activity or in love or in intellectual distraction, results in only so much frustration. For melancholy is a reflexive emotion. Emotions are generally directed outwards, toward some object (as in love, hate, etc.). Melancholy has no object, in two senses. First, it has no object because the Absolute, the Infinite, is an impossible object for it (understood in the external sense). The finite personality cannot encompass or even reach the Absolute in an external sense. Second, it has no object

---

[89] (Paris, 1953), translated by Jeanne Ancelet-Hustache, p. 80.

80 MELANCHOLY

because the "object" which is ultimately the solution is the self and is not properly an object. Melancholy is an emotion which is "about" the self, which seeks the incorporation of an element of the Absolute, of the Eternal, in which it already participates in a nascent sense. We recall that the aesthete of *Either/Or* recognized a desire for the Absolute as being at the root of melancholy (*Melancholi*), and that in Part II Judge William stated that the solution for melancholy (*Tungsind*) is despair in which one chooses the self, thus affirming the spiritual dynamism within the personality by an act of the will. This affirming act of the will is the *sine qua non* for the cohesive movement underway in the personality.[90]

INTO *TUNGSIND*. While there is no clear line of demarcation between the two degrees of melancholy, *Tungsind* indicates that the state of melancholy is taking on a new seriousness and is more urgent in its demand for solution. *Tungsind* is a natural development of the state, as spirit begins to stir very actively. A new degree of reflection enters in. One perceives the problem in a new seriousness; one begins to recognize that one's present state is responsible for the continuation and aggravation of this "wound." Guilt enters into consciousness as well, as one recognizes that no outside agent is responsible for this suffering, that indeed only oneself is responsible, so long as no solution is found.

The heaviness of melancholy, of which the image in *Tungsind* speaks, is constituted by the "burden of the self" which is felt more and more. The refusal to will is the refusal to lift the weight. One senses the task to become a centered personality, to allow and affirm centripetal movement in the personality. As long as this is refused, the more the heaviness presses down. At the same time, a tension mounts so long as this energy toward transformation is not properly channelled, as it can be only by an act of the will. The result of this unspent energy is chaos within the personality in which centrifugal movement is brought about, in which eccentric movement develops (and eccentricity emerges).

There is no automatic resolution of the mounting crisis in the personality, except the choice involved in an act of will. To return to the image of childbirth, we here view a situation in which the labor pains continue rather indefinitely, fluctuating in intensity. Only the highly gifted and highly sensitive nature feels the problem acutely. Those of little sensitivity are relatively untroubled, although there are minor periods of moodiness. The sensitive nature will feel the problem in recurring periods of intensity so long as it does not resolve it.

CONSEQUENCES OF NON-RESOLUTION. One consequence of the refusal to will is the enfeeblement of the will itself. Melancholy has an aspect of passivity about it, but the longer it continues the more spiritual lethargy grows. Correspondingly, the gloom of melancholy increases. Refusal to move toward cohesion of the personality leaves one fragmented, and

---

[90] This makes sense of the comment by Judge William, "I am the Absolute." This can be translated "I am the absolute which I desire," "I am the absolute which I choose." For it is the self, as participating in the Absolute, in the Eternal, of which he is speaking.

MELANCHOLY 81

this state is aggravated by mis-channeling of the energy of transformation. Enfeebled in will, one is ever more the victim of moods, riding crests of enthusiasm and despair. At the same time, this objectless, reflexive emotion increases one's isolation so long as it is not resolved. Thus one is not only the prisoner of moods but prisoner of oneself, locked in upon oneself, closed-in and unable to get outside. One is driven ever deeper into oneself. The sole exit from this problem remains the same: despair issuing from an act of the will (and meaning choice of self, of the ethical and the social). The fact that the aesthete of *Either/Or* refuses to make the act of the will leads him to speak of "empty birthpangs, sensual and tormenting" precisely because he refuses the childbirth of the eternal in the personality.

In Kierkegaard's analysis, we have dealt with characters who refuse to choose the only possible solution. The solution itself is to be far more complex than the simple word "despair" might suggest. For the solution too is one of degrees. In this section, we have spoken of the solution of melancholy as it applies to the aesthetic life. But we have already suggested the solution, viz. the religious, which begins beyond the aesthetic and which ultimately is the solution for despair as well.

CHAPTER IV

DESPAIR

In the strictest sense, the discussion of despair cannot be separated from that of anxiety, for the analysis of anxiety leads naturally into the consideration of this, its intensified form. Thus in one sense the discussion of despair should have followed that of anxiety. However, the ordering here is meant to correspond to the order in which the crisis phase of each mood arises, a matter which will be more fully set out in Chapter Six.

Anxiety and despair are more integrally allied than are any of the other moods here considered. They can and should be considered separately, since indeed they are not identical. But in allowing pen and ink to reflect the separation which abstraction can make between these two degrees of the experience of potentiality, we must in fairness smudge the ink, as it were, in order to show that the separation is less than entirely neat. There are of course differences between the two, but these are rather in the nature of refinements.

Gregor Malantschuk, in *Kierkegaard's Thought*, says that *The Sickness Unto Death* may be regarded as a dialectical continuation of the discussion in *The Concept of Anxiety*.[1] In addition, Professor Malantschuk notes in Kierkegaard's *Papirer* the frequent references to the relationship between anxiety and despair.[2]

Our discussion of despair will be based principally upon *The Sickness Unto Death*, with further insights offered by the earlier *Either/Or*, Part II. The Journals and Discourses provide yet additional material. However, the mood receives its direct and sustained presentation in the thinly pseudonymous work of Anti-Climacus. More than any of the other three cardinal moods here considered, it is directly and exhaustively treated in a single treatise. (*The Concept of Anxiety*, we recall, despite its title, begins not as a treatise on anxiety but rather as a psychological investigation oriented toward the dogmatic problem of original sin.)

---

[1] Page 339.
[2] Cf. VIII[2] B 166 ff.

DESPAIR

83

In the consideration of despair, while we move along the same land mass to a higher plane, we move, as in anxiety, in a hitherto seldom charted region. And while Kierkegaard-Anti-Climacus' treatise exhibits impressive dialectical organization, the terminology is once again not entirely clear. In the writings, the term "despair" has two senses as action: 1) the initial saving act of choosing (to become) the self and 2) the taking on of sin-consciousness. Despair is, in addition, an enduring structure in the depths of the person which reflects the level of self-realization.

Despair as a structure has basically to do with the quality of interrelation among the elements constituting the human synthesis, with the added element of a relationship to the Constituting Power of the synthesis. The existential interest of despair clearly revolves around, first, the initial saving act of despair and then, secondly, the later critical despair experience before forgiveness. Both these phases constitute the crisis in the state of despair where a higher phase of spiritual evolution and consciousness is at stake.

But the crisis moment of despair stands at the very boundary line of the aesthetic sphere which has been the principal terrain of this study. The act of despair, which is Judge William's passionate counsel to the aesthete (cf. Chapter Five for the analysis of the aesthete) takes one beyond the aesthetic and into the ethico-religious as soon as the choice of the self is made.

The higher crisis and wrenching experience in a higher consciousness that one is in despair – that one is not the self and not merely responsible *to* oneself for this condition but also responsible *before* God – is firmly within the sphere of the religious, and thus well beyond the aesthetic. However, a consideration of the full scope and many degrees of despair is in order, by way of outlining phases in the rise of the subjectivity toward which despair presses one. Aesthetic existence is profoundly in despair from the first moment of fall into sin, in primal anxiety. Then the non-synthesized self is, as it were, stirred potentially toward higher personal evolution and consciousness.

It is interesting and noteworthy that the pseudonymous author of *The Sickness Unto Death* never offers a solution to despair. Vigilius Haufniensis, even if only indirectly, suggested the solution to anxiety by emphasizing it as a phase and positing a higher phase to be gone through, by which anxiety would be overcome. And the final section of *The Concept of Anxiety* announces clearly the direction in which the solution is to be sought, although it does not say how one is to arrive at it (cf. Chapter V, "Anxiety as a Saving Experience by means of Faith").

Anti-Climacus, of the *Sickness Unto Death*, although a religious pseudonym, offers no solution to despair when experienced at its highest and most intense levels. The cure for despair is rather proposed in the *Edifying Discourses in Various Spirits*, especially "Purity of Heart."[3]

---

[3] Cf. Malantschuk, *Kierkegaard's Thought*, p. 347.

84 DESPAIR

For with the higher phases of despair we reach the limits of the natural man. The natural evolution represented by the movement of spirit and the stirring of the eternal will not take one through the final crisis to a resolution. A natural growth of consciousness and inwardness takes one from the waking moment after first sin through the infinite negativity of irony, the crisis of the vague experience of possibility in anxiety, and the crisis of *Tungsind* – finally into the experience of specific possibility in despair.

But the specific possibility experienced in despair, viz. that of a God-relationship for one who is a sinner, cannot be realized simply by the evolution itself. It is as if one has moved to the edge of a cliff and experiences the call and destiny to reach the other side, but no natural leap can take one to this new ground. The evolution has taken one through to the highest level of natural consciousness (within the epoch of Christian Revelation), viz. sin-consciousness. But for resolution and further advance, outside and super-natural help will be necessary, viz. the grace of forgiveness. And even if the Christian man presses forward supported by the promise of such grace, he no longer moves on his own power, for he experiences here intensely the helplessness of his finitude in the face of destiny characterized by infinitude.

A. PRELIMINARY CONSIDERATIONS

In addition to the natural conceptual links which ally the moods of anxiety and despair, according to which despair is viewed as an intensification of anxiety, there exist stylistic links within the respective treatises, which strengthen theoretical and existential connections. *The Concept of Anxiety* was published about mid-way within the aesthetic authorship proper by the pseudonym Vigilius Haufniensis. *The Sickness Unto Death* (hereafter referred to as *Sickness*) is written and published much later, relatively speaking, within the authorship: *The Concept of Anxiety* was published in 1844, *Sickness* was written in 1848 and published in 1849. In terms of the brief authorship of Kierkegaard, this is a large time gap between two works which we maintain are integrally related. Nonetheless, observing the style of the works reveals the conceptual continuum which embraces both.

We remarked above that, in Haufniensis' treatise on anxiety, the discussion constantly moves back and forth between sin and anxiety. Formally, *The Concept of Anxiety* opens with a consideration of original sin and then evolves into a discussion of anxiety, with its relevance to sin pointed out. *Sickness*, on the other hand, after a long discussion of despair which is a heightened form of anxiety, closes with a discussion of sin and the offense. Taken together, the two treatises may be considered treatments of sinfulness and related psychological states. For in relation to sin, anxiety is the state in which sinfulness arises, and despair is the state of continuation in sin as well as ultimately the state in which sin

DESPAIR   85

can be vanquished. From the psychological point of view, anxiety is essentially the experience of possibility, and the state of despair is the avoidance of one's authentic, specific possibility (viz. of being a self grounded in a God-relationship). Anti-Climacus completes, as it were, the discussion inaugurated by Haufniensis. Anti-Climacus, as the Christian pseudonym, brings the Christian perspective with its basis in Revelation, a perspective which is subsequently articulated in *Training in Christianity*.

Before turning to study the uses of the term despair and then proceeding in the direction of formulating the concept of despair, let us reflect briefly upon the word itself, in Danish and other languages, for the suggestive associations that may thereby be uncovered. In short, we pause for the *word* before advancing to the *idea*.

The Danish term used by Kierkegaard is *Fortvivlelse*. The root of this word is *Tvivl (For -tvivlelse)*, which is the Danish word for "doubt." The prefix "for-" in this usage serves to indicate continuation unto completion, as is also the case and more readily seen perhaps in the German parallels of *Zweifel* (doubt) and *Verzweiflung* (despair). The root *Tvivl* also suggests two-ness, or a split – an idea despair will develop.

The relation of doubt to despair is quite relevant here, for the etymological connection is in no way accidental. Doubt figures prominently as a topic in the authorship, and the *Papirer* contain an unpublished treatise by the pseudonym Johannes Climacus on doubt, *De Omnibus Dubitandum Est*, in which the young pseudonym begins his philosophical life with this famous refrain from Descartes and then moves on to apply it to everything.

But doubt is entirely intellectual, and it has little application in constructing a life-view, or life-philosophy. The intensification and extension of *Tvivl* with which *Fortvivlelse* is associated has, not *intellectual*, but rather *existential* application. Doubt : philosophy: :despair : existence. Just as (a certain kind of) philosophy begins with doubt, so a life-philosophy begins with despair. Had *De Omnibus Dubitandum Est* been published, it might later have found pseudonymous development and extension in a work perhaps entitled *De Omnibus Desperandum Est*. For this latter refrain is the cry of the philosopher of existence, concerned with moving toward a viable life-view constructed on firm foundations.

The association between the two words, *Tvivl* and *Fortvivlelse*, is not to be overlooked. Kierkegaard's pseudonyms associate the two time and again, and with the purpose of contrasting the type of philosophy which issues from each: from the one, exclusively intellectual, academic philosophy; from the other, a philosophy grounded in the whole person and still intellectually solid but with passionate, subjective concern for existence.

The imagery which exists in Danish and which has its German parallel is, unfortunately, lost with translation into English. (In acquiring so many non-Germanic words in its evolution, English has been enriched from the point of view of vocabulary but has lost much from the point of view of imagery.) Our own English word despair is linked with the

86   DESPAIR

French *desespoir*. However, the French word immediately suggests its opposite, *espoir*, hope.

Thus, in the French, the word despair summons up more clearly what the English word connotes: the negating of hope. While in no way does this study suggest that Kierkegaard had French or English in mind, it can affirm the relevance of the association (viz. loss of hope) to Kierkegaard's understanding of despair. For when the relation of hope to the future and to possibility is seen, the aptness of the word association is also seen.

The sickness of despair is the state of being cut off from the future, from possibility (first in a general way, and then, in the critical higher despair experience, from specific possibility). "Without a future," one is self-condemned to an ever-repeating present, in the sense that one has denied oneself a "future" insofar as one has hindered or refused the process of spiritual evolution within the personality. The self-denial of future, including the specific possibility of a God-relationship, is nothing less than hope-lessness: despair. The English and French associations are not without relevance for understanding Kierkegaard's meaning. But in this study of despair, the Danish word must be kept in mind first and foremost, with its contrast term "doubt."

B. DESPAIR IN *EITHER/OR*

Following a chronological order of the publication of the works, it is natural to consider the presentation of despair in *Either/Or* before *Sickness Unto Death*. However, the scope of despair presented in *Either/Or* is quite narrow. Part I depicts the despair of the aesthete rather than an explicit understanding of despair. Thus the insight into one man's despair is more appropriately considered in Chapter Five below. Part II of *Either/Or* presents the understanding of Judge William, but, it must be noted, from his own standpoint of ethical humanism. He does not have the larger religious perspective in which to see the whole of despair as a state. He can, from his standpoint, view the problem of the aesthete and his despair. But, his remedy consists of imitation of himself. However, since in the characterization of Judge William his own despair is different in form from that of the aesthete, we might suppose that a different remedy is required. This is precisely the case and is the reason why Judge William's advice is inadequate for the problem of the aesthete.

In the normal meaning of the word, one would tend to characterize the "Dispsalmata" as despair in the sense of hopelessness. In a deep sense this is the problem of the aesthete: loss of hope, loss of potentiality, as he himself expresses it:

If I could wish for anything, I should ... wish ... for the passionate sense of the potential, for the eye which, ever young and ardent, sees the possible.[4]

[4] *EO* 1, p. 40. Danish text reads: "Skulde jeg ønske mig Noget, da vilde jeg ... ønske ... Mulighedens Lidenskab, det Øie, der overalt evigt ungt, evigt brænende seer Muligheden." *S.V.*, I, 25.

DESPAIR 87

Judge William, in Part II, sees the young aesthete as a victim of the despair of thought, as intoxicated with despair.[5] On several occasions,[6] William associates the root problem of melancholy with the despair of the aesthete and he recommends the solution for both as despair. "Despair" as the cure for "despair" – clearly two different senses of the word are used here. Judge William never explicitly and fully defines the meaning of the word which he uses so frequently. Every aesthetic view is despair, he says.[7] The reader has come no doubt to this opinion about the aesthete of Part I, and he can concur with the judgement without reflecting upon its precise meaning. However, in prescribing a remedy for his young friend, Judge William does partially indicate his understanding of the mood. The "despair" which characterizes the existence of A is the evasion of choice. What William counsels is an act of the will which recognizes that the aesthetic life is "despair" (in the sense of being without a self) and which chooses the self in its eternal validity.

Willing choice constitutes the initial act of despair: the first saving act which rescues one from the hopelessness of aesthetic existence and is the decisive move into ethico-religious categories. The more detailed schematization of *Sickness* will be needed to place this phase within larger perspective. The initial saving act of despair constitutes the first affirmation of the self and movement towards higher consciousness of the self and its destiny. *Sickness* will show that the active *prise de conscience* continues well beyond this point.

Judge William does not speak of a further crisis in the personality requiring one to act again, because the character of Judge William has not (yet) advanced beyond its ethical humanism. He himself has not entered into the higher sin-consciousness which is the path by which the state despair (viz. being a self not wholly synthesized and grounded in the God-relationship) is essentially overcome. And this is spite of the enclosure in the third letter of Part II: the "Ultimatum" with the sermon entitled "The Edification Implied in the Thought that against God We are Always in the Wrong." Judge William counsels despair for the aesthete. But Anti-Climacus in the Preface to *Sickness* says that despair is the sickness and not the cure.[8] Clearly then Anti-Climacus and William do not have entirely the same perspective on it.

The counsel of William is an inevitable first step toward the resolution of the essentially spiritual problem of the aesthete. But William's understanding (as he is drawn as a character) is limited to his own (as yet) incomplete development into the religious. It will be left for the religious pseudonym Anti-Climacus to give the complete presentation. While Anti-Climacus is not drawn as a character within the authorship,

[5] *EO* 2, p. 199; *S.V.*, II, 176.
[6] *EO*, p. 212, p. 223 et al.; *S. V.*, II, 187, 196 et al.
[7] *EO* 2, p. 197; *S.V.*, II, 173–174.
[8] *SUD*, p. 143; *S.V.*, XI, 118.

88 DESPAIR

he is posited as a religious author, with the benefit of the understanding which has come from both Revelation and fuller Christian development.

C. DESPAIR IN *THE SICKNESS UNTO DEATH*

Sickness, as the subtitle proclaims, is intended to be psychological in approach, but with an edifying purpose. It is, of course, more our interest to explore its psychological character than its edifying purpose. *Sickness* is a work so profound that the edifying purpose may even have become obscured. Its style and procedure have little to do with the more simply composed Edifying Discourses addressed to the common man. But even the psychology will leave some bewildered – especially those for whom the word psychology is narrowly empirical.

Sickness, perhaps more than any other psychological work in the authorship, leaves itself open to the charge of being a "metaphysical psychology," a charge which we have entertained elsewhere. But here as well we contend that the charge can finally be answered. A great portion of the work deals with forms of despair which arise from misrelations in the human synthesis. And how are the elements of the synthesis arrived at and formulated if not by metaphysical abstraction? Finitude and Infinitude, Possibility and Necessity – these are certainly metaphysical rather than empirical categories. However, despite the terminology, one may say that such terms are the attempt to express something deeply empirical: the conflicting elements in the depths of the personality. Experience, in the end, is at the base of this psychology which dialectic unfolds. This is clearly borne out by the description the author gives, and confirmed by the author's intention to address the problems of existence rather than merely those of thought. The Preface proclaims that the book is written in the spirit of "Christian seriousness" because it represents not indifferent learning but rather relates to existence.

The high aloofness of indifferent learning is, from the Christian point of view, far from being seriousness, it is, from the Christian point of view, jest and vanity.[9]

For those capable of the rigor, the author is concerned to stimulate the growth of consciousness by the reminder that growth is already taking place and by indicating, through psychological exposition, that the direction is the same as that announced by Christianity: the overcoming of sin and the establishment of a relationship of faith to God.

---

[9] *SUD,* pp. 142–143. Danish text reads: "... den ligegyldige Videns Ophøiethed er, christelig, langt fra at være mere Alvor, den er, christelig, Spøg og Forfængelighed ." *S.V.,* XI, 117.

DESPAIR

RELATION BETWEEN ANXIETY AND DESPAIR

The relationship between anxiety and despair has already been mentioned above. Similarities and differences are referred to in Kierkegaard's first draft for *Sickness*.[10] They are further suggested by comments in the published version of *Sickness*. And they are important enough to pause for and consider.

Anxiety, we recall, treats of man on the mental-emotional plane. In *Concept of Anxiety*, man was considered within the mental-physical synthesis. Confrontation with the eternal, in so far as it can be spoken of at this point, is confrontation with the eternal *outside* man. The eternal within is present only potentially. However, in the section on the exclusion of inwardness, Vigilius Haufniensis, in speaking of the inwardness of man, implied the eternal *within* man which is subsequently excluded, and in this he reached the borderline between anxiety and despair.[11]

Despair emerges as a distinct category from anxiety, although always of the same essence (i.e. the confrontation of possibility), because of the addition of the eternal, the eternal *within* man. In delineating the realm of despair, Anti-Climacus too comes to a borderline form in which one is close again to anxiety. This form is unconscious despair, a despair which exists without knowledge of the eternal. Because the specific nature of despair is the eternal within man, Malantschuk has called this form of despair in ignorance of the eternal "figurative despair."[12] The obvious implication of this is that despair proper is despair not only because of the *presence* of the eternal, but also in *consciousness* of the eternal.

In despair, the additional synthesis of the temporal and the eternal is stressed, thus emphasizing man as a higher synthesis. Despair, as a misrelationship within the elements of the human synthesis, is a sickness within spirit which becomes evident as despair proper only when a definite growth-point in the personal spiritual life has been attained. Thus the sickness can be spoken of as a sickness within the spirit and manifest in the life of the spirit for those capable of discerning it.

In addition, however, to spiritual manifestation, despair is manifest on the mental-emotional plane, as was anxiety. Here the psychologist will first observe the manifestation. Only as he makes closer observations and refinements will he see the difference between anxiety and despair. And, according to Kierkegaard, in this he will have to be a *Christian* psychologist in order to make the detailed refinements, to penetrate into the full depths of the problem.

[10] VIII² B 166 ff.

[11] Cf. Malantschuk, *Kierkegaard's Thought*, pp. 340 ff.

[12] *Ibid.*, p. 345.

90 DESPAIR

THE DEFINITION OF THE SELF

The first part of *Sickness* opens with a celebrated and puzzlesome definition of the self (which we retranslate, in the interests of clarity):

Spirit is the self. But what is the self? The self is a relation which relates back to itself; or it is the fact that, in the relation, the relation relates back to itself; the self is not the relation, but the fact that the relation relates back to itself. Man is a synthesis of the infinite and the finite, of the temporal and the eternal, of freedom and necessity, in short a synthesis. A synthesis is a relation between two [factors]. Looked at in this way, man is as yet not the self.[13]

"Man is spirit, and spirit is the self." But man is not the self – not yet. It is not total equation (man = spirit = the self), because of the state of spirit. There is a sickness in the spirit, reflected as a loss of equilibrium among the factors which constitute the relation. In examining the sickness, Anti-Climacus will first consider the dis-equilibrium among the factors, and then he will consider the sickness more properly as it relates to the eternal. That is, Anti-Climacus will first examine the manifestation of dis-equilibrium in paired elements of the synthesis, and then he will turn to the examination of the root-reason, viz. misrelation to the Constituting Power. Were there a proper relation to the Constituting Power, the synthesis would be firmly united and properly self-related; there would be equilibrium among the factors, and in such a case, man would be the self.

In the speculative and probing examination of the dis-equilibrium in the human synthesis, Anti-Climacus does not suggest directly and explicitly how the lack of the respective paired opposite came about. For example, the despair of finitude is due to the lack of infinitude. But how does this lack come about? How does the root imbalancing force come about which prevents equilibrium? Anti-Climacus does say that despair is sin and it will be seen that sin is this imbalancing force. Sin and its dis-equilibrium can only be overcome by taking on sin-consciousness, and then by forgiveness and hence a restoration of a right relation to the Eternal, Constituting Power of the synthesis.

Despair proper is refusal to be the self, refusal to make the movements towards the enhanced restoration ("repetition") of the self which is promised by the Christian forgiveness of sins. And this refusal to become the self, which is sin and which creates the imbalance in the elements of the synthesis, is refusal to relate to the Eternal.

Anti-Climacus declares, before his exploration which will prove it, that one cannot get rid of the Eternal.

---

[13] *S.V.*, XI, 127. Cf. Lowrie's translation, *SUD*, p. 146. Danish text reads: "Aand er Selvet. Men hvad er Selvet? Selvet er et Forhold, der forholder sig til sig selv, eller er det i Forholdet, at Forholdet forholder sig til sig selv; Selvet er ikke Forholdet, men at Forholdet forholder sig til sig selv. Mennesket er en Synthese af Uendelighed og Endelighed, af det Timelige og det Evige, af Frihed og Nødvendighed, kort en Synthese. En Synthese er et Forhold mellem To. Saaledes betragtet er Mennesket endnu intet Selv."

DESPAIR 91

But the eternal he cannot get rid of, no, not to all eternity; he cannot cast it from him once for all, nothing is more impossible.[14]

But despair, in its essence, is precisely the attempt. It is an attempt at spiritual suicide, the self-inflicted wounds of which are witnessed in the character Johannes, the aesthete of the "Diapsalmata." Such an attempt is "an impotent self-consumption which is not able to do what it wills."[15] Thus Anti-Climacus warns the reader whom he hopes to edify that all such attempts are doomed to failure. To refuse the eternal is to struggle constantly against it, and always to lie in defeat. Such defeat constitutes the festering sickness in the spirit, in its manifold forms. Having given this warning, Anti-Climacus now gives the result of his exploratory surgery upon the human spirit. He first explores the four forms of dis-equilibrium and then the two forms of refusing to be the self, which constitute despair proper.

THE FOUR FORMS OF DIS-EQUILIBRIUM

Despair without Reference to Consciousness	*Aspects of the Synthesis*
Despair of Infinitude Despair of Finitude	Infinitude-Finitude
Despair of Possibility Despair of Necessity	Possibility-Necessity

DESPAIR OF INFINITUDE. "The despair of infinitude is due to the lack of finitude."[16] But what is the exact nature of the imbalance here? Anti-Climacus writes, "For the self is a synthesis in which the finite is the limiting factor, and the infinite is the expanding factor."[17] In speaking of the infinite as an expanding factor, he is essentially speaking about the power of imagination to carry one beyond oneself towards a "something more." The imaginative power to posit a "something more" which one can become, however, needs to be limited. Otherwise one simply becomes carried away in imagination, intoxicated with the idea of a fantastical self which is entirely abstract and never to be concretized (i.e. actualized). (It should be noted here that Kierkegaard-Anti-Climacus plays on "imagination" and the "fantastic" as the two senses of a single (Greek) root in Danish, viz. *Phantasien* and *Det Phantastiske* respectively.)

[14] *SUD*, p. 150. Danish text reads: "Men det Evige kan han ikke blive af med, nei, i al Evighed ikke; han kan ikke een Gang for alle kaste det fra sig, Intet er umuligere ..." *S.V.*, XI, 131.

[15] *SUD*, p. 151. Danish text reads: "... men en afmægtig Selvfortærelse, der ikke formaaer hvad den selv vil." *S.V.*, XI, 132.

[16] *SUD*, p. 163; *S.V.*, XI, 143.

[17] *Ibid.* Danish text reads: "Thi Selvet er Synthesen, hvor det Endelige er det Begrændsende, det Uendelige det Udvidende." *S. V.*, XI, 144.

92 DESPAIR

Imagination has three aspects, viz. feeling, knowledge and will. Flight into imagination is flight into one or more of these aspects. Thus in this form of despair, feeling, knowledge and will get carried away and become "fantastic."

FEELING. Feeling becomes fantastic in the form of abstract sentimentality, so that one feels deeply and "inhumanly participates feelingly, so to speak, in the fate of one or another abstraction, e.g. that of mankind *in abstracto.*"[18] One expands oneself through feeling, and applies feeling on the grand scale: to mankind *in abstracto*, while the concrete problems of mankind are left far below, still lower the problems of individual men. Were there an equilibrium, the expansion of feeling should enable one to participate more sympathetically in the problems of men. But because it has not been checked by finitude, feeling here is only imaginary, and abstract, i.e. it is directed only to the idea of men and not to men themselves.

KNOWLEDGE. Knowledge becomes fantastic when it is acquired only for its own sake, when it has no relevance to concrete existence. In this aspect of the despair of infinitude, one expands oneself through the acquisition of knowledge; but because this acquisition is never directed toward knowing the self, the self is lost. Were there equilibrium, i.e. were the passion for knowing directed also toward knowing oneself, there would be a corresponding increase in self-knowledge along with the increasing degree of worldly knowledge.[19] Knowledge which does not include knowledge of the self is thus viewed as vain, empty, and imaginary (*phantastisk*).

WILL. Will becomes fantastic when it does not bother to accomplish on the small scale, and in the instant at hand, the great plan it wills abstractly with purpose and resolution. This aspect of despair lets imagination run away with itself, so that one wills a great, abstract destiny one has fantasized for oneself, but forgets the everyday in which concrete action is called for.

The despair of infinitude may be either active or passive, i.e. one may either rush into the fantastic or be "carried away."

The self thus leads a fantastic [in the sense of "imaginary"] existence in abstract endeavor after infinity, or in abstract isolation, constantly lacking itself, from which it merely gets further and further away.[20]

It is this form of despair to which the Romantics are prone, according to Kierkegaard, and it is into this form that the aesthetic characters fall as

---

[18] *SUD*, p. 164. Danish text reads: "... umenneskeligt saa at sige følsomt participerer i et eller andet Abstraktums Skjebne, f. Ex. Menneskeheden *in abstracto.*" *S. V.*, XI, 144.

[19] *SUD*, p. 164; *S.V.*, XI, 145.

[20] *SUD*, p. 165. Danish text reads: "Selvet fører saa en phantastisk Existents i abstrakt Uendelig jørelse eller i abstrakt Isolation, bestandigt manglende sit Selv, hvorfra det blot kommer mere og mere bort." *S.V.*, XI, 145.

DESPAIR 93

they lead a "poet's existence." There is in addition, as Anti-Climacus points out, a religious manifestation of this form of despair. A man may become inebriated with the infinitizing brought about by a God-relationship – drunk and overwhelmed with the idea of being a self existing before God.

In a state of equilibrium, finitude would balance the fundamentally good function of expansiveness represented by infinitude. Positively, finitude means that one is limited as an individual with a concrete, ethical task in relation to oneself. Obliviousness to this fact leads to flights of fancy in which one directs knowledge, feeling and will to quite other, imaginary and un-realizable ends.

DESPAIR OF FINITUDE. "The despair of finitude is due to the lack of infinitude."[21] This form of despair consists in the self's letting itself be trapped in the realm of the finite, in the narrow confines of an existence which is ignorant of a higher calling. Thus the despair of finitude consists in becoming worldly, in becoming overly attached and caught up in the things of this world. It is manifested as ethical closed- and narrow-mindedness more than aesthetic or intellectual narrow-mindedness, in ignorance of a higher spiritual calling. The despair of finitude, in contrast to that of infinitude, represents narrowness of feeling, knowledge and will. Rather than expanding himself in growth of these faculties, a person stays as he is and merges into the crowd and never develops as an individual. And no one is potentially as insensitive, ignorant and weak-willed as the crowd.

In being cut off from infinitude, which posits and calls one to a higher self, one bars oneself from personal expansion and growth in the spiritual. The result is that one becomes just one more number in the crowd; and even if one attaches some importance to the destiny of the world-historical crowd with which one marches, one is still in despair for having lost one's own personal destiny. In other writings, Kierkegaard has given voice to his passionate feelings about this form of despair into which the crowd has fallen. He has especially pointed castigations in the essay entitled "The Present Age" (*To Tidsaldre*, 1846).

One sees in both forms of despair above the two possible extremes toward which the imbalance in the human synthesis leans. In the first instance a fantastic and imaginary individual emerges, in the second the faceless number in the crowd. In neither instance is the one specific and attainable human spiritual destiny known. The despair of infinitude, on the one hand, posits a destiny whose sole and specific content is enthusiasm; on the other hand, the despair of finitude posits at most unimaginative variations of the present human condition, with perhaps quantitative ameliorations, but none qualitative.

DESPAIR OF POSSIBILITY. "The despair of possibility is due to the lack

---

[21] *SUD*, p. 166; *S.V.*, XI, 146.

94   DESPAIR

of necessity."[22] Anti-Climacus writes that

> The self, *kata dynamin*, is just as possible as it is necessary; for though it is itself, it has become itself. Inasmuch as it itself, it is necessary, and inasmuch as it has to become itself, it is possibility.[23]

The self is viewed as both being and becoming: there is the actual self and the self which one is called to become. The actual self is the present realization in the personality of certain possibilities. Thus it represents limitations and concretion. The self which one is called to become, on the other hand, is abstract. But it too will have limitation and be specific when concretized.

Necessity in the human self means that the self which one is influences the self one can become. And it is this aspect of the self, with its conditionality and structure, which is forgotten in the despair of possibility.

Anti-Climacus talks about moving from the spot where one is. This "spot" (*Sted*) is the actual self, and upon this self one builds the higher self. Anti-Climacus writes that to become oneself is movement *at* the spot where one is,[24] and movement *from* that spot. To forget this spot is to lose one's roots in concretion and to launch off into abstraction, to attempt creation of some new self *ex nihilo*.

In the first level of the consciousness of possibility, one is directed toward an unspecified higher self which one can become. (As one moves toward sin-consciousness, the higher self becomes more specific. But we are as yet still far from that realm.) The new self which one is to become, in order to become actual, must be a unity of possibility and necessity.[25] But when necessity is forgotten, one gets carried away in an endless series of speculative possibilities which have no relation to the type of self one *can* become. One can imagine for oneself whatever destiny one wishes. And this is exactly what the despair of possibility does. Because one forgets necessity, possibility seems greater and greater; more and more things seems possible, because nothing becomes actual.[26] One moves from one possibility to another, or out to infinite possibility. And there is nothing to impede one. One is as light as air and has no more substance than air, for this self is totally ethereal, totally abstract. One forgets oneself firmly footed at a definite spot and allows one's mind to wander off. And then one becomes so oblivious, in the extreme case, to the real that one denies the self one is and identifies with the abstract, chameleon self of fantasy.

---

[22] *SUD*, p. 168; *S.V.*, XI, 148.

[23] *SUD*, p. 168. Danish text reads: "Selvet er *kata dynamin* lige saa meget muligt som nødvendigt; thi det er jo sig selv, men det skal vorde sig selv. Forsaavidt det er sig selv, er det Nødvendigt, og forsaavidt det skal vorde sig selv, er det en Mulighed." *S.V.*, XI, 148.

[24] *SUD*, p. 169, *S.V.*, XI, 149.

[25] *Ibid.*

[26] *Ibid.*

DESPAIR   95

DESPAIR OF NECESSITY. "The despair of necessity is due to the lack of possibility."[27] In this form of despair, Anti-Climacus points out, all has been reduced either to fatalism or to triviality (philistinism), including the self.

With relation to the self, what happens (to continue the simile used just above) is that one is overwhelmed and weighed down on the "spot" where one is as the actual self and one cannot move. In this form of despair, consciousness of the actual self so overtakes one that one cannot believe in the possibility of a higher self. Here the real limits of the self are seen, as well as the real limits of the human. But the great depths of the self are *not* seen. One realizes that with human power alone one cannot become an actual, higher self. Here the person is not distracted by an endless series of possible selves. He sees only too well how abstract, unreal and unattainable they all are. But he so limits the scope of possibility that he closes *all* possibility out, and reduces himself to impossibility. And should he envision the possibility of the higher, spiritual self, he calls it impossibility because he cannot believe that there is a way to attain it.

Viewed from a more complete perspective, what is lacking is deeper consciousness. He lacks the Christian Revelation which would enable him to see that the laws of necessity have already been altered, that there is a higher possibility for man in sonship to God. On the individual level he lacks belief in the forgiveness of sins which would allow him to see that what is humanly impossible is nonetheless still possible by the grace of a higher Power. And so he remains closed into the consciousness of the actual self and closed off from the one possible self which is supra-humanly attainable. He identifies with the course of his fellows in the march of history, according to the laws of necessity, with no extra-human upturn possible either on the collective or individual levels.

In the despair of possibility one had forgotten the concrete, actual self and drifted off into the abstract creation of possible selves and consequently has no way to move from possibility to actuality.

In the despair of necessity, consciousness of the actual self so overwhelms one that one cannot envision change wrought upon the actual.

In these two paired forms of despair, we have analyses of two tendencies which Kierkegaard observed in his day: on the one hand, the Romantics (despair of infinitude, despair of possibility) and, on the other, the crowd (despair of finitude, despair of necessity).

In following the order of Anti-Climacus' treatise, we have so far only considered the forms of dis-equilibrium. We turn now to consider the two principal forms of despair, to which all forms may be reduced. Despair is now to be regarded from the viewpoint of consciousness of the eternal. For one's stance in relation to the Eternal, the Constituting Power of the synthesis, is at the base either of dis-equilibrium in the human synthesis or, more rarely, of true equilibrium. Up to this point

[27] *SUD*, p. 170; *S.V.*, XI, 150.

96 DESPAIR

we have considered but the surface symptoms of despair. The essence
and cause of despair must be sought at deeper levels – in consciousness
and in the will. For from these depths sinfulness (and thus despair)
comes forth.

UNCONSCIOUS DESPAIR: THE COMMONEST FORM

In the section of *Sickness* entitled "Despair viewed under the Aspect
of Consciousness," Anti-Climacus first deals with unconscious despair.
Unconscious despair is paradoxical. On the one hand it is the
commonest form of despair.[28] On the other hand, in the strictest use of
the term, it is hardly despair at all, for despair proper involves consciousness of the eternal.

The analysis of unconscious despair has no bearing on the edifying
purposes of *Sickness* but as a dialectician, Anti-Climacus must concern
himself with all varieties. Thus in the section on conscious despair, he
includes a smaller section on the unconscious form. As a dis-equilibrium
with symptomatic manifestations, there is no question but that unconscious despair partakes of the structure of despair. However, it precedes
both the initial, saving act of despair by which one moves into ethico-
religious categories and the later act of despair which consists of
assuming sin-consciousness. In terms of a larger schematization, unconscious despair stands at the borderline between anxiety and despair, in
that hazy and ill-defined realm in which spirit is already asserting itself,
but in which there is as yet no true consciousness of the eternal self. It is
a form of spiritlessness in which spirit is yet actively present. (Spirit may
also be present in a movement away from spirit, as Kierkegaard thinks
Romanticism illustrates, constituting according to him "paganism within
Christianity.")[29]

Anti-Climacus asserts that every existence not conscious of itself as
spirit and as standing before God is in despair.[30] This then is despair's
commonest form. For it includes the vast majority of mankind who do
not have a deeper consciousness of the self and its density. To the extent
that one is unconscious of the eternal, one is unconscious that the actual
self is in despair. The underlying state of despair remains, for the
imperfection of the synthesis prevails and dis-equilibrium will show up
as phenomena in the personality. One is unconscious of the possibility of
the eternal self. It is an unconscious despair, but despair nonetheless.

CONSCIOUS DESPAIR: THE PRINCIPAL FORMS

The two forms of despair to be considered are located at the threshold
of the ethico-religious. They represent awareness of the Eternal but
either hesitation or refusal to make the act of choice for reasons now to
be considered. Because these forms are conscious of the eternal self,

[28] *SUD*, p. 178; *S.V.*, XI, 157.
[29] *SUD*, pp. 178–180; *S.V.*, XI, 157–159.
[30] *SUD*, p. 179; *S.V.*, XI, 158.

DESPAIR

they are dialectically closer to a resolution than is unconscious despair. But at the same time, the intensity of despair which they represent is all the greater because of consciousness. With consciousness of the Eternal comes a corresponding deeper consciousness of the self, and, with this, awareness that the actual self is not the self one is called to become. Thus the two forms of despair are self-conscious of being in despair. And this self-consciousness intensifies again despair in the stance of non-resolution.

DESPAIR OF WEAKNESS: NOT TO WILL TO BE ONESELF. The despair of weakness is the dialectical opposite of the despair of defiance; but at the same time, Anti-Climacus notes,[31] there is only a relative difference between the two, since "not to will" already contains an element of defiance within it. In the course of the treatise, Anti-Climacus supplies an instructive footnote on the difference between "despairing *over*" something and "despairing *about*" something. He writes,

One despairs *over* that which fixes one in despair, over one's misfortune, for example, . . . but *about* that which, rightly understood, releases one from despair, therefore about the eternal, about one's salvation . . .[32]

With this in mind, we can now turn to two aspects under which one can view the despair of weakness. And these are nothing more than slightly different ways of looking at and articulating the one same phenomenon.

DESPAIR "OVER" THE EARTHLY. Despair "over" the earthly consists in the self's being rooted in pure immediacy, in the worldly and in the temporal[33] – in that which must be broken out and away from in order to overcome despair. Its categories are the agreeable and the disagreeable; its concepts are good fortune, misfortune, and fate. But in this aspect, there is still present some degree of consciousness of the eternal self from which one shies away. One is, however, tied and fixed in the world of sensation, in the cultivation of the agreeable and the avoidance of the disagreeable. The weak-willed self is seen to be rather passive; and thus the call to become the self is regarded as an exertion that one would avoid or have reduced to some self which requires less effort, less painful transformation.

DESPAIR "ABOUT" THE ETERNAL OR "OVER" ONESELF. As has been said, despair over the earthly and over oneself are not really different. In the despair over the earthly, it is an earthly self that one confines oneself to being, because of overly strong ties to the earthly. And if we recall that that *over which* one despairs is that which fixes one in despair, then we see that to speak of despairing over oneself is to localize more clearly the obstacle: the actual self which must be surmounted in order to

---

[31] *SUD*, p. 182; *S.V.*, XI, 161.

[32] *SUD*, p. 194. Danish text reads: "Man fortvivler *over* Det, som sætter En fast i Fortvivlesen: over sin Ulykke . . . o.s.v.; men *om* Det, der, rigtigt forstaaet, løser En ud af Fortvivlelsen: om det Evige om sin Frelse . . ." *S.V.*, XI, 172–173n.

[33] *SUD*, p. 184; *S.V.*, XI, 162–163.

98 DESPAIR

overcome despair. In the sense, Anti-Climacus also refers to this aspect of the despair of weakness as "despair over one's weakness." For it is equally one's weakness which must be overcome in order to overcome despair. And in this sense, all despair is despair of weakness. In every form of despair, there is a weakness which must be overcome and which can be overcome only with an outside aid (grace, forgiveness).

That *about which* one despairs is that which releases one from despair. Thus to speak of despair *about* the eternal is also to indicate the source for overcoming the despair of weakness.

The despair of weakness indicates the area where the actual self is held prisoner: in the earthly, in the actual self defined in earthly terms. This weakness saps the will, just as the continuing refusal to exert oneself in an act of will further weakens the will. In this weakness, one does not will the self one is called to become. Thus, here, in the phrase "not to will oneself," "oneself" is not to be understood as the "actual" but rather the higher self.[34]

THE DESPAIR OF DEFIANCE: TO WILL TO BE ONESELF. Despair here is the desire to be "oneself" in the sense of being a self of one's own creation. And, in this, we come to the extreme form of despair. (But note that this is the extreme *form*, not the extreme *act* of despair.) In this form, the self is conscious of the infinite self, but moreover it is conscious of why it does not want to be itself,[35] and herein lies the defiance.

For here a self is chosen, but a self of one's own creation (the sense of "oneself" used here). On the one hand, consciousness of the infinite self is present, as is consciousness of the eternal; and on the other hand a clear choice of self is made. But the self chosen is the abstract, infinite self. One cuts oneself off from the Constituting Power, out of defiance which will not choose a self except of one's own creation. Thus the point of Anti-Climacus' remark[36] that here the despairer wills to begin not *with* the beginning, but *"in* the beginning" – he wishes to play the role of self-creator.

In brief, he refuses to accept the fact of "creaturehood," the fact that one has not created, as well as the fact that one cannot create, oneself. In the consciousness reached, one knows this, but refuses to accept it. The despairer refashions the self to one of his own making, and he rejects any self which is brought into being by a Constituting Power.

This, in effect, relegates him to a defiant poet's existence. For this self which he wills is an imaginary self, and he knows it by virtue of the consciousness which he has reached. But he will be "lord over himself" by rejecting the Constituting Power. And thus he becomes "a king

---

[34] Kierkegaard's terminology is confusing here and is rather a mind teaser. Where he uses the terms "self" and "oneself," one must understand "actual self" or "higher (eternal) self" or "imaginary (fantastic) self," depending on the context.

[35] *SUD*, p. 210; *S.V.*, XI, 191.

[36] *SUD*, p. 202; *S.V.*, XI, 179.

DESPAIR 99

without a country,"[37] for he is a ruler, but over no self, since without the Constituting Power there is no concrete becoming of self.

He wills a poetical self which has no possibility of moving from abstraction to concretion, and he will accept no other. Dialectically, there is a clear advance here upon the despair of infinitude discussed above. For here the key difference is a higher consciousness. There is no question of simply being carried away with one's poetic imagination, holding before oneself an endless series of ideas of selfhood and then becoming oblivious to the difference between abstraction and concretion. No, consciousness is clearer in this instance. And choice of an abstract self which excludes the Constituting Power can only be judged absurd. Here is expressed the important difference between Christian (Anti-Climacus) and pagan (Socrates) philosophy in the matter of choice of the good. Socrates affirmed that if a man knew the good, he would choose it (hence evil would be ignorance of the good). Anti-Climacus points out a situation in which "the good" (the infinite self grounded in the Constituting Power) is both known and rejected, in what can only be judged absurd defiance. And thus we see that, for the Christian pseudonym Anti-Climacus, evil and sin have roots not in the problem of knowledge vs. ignorance, but in the will.

The end result of the defiant choice of an impossible self (over against the only possible higher self) is self-torment. Anti-Climacus suggests that defiant despair keeps itself suffering in order to prove the wretchedness of existence, as if what it has wrought for its own existence can be generally or universally applied:

Revolting against the whole of existence, it thinks it has hold of a proof against it, against its goodness. This proof the despairer thinks he himself is, and that is what he wills to be, therefore he wills to be himself, himself with his torment to protest against the whole of existence.[38]

In this highest form of despair, then, we have deep consciousness of the nature of the self: a becoming, grounded in the Constituting Power of the synthesis; and at the same time a forceful refusal to accept what it knows to be true. It is a defiant decision to remain in sin, and in suffering, rather than accept forgiveness from an outside source. An absurd pride has discovered the fact of creaturehood and tries to go against it, has discovered something essential to human nature and then attempts to live "un-naturally." In its magnitude, one can perhaps understand why Christians have called despair the "Sin against the Holy Ghost," the one unforgivable sin, for it is rejection of forgiveness and the possibility of forgiveness. And although Anti-Climacus says that

[37] *SUD*, p. 203; *S.V.*, XI, 180.

[38] *SUD*, p. 207. Danish text reads: "Den mener, oprørende sig mod hele Tilværelsen, at have faaet et Beviis mod denne, mod dennes Godhed. Dette Beviis mener den Fortvivlede sig selv at være, og det er det han vil være, derfor vil han være sig selv, sig selv i sin Qval, for med denne Qval at protestere hele Tilværelsen." *S. V.*, XI, 184.

100 DESPAIR

cases of such despair are rare, he affirms that such despair is met, outside the poetical creations of man as well, in the world of men.[39]

D. THE IDEA OF DESPAIR

THE STATE AND STRUCTURE OF DESPAIR

SOURCE. For any understanding of despair, it must be clear that the source of despair lies in the self itself. No external cause, no external agent brings one to despair. And no external analysis will bring any deeper understanding of the state. To understand despair, the self from which it comes forth must be examined, in its structure and in its directionality.

THE ISSUE. In despair, the self is *en cause*. The sickness is lodged in the actual self, and in overcoming this actual self, in freeing up the evolving dynamism of the human spirit once again to go forward toward its appointed goal, the "cure" comes about. But despair raises clearly the spectre of the higher self, which it posits and which it requires for the cure. Thus despair treats of the actual self and requires an understanding of the becoming process by which the actual self moves toward becoming the higher self. (Obviously, there is no sense here of "replacement" of the actual by a higher, different self. This is the folly of the despair of possibility.) The issue in despair is the overcoming of sin, so that the higher self may come to be.

CONSCIOUS AND UNCONSCIOUS DESPAIR. We have pointed out above that the commonest form of despair is unconscious, but that this is really a borderline form, a "figurative despair." For despair proper presumes a consciousness of the eternal and of human destiny over against which the actual self takes up a stance. The stance in unconsciousness is still a stance, and to that extent is despair.

But with consciousness comes the understanding that the root of despair lies in the will. The will brings one into sinfulness (cf. *Concept of Anxiety*) and the will keeps one in sinfulness. And only the will can begin the process of release. In both the despair of weakness and the despair of defiance, there is a conscious, will-ful turning from the sole resolution possible for the sickness of the spirit.

DESPAIR AS MISRELATION, DIS-EQUILIBRIUM. The result of refusal to choose the becoming process which leads from the actual to the higher self is the disequilibrium of sin. The self willfully turns away from the Constituting Power which brings it into being and which posits the elements in the human synthesis which it has created. Turning away constitutes rejection of the source of equilibrium in the personality. The result is not only misrelation to the Constituting Power and to oneself, but also dis-equilibrium reflected in the personality (cf. section above on the forms of dis-equilibrium).

[39] *SUD*, p. 206; *S.V.*, XI, 183.

DESPAIR 101

Despair is disharmony in the actual self, resulting from misorientation to the higher self. And this misorientation constitutes the attempt to escape from one's spiritual destiny.[40] In addition, it is the more intense to the degree that it is conscious.

Escape from one's spiritual destiny blocks re-integration of the personality ("repetition") after the breakdown which sin has brought about. It effectively chokes off the growth process in the personality, and rechannels the energy of growth which it cannot otherwise marshal into the sole remaining possibility: wreaking havoc within the personality, about which the "Diapsalmata" bear witness.

But the despair of which we have just been speaking is the state of remaining in sin. This is the issue which confronts the *reader* of Anti-Climacus' treatise and is central in his edifying concerns. However, underlying the issue of remaining in despair or not is the fact that one is in despair "from the beginning" as it were: the state in which one finds oneself is *always already* despair. Despair enters furtively, after the primal anxiety from which one arises to discover that one is in sin – and hence in despair. For despair is sin, sin is despair. Prior to the despair which is the *state* of remaining in sin is the despair which is the *fact* of being in sin, whether or not one is conscious of it. When the issue of remaining in sin or overcoming sin is raised, the dis-equilibrium, which exists by the fact of sin, becomes manifest and heightened, calling for a resolution. But the dis-equilibrium has existed all the time, for one has always been in despair. The synthesis is incomplete from the very first moment of existence after primal anxiety until the final resolution of sinfulness. (And even the higher act of despair, while essentially solving the problem of despair, does not solve it finally. Such final solution is theoretically possible within existence but is reached only by degrees in actuality.)

THE EXPERIENCE AND ACT OF DESPAIR

DESPAIR AS EXPERIENCE. As experience, despair is first felt as the dis-equilibrium described above, with its consequences. However, since the spirit is not static, despair also interacts with the dynamism of growth within the person. Experienced as part of this process, despair is not really distinguishable from anxiety in terms of its surface characteristics. The psychologist will tend to identify it as anxiety: facing possibility. Unless he is a religious psychologist, however, he will not see that despair concerns the possibility of continuing in sin or overcoming it, and that in its highest phase it is a matter of taking on sin-consciousness – an advanced point consisting of facing a *specific* possibility.[41]

---

[40] Kreston Nordentoft, *Kierkegaards Psykologi* (Copenhagen, 1972), p. 498.

[41] However, even the non-religious psychologist will be able to observe the forms of disequilibrium in the human synthesis, although he may not connect them to the underlying problem of despair, viz. sin. For example, the Heideggerian analysis of basically the

102 DESPAIR

THE ACTS OF DESPAIR: OVERCOMING DESPAIR. The sole possibility for overcoming despair is to "recite the spell backwards," i.e. step by step to undo what despair is. Questions of equilibrium in the personality are matters of symptoms and results, and not the essence of despair. Thus they will disappear just as they appeared, when and as despair is undone.

Clearly in this treatise, the undoing of the spell revolves around an act of will and the establishment of a relationship to the Constituting Power built upon the prior choice and affirmation of eternal, higher self, in so far as the self can choose itself. With that choice, a decisive break is made with exclusively aesthetic categories, and one enters the ethico-religious where the final destiny of the self is to be attained.

The first act of choice (made from within the aesthetic) frees the previously blocked growth process in the personality. For while the process is natural, it is not automatic. In order to function, it requires active cooperation, in the form of an act of will. The act of choice properly channels the dynamism of growth away from self-destruction and toward self-fulfillment. Growth brings one into a higher and deeper consciousness of the nature of the self, and an ever clearer vision of final spiritual destiny.

However, the evolution of consciousness also brings one to consciousness of the extremes of human finitude: that one is a sinner before God. And the natural process alone cannot restore the ruptured relation to the Constituting Power. A second, higher act of despair is required wherein one takes on the painful consciousness of being responsible before God for the fragmented self and being helpless to restore a right relation to God. It is at the very limit and brink of the natural where re-integration and restoration come about by the supernatural act of the

---

same problem – although to be sure stated in particular Heideggerian terms of *Verfallenheit* and *Verschlossenheit* and making the claim to be non-religious – connects the anxiety experience (*Angst*) to a process of overcoming the fallen state in which the human self (*Dasein*) finds itself, and connects the anxiety experience to a process of recovery of authentic possibility. While Heidegger, who is certainly more influenced by Kierkegaard than he will admit, has the category of *Angst*, he does not have a category corresponding to despair. For the analysis of despair posits a religious perspective. Both Kierkegaard and Heidegger speak of *Angst* and taking on responsibility for the state of the self (in guilt). But Kierkegaard goes on to speak of sin-consciousness and the torturous experience of human incapacity totally to recover itself.

Were Heidegger religious, he would probably be "Pelagian" by Kierkegaard standards, for Heidegger believes in a restored relation to Being solely on the basis of human initiative. Heidegger speaks of taking on guilt, but in his schema the next step is "self-absolution." Anti-Climacus–Kierkegaard's perspective is religious – is Christian, is more "Augustinian."

The difference of perspective finally means a different schematization of data. For the Heideggerian humanist, the dis-equilibrium stems from man's fallenness which is faithlessness to himself. For the Kierkegaardian Christian, the faithlessness is not only faithlessness to oneself but also to the Constituting Power. And this in turn bespeaks a differing conception of the self.

DESPAIR 103

Constituting Power bringing forgiveness and establishing the God-relationship of faith.

ADVANCE IN CONSCIOUSNESS. The second phase of the act of choice in despair is a true *prise de conscience*: taking on of consciousness. For on the one hand it represents the evolution of consciousness and on the other it means taking on this consciousness. At this higher phase, the consciousness taken on, as in anxiety, is the consciousness of oneself as having possibility. However, in the higher choice of despair, the possibility has become specific: one sees one's own specific, realizable possibility, viz. sin-consciousness and the relationship of faith to God.

The specific, clear consciousness of the one true concrete human possibility represents the advance in consciousness of despair over anxiety. In anxiety, possibility, in its vaguest sense, was experienced and brought to consciousness. But despair presumes also the presence of *Tungsind* – a crisis whose sole solution can be in the religious. In the higher act of despair, in which one takes on sin-consciousness and disposes onself to a God-relationship, a step has been taken in the direction paved by both anxiety and melancholy: possibility, religious direction. But not until the higher choice of despair do the possibility and direction become entirely explicit.

E. DESPAIR AND THE AESTHETIC LIFE-VIEW

We have heard from Judge William that all aesthetic existence is despair, and in the sense of the essence of the state of despair this is readily seen: aesthetic existence is in sin and represents avoidance of the choice of the eternal self.

However, among the several various modes of avoiding the choice of self, not all apply to aesthetic existence as Kierkegaard presents it. Indeed, among the forms of the dis-equilibrium, the paired forms exclude each other. Thus aesthetic existence in refusing to choose the self in its eternal validity effects a dis-equilibrium, the forms of which, for Kierkegaard's aesthetic characters, are the despair of infinitude and the despair of possibility. (In the next chapter, we shall point out that the particular despair of the aesthetic character A is a further development of and refinement upon this basic despair-form in aesthetic existence.)[42]

The aesthetic life-view, by which Kierkegaard means Romanticism and Idealism and in its widest sense all existence which is not under the

---

[42] The despair of finitude and the despair of necessity are the despair of the crowd, and in the strictest sense are still part of aesthetic existence. However, such an existence de-humanizes itself by defining itself in entirely external terms, by abandoning itself to the crowd. While Kierkegaard denounces this abandonment, particularly in "The Present Age" (*To Tidsaldre*), it is not his particular concern in his attack upon aesthetic existence. There he is more concerned with the continuing active existence involvement of individuals, and particularly with sensitive, developed existences in need of and on the edge of higher development.

104   DESPAIR

category of the ethico-religious, is time and again criticized for not knowing its own limits. Thus in the mind of Kierkegaard, Romanticism represents a flight of fancy, an illusory adventure of the imagination, a poetic existence which has no concrete reality to it. In the three fantastic forms of knowledge, feeling and will, Kierkegaard's literary and intellectual targets can be seen as comprising the despair of infinitude, which is defined as the lack of finitude. The lack of finitude here means obliviousness to the ethical taks of becoming a concrete individual. The Romantic lives in his infinite possibilities which imagination conveniently varies for him in the battle to stave off boredom.

Aesthetic existence is under the despair of possibility (which is the lack of necessity) because it exists in ignorance of the actual self. For all the psychological acumen of Constantine Constantius, the understanding which aesthetic existence has of the individual self is very limited in nature. (And, it has been seen, the ethical humanism of Judge William has a limited perspective as well.) Romanticism and Idealism do not begin with the actual self as starting-point; that would be too pedestrian. Rather they begin with the possible self and vary this to infinity. Having severed roots with actuality, the despair of possibility has of course no way to move from abstraction to concretion. The possible, abstract self which it has intellectually fashioned for itself is a "nothing." And creation *ex nihilo* cannot here be successful.

Aesthetic existence is conscious of the infinite and the eternal, even if it has not made an act of choice. Thus Kierkegaard locates the aesthetic life-view among the essential forms of despair. In an extended sense, unconscious despair is of course still part of aesthetic existence. But the aesthetic existence which Kierkegaard constantly criticizes as a life-view is the higher form of Romanticism and Idealism which he did indeed consider conscious of the eternal, but moving in a direction away from it.

A discussion of the "despair of weakness" and "despair of defiance" with reference to the aesthetic life is not appropriate here, for the analysis of these two conscious forms of despair apply only to an existing individual. Thus we leave them until the consideration of the aesthete A, who while not a concrete individual at least approaches one as character and "idea clothed in the flesh."

Despair as a mood in the aesthetic life first means the experience of dis-equilibrium which sin is. Thus the four forms of dis-equilibrium, although stated in terms of the abstract elements of the human synthesis, refer to experiences of imbalance within the personality: captivation by one's own imagination and bondage to one's limited understanding of the nature of the self.

Despair in the aesthetic life is always one and the same: it is sinfulness, it is the continuation in sin. But continuation in sin cannot be viewed as some abstract state which has nothing to do with one's existence. On the contrary, it has everything to do with one's existence, with one's existence in its deepest strata. But its manifestations may be

DESPAIR

diverse. Thus the several forms of dis-equilibrium discussed. However, even these are not always mutually exclusive, as will be seen in the analysis of the aesthete in whom opposite forms seem to alternate.

Despair as a mood in its higher phase is a distorted view of the self in the world, the continuing experience of the dis-equilibrium sinfulness is and also the experience of the need for re-integration: the need first to choose the self in its eternal validity and then at its yet higher point to choose the self in relation to its Constituting Power. In its higher phase, the mood of despair includes both the sense of dis-equilibrium and the need for reintegration, based on an awakening understanding of the spiritual dynamism present in the psyche.

Having considered the presentation of the four key moods in Kierkegaard's thought, their scope, and then their application to aesthetic existence, we now turn to a more specific exercise in studying the authorship (and one slightly less abstract as well): observing the moods of the aesthete Johannes and what they mean in his troubled existence, as religious subjectivity presses to be born. At the same time the exercise allows us to test the schematization of moods by applying it, in this instance, to the principal aesthetic character of the authorship. We hope to understand Johannes better for the effort, but more importantly we seek to show that the schematization provides a scale for measuring the appearance of subjectivity and the manner in which religious subjectivity is born.

CHAPTER V

THE MOODS AND SUBJECTIVITY OF
THE YOUNG AESTHETE JOHANNES

> I am an aesthete, an eroticist, one who has understood the
> nature and meaning of love, who believes in love and knows
> it from the ground up, and only makes the private reserva-
> tion that no love affair should last more than six months at
> the most and that every erotic relationship should cease as
> soon as one has had the ultimate enjoyment.
>
> – *Either/Or* I, pp. 363–364; *S.V.*, I, 337.

> When one skims a stone over the surface of the water, it
> skips lightly for a time, but as soon as it ceases to skip, it
> instantly sinks down into the depths; so Don Juan dances
> over the abyss, jubilant in his brief respite.
>
> – *Either/Or* I, p. 129; *S.V.* I, 108.

The aesthetic writings originate and revolve in large part around the
young aesthete who is the anonymous-pseudonymous author of
Either/Or Part I. In addition, much of the analysis of the aesthetic life
and the moods described there originate in a critique of this young
aesthete (pseudonymously, of course, by himself and others). Thus it
seems appropriate to apply the general psychological critique of the
aesthetic to the central aesthetic character, in order to observe the
breakdown of an attempted aesthetic life and to examine the subjectivity revealed in his moods.

However, since this involves moving back and forth between several
layers of abstraction, with anonyms and pseudonyms, it might be best to
pause a moment to consider our study's *whence* and *whither*, as well as
Kierkegaard's. To any not fully initiated into the Kierkegaardian
labyrinth, we hold out an Ariadne's thread, with the hope that it may
help the reader find his way rather than further entangle him.

As has been pointed out, Kierkegaard's writings develop a critique of
the aesthetic life in the form of novels and treatises by various
pseudonymous writers who in some instances also analyze fellow
pseudonymous authors. Thus, for example, *Either/Or* Part I is an
autopresentation and unconscious auto-critique of the aesthetic life by
the pseudonymous author Johannes who attempts to remain anonymous.[1] Johannes' analysis is complemented by that of Judge William in

---

[1] In this study, we follow the interpretation of the pseudonymous editor Victor Eremita
who believes that "A" is the Johannes of the "Diary of the Seducer," but that he has
become a poet afraid to acknowledge his creation (*Either/Or* I, p. 9; *S.V.*, I, x.). For
reasons which are unclear to this writer, Lowrie, in his Preface to his translation of *Stages*,
identifies the young aesthete of *Either/Or* with the young man of the Banquet rather than
with Johannes who is also in attendance. We believe that Victor's interpretation is to be
preferred.

THE MOODS AND SUBJECTIVITY OF JOHANNES 107

Part II. Within the authorship as a whole, Johannes clearly emerges as the principal aesthetic character. (The other aesthetic characters are Victor Eremita, Constantine, the "young man" of the Banquet, the "young man" of *Repetition*, and Ladies' Tailor.) The complete presentation of the philosophy and critique depends upon *all* the characters, in the several works in which they appear. And any complete presentation, or collection of the fragments, of the philosophy and critique clearly comprehends more than the stance and life-view of the young aesthete Johannes. Johannes is situated at a certain point of development. He does not represent aesthetic existence fully or purely. The general analysis remains general and can be applied to any of the characters, so long as room is left for individuality – in this case pseudonymous individuality.

Having sketched above Kierkegaard's analysis of the four critical moods of aesthetic life, we return briefly here to the individual level. One might take other characters, or, time and space permitting, all the aesthetic characters. However, our purposes, in emphasizing the difference between the abstract general critique and the individual less-abstract critique, are well served in scrutinizing the single character Johannes. He is fully enough drawn to make analysis of him fruitful, even though to some extent he too always remains abstract.

What we propose is to apply the schematization of moods – the chart of an evolution of consciousness which we have explicated – to Johannes in order to see where he stands. We propose to analyze his irony and melancholy (moods in which he as an author has already contributed to the general diagnosis) and then his anxiety and despair. In the latter, we will be applying the analysis contained in the respective treatises on anxiety and despair.

In effect then, we seek to apply the analysis of moods in the aesthetic life to the character who embodies the aesthetic life-view and who represents *par excellence* the moods which seek to transform it. Having systematized Kierkegaard's analysis of aesthetic life from amidst its diverse and even fragmentary sources within the authorship, we now simply apply it to Johannes. Complications arise because of the type of character Johannes is, because of his semi-patient role for Judge William, and because of the array of pseudonyms and the deliberately unsystematic form in which Kierkegaard presents portions of the analysis. Whatever its puzzlesome form, the analysis of moods and subjectivity in the aesthetic is comprehensive and fully developed. Ours is but the dialectical task of seeing the connections between purposeful fragments.

All the aesthetic characters are preoccupied with romantic love, and love always provides the catalyst for self-analysis. Behind the character of Johannes in *Either/Or* stands the mythical character Don Juan, and it might be well to dwell on the differences between them before proceeding.

For the reader of *Either/Or*, there is an evident natural association of the two. First of all, "Johannes" and "Juan" are forms of the same

108 THE MOODS AND SUBJECTIVITY OF JOHANNES

name. Secondly, there is the theme of seduction which is essential to the Don Juan myth and to the "Diary of the Seducer." The "Diary" obviously models itself on Don Juan, but with important differences.

Johannes refers to the Don Juan myth in the essay "Immediate Stages of the Erotic." He writes, "The immediate Don Juan must seduce 1,003; the reflective need only seduce one, and what interests us is how he did it."[2] Johannes himself in the "Diary" is precisely this reflective seducer who emphasizes the *how*.

Don Juan is the pure idea of the erotic and remains mythic. He is pure immediacy, and he can, according to the author of the essay, be best presented in the abstract medium of music. He loves only in the moment; he loves woman in the abstract;[3] and any girl will satisfy him.[4] The erotic takes the form of seduction in him, but without intrigue and cunning, according to Johannes who in the "Diary" distinguishes himself by intrigue and cunning in manipulating a relationship with the unfortunate Cordelia. Johannes is one step at least removed from the abstract, but he is still an idea. He remains one of the "ideas clothed in the flesh" who incorporate the aesthetic life.

A. JOHANNES' IRONY

Johannes knows how to employ irony as a tool, but more importantly he is a personality whose entire existence-stance is pervaded by irony. Among the pseudonyms, it is Constantine Constantius who is called the ironist, but the quality is surely not lacking in Johannes.

Since Johannes is so very passionate, in contrast to the cool Constantius, his irony is sharp and biting. In ancient Roman satire, scholars make a distinction between Juvenalian and Horatian: on the one hand, Juvenal as the passionate despiser of his time, on the other, the more tolerant Horace who poked fun and chuckled at human foibles. Following a parallel schema for irony, one would have to say that Johannes is thoroughly Juvenalian – perhaps going far beyond the Juvenal who decried the decline of the great Roman people to "panem et circenses" to intimate that his own contemporaries have never been above them.

The "Diapsalmata" open with the simile of Phalaris' bull which compares the poet's sufferings to those roasted in the brazen bull and compares the audience to those who only listened to the entertaining sound and not the inner reality. The ironist knows the surface phenomenon is not the inner reality and seeks to sting his fellows with his discovery. The irony of the "Diapsalmata" provokes a laugh and a cringe in him who has been amused and wounded simultaneously. In the witty "Rotation Method" the young aesthete gives his advice against

---

[2] *EO* 1, p. 107. Danish text reads: "Den umiddelbare *Don Juan* maa forføre 1003, den reflekterede behøver kun at forføre een, og det, der beskjeftiger os, er hvorledes han gjør det." *S.V.*, I, 88.

[3] *EO* 1, p, 94; *S.V.*, 76.

[4] *EO* 1, p. 96; *S.V.*, I, 78.

THE MOODS AND SUBJECTIVITY OF JOHANNES 109

friendship and marriage, reducing all men to bores and positing boredom as the root of all evil. The "Diary" sees the irony of Edward's gratitude to the Johannes who will, and then does, seduce Cordelia – a seduction that comes about through the power of irony to captivate the young girl. In the banquet of *Stages*, Johannes is the sole to advocate accepting woman "as she is," without ever defining her. By his references to Aristophanes' myth at Plato's Banquet, he posits the essence of woman as a deception and ruse on the part of the gods, a bait he is willing to dine on but not be hooked on.[5] His ironic conclusion, which is meant to justify his conduct, is that woman wants to be seduced and that the gods want it too, in their case to distract humankind from designs upon heaven.

More than a technique, or tool of disclosure, Johannes' irony is his existence-stance, and it is this which chiefly concerns us. The "Diapsalmata" indicate an underlying ironic existence-stance which is fueled with passion against phenomenal existence. Johannes evidences pain and bitterness as he suffers through to the realization of the wide gap between phenomena and essence. Thus he scorns present attitudes about marriage and friendship (something which even William agrees with him on, although William sees the possibility of more substantial ethical relationships), scorns too ambition in life, and attempts to find meaning. The wide gap between phenomena and essence, rather than the essence itself, is foremost in Johannes' consciousness. For while he has moved in suffering beyond the phenomenal, he is still far from clear about the essential.

SEEKING THE IDEAL

Johannes is seeking the Ideal. The first result of this is *Melancholi*, as he yearns for the One ideally. He moves further, further than the third stage of desiring (cf. "Immediate Stages of the Erotic") which desires the particular absolutely. Johannes has advocated just such desire, but ironically as part of the "art of the arbitrary" in which one elevates *any* particular to the Absolute and then desires it absolutely. However, he is already beyond this position which he ironically advocates. He has realized the impossibility of having his desire for the Ideal satisfied by anything within the phenomenal world. The realization has rendered him ironic to a high degree, after he sees the impossibility of fulfillment in the external toward which desire is presently directed. But he has not come to the more advanced state of the ironist Constantine who realizes that what is to be sought can be found only internally.

Johannes is more passionate than the detached Constantine, and so the realization brings about an agonizing sense of meaninglessness. All false meanings have been stripped away. Johannes, as he indicates in the "Diapsalmata," finds himself estranged from existence: estranged from

---

• [5] *SLW*, p. 84; *S.V.*, VI, 74.

110 THE MOODS AND SUBJECTIVITY OF JOHANNES

his contemporaries and from the illusions which comprise their life-views. Johannes' innards are churning as he as-yet-unconsciously experiences the impulsion toward something higher. He seeks new positivity, but he is as yet still fumbling in the darkness. He is not content to negate; he knows he requires a new positivity even if he does not know how to attain it.

NEGATIVE AND POSITIVE IRONY

Beyond the illusions of his fellows and beyond the illusion of reaching the Ideal, Johannes soars in the negative freedom of the ironist. He is beyond the hold of the immediate (a development represented in the presence of reflection). Johannes is also beyond the Romantics and their life-view. In contrast to their misdirected irony (cf. *Concept of Irony*), his irony is directed toward the spiritual. However, while it is directed (and his *Tungsind* will confirm this), it is not in movement. Along with the Romantics, he uses negative irony to free himself. But his irony also has a positive dimension, searching for the new – even if hope-lessly.

Johannes is at the threshold of developing positivity, of giving new content and meaning to his existence. However, he is not conscious of this. And he cannot move further until he makes the act of the will which will also resolve the problem of his melancholy: the act of the will in which he chooses himself, and allows a transformation of personality to come about.

Because he will not will, he lives in abstract possibles; he lives poetically, as Judge William who much appreciates him points out. Because his existence has no content, it has no stability either; and he is thus the victim of the passing moods to which the "Diapsalmata" attest. In addition to being emotionally unstable, the ironic stance of Johannes is prone to be immoral. For his irony represents the affirmation of self-ish individuality – an individuality which has not moved on to affirm the individuality of others. The Johannes of the "Diary" is profoundly selfish. And in his attitudes toward women at the Banquet, he is older but unchanged in this. While discovering subjectivity is always individual and personal, the conduct of the seducer would imply that subjectivity is his own original discovery and that no others possess it, even potentially. Thus he takes advantage of and abuses his relationships with others, in a fashion that not only renders him immoral but demonic.

THE STANCE OF JOHANNES

Where, in summation, does the ironic stance of Johannes situate him? He possesses an ironic consciousness which is directed, but not moving, toward the religious. He is on the threshold of the ethico-religious but takes no step. He is impelled toward a more essential humanity – a goal which can only be reached within the sphere of the religious, yet he is unconscious of the direction of the impulsion.

THE MOODS AND SUBJECTIVITY OF JOHANNES 111

Johannes is negative enough to be beyond the finite, and positive enough in his groping to be beyond the Romantics, but he has not answered irony. He has not moved so far as to negate his ironic stance and thus to posit some higher stance beyond the ironic. Johannes is seemingly far from this. For mastered irony requires movement into ethical categories, a sphere into which Johannes will not cross. He contents himself to rage in negativity against his age and against himself. His irony has served to check the illusions of finitude, but has not yet checked the subtle illusion of non-mastered irony which, by positing nothing beyond itself, posits itself by default as a final end. Those conscious of existence-spheres beyond the ironic can recognize the ironic stance as standing on a threshold. For Johannes, his irony represents the passionate rejection of the illusions which are behind him, but not (yet) the commitment to what lies ahead.

Paradoxically, however, there is a sense in which the irony of Johannes is already beyond the ethical humanism of Judge William because it is infused with a melancholy demanding a solution higher than the ethical. Johannes is not conscious of this, but the failure of William's appeal to his young friend can be traced to the fact that his problem is deeper than William himself can see.

B. HIS ANXIETY

The major source for the analysis of Johannes' anxiety is the "Diapsalmata," those effusions so colored with mood. Tremors of anxiety pervade them. Some vague, black crisis faces Johannes at the same time as he has some intuitions of its nature (cf. his comments on melancholy in this regard). Additional evidence of anxiety is found in his quest for adventure, in the "Diary," for Vigilius Haufniensis says that this is a sure indication of anxiety.[6]

JOHANNES' ESSENTIAL ANXIETY

The Johannes depicted in *Either/Or* and in the Banquet is a fallen subject: one who is deeply in sinfulness which is selfishness and consequently also self-lessness. But while he is fallen, he is not lost. The movement of recovery is possible for him, although when we leave him as a character he seems to have refused it.

An energy is at work within the deeper recesses of Johannes which he is aware of but whose significance is vague to him. Ironically, at the same time as he laments the absence of the sense of possibility in his life, he is experiencing the first tremors of possibility. He speaks of his fight with pale, nocturnal shapes;[7] he refers to a movement within him which presages an earthquake; he speaks of being bound in a chain of

[6] *CA*, p. 38; *S.V.*, IV, 314.
[7] *EO* 1, p. 23; *S.V.*, I, 8.

112 THE MOODS AND SUBJECTIVITY OF JOHANNES

inexplicable anxieties.[8] We who have seen Haufniensis' explanation of these anxieties are in a position to view Johannes with a clarity and perspective which he himself does not have, because he is limited to the perspective of the aesthetic.

His inexplicable anxieties are rooted in the problem of his self, which is where they are experienced. The shudder of anxiety which moves through him is an objectless fear because it has reference to himself as subject. There is no object strictly speaking, and hence the fear points back, for resolution, to the subject in whom it originates.

The "nothing" of his anxiety is the potential, higher self from which he is still distant. But he has a vague intuition of a transformed self, although the content of that self remains unclear. In the face of the movement at work deep within him, Johannes evidences the antipathy and sympathy which is characteristic of anxiety. He both likes and fears what is going on. He likes it, because he is fascinating to himself and he enjoys scrutinizing himself as much as he does doing the same to others. Thus his "Diapsalmata" dissect himself and his emotions much more thoroughly than he ever does to Edward or Cordelia. But at the same time he fears himself more than he fears any other subject. For ultimately he knows that he cannot entirely control the movement which he can observe. It pulls him along, and he has only the choice to cooperate or resist. This poses no small challenge to his pride.

He knows that the movement within is about himself, although he does not yet know that it is about his "self." It is a movement in conflict with his espoused philosophy of the moment and of repeated moments. And his resistance merely confirms the impotence of the life-view he holds to, as he experiences the self-inflicted tortures of defeat resulting from the conflict of his life-view with the reality stirring deep within him.

HIS STANCE IN ANXIETY

We know from Johannes' self-revelations that he has not resolved, nor will he resolve, the problem which is revealed by his anxiety. At the same time as he laments the absence of possibility, he experiences and refuses its meaning for him. He is in a clear mis-relation to time, as he attempts to freeze an instant of the temporal and to block out the eternal which is asserting itself. And "That man sins who lives in the instant abstracted from the eternal."[9]

Johannes attempts to live in the moment, in repeated present time, in order to avoid a future of which he is not entirely master. The consequence is that he experiences the barrenness of an exhausted present, as he holds himself back from the future. Johannes is in "anxiety for the good" – he attempts to refuse the movement of possibility from its very

---

[8] *EO* 1, p. 33; *S.V.*, I, 18.

[9] *CA*, p. 83. Danish text reads: "Derfor synder den, der blot lever i Øieblikket som Abstraktion fra det Evige." *S.V.*, IV, 363.

THE MOODS AND SUBJECTIVITY OF JOHANNES 113

inception. He cannot refuse the experience of possibility, and so he is always subject to inner eruptions. But he can refuse possibility itself. He does not go part way, as does the man in "anxiety for the evil" who moves but refuses to go the whole route into characterization as sinner. No, Johannes refuses the entire movement; he turns himself from the future continually.

He is clearly in the demoniacal – the sudden, cut off from continuity with time. He is closed-in as is the man who attempts to refuse the dynamism of possibility. By his stance – his refusal to will the self in its eternal validity – Johannes leaves himself the perpetual victim of the terror of anxiety. His experience of the bankruptcy of his life-view is thorough; he has intensely experienced its barrenness. For this reason, his irony is so sharp, being an irony reached by experience rather than reflection. For this reason is his melancholy so critical, being a call to the new. And for this reason is his anxiety so terrible, that he refuses the possibility which he craves.

C. HIS MELANCHOLY

The sources for a discussion of Johannes' melancholy are principally his "Diapsalmata" and then information filled in about him by Judge William. Johannes tells us that he is melancholy, and that he is attached to his melancholy. But note, a melancholy of a critical kind. "My melancholy [Tungsind] is the most faithful mistress I have ever known; what wonder then that I love in return."[10]

Johannes is both aware of and testifies to the presence of an energy within him, deep beneath the surface, which is in a state of agitation. He refers to a spiritual battle and, in comparing it to the trolls of romances, he says,

What are all such enemies taken together, compared with the pale, bloodless, tenacious, nocturnal shapes with which I fight, and to whom I give life and substance?[11]

Another entry confesses, "Over my inmost being there broods a depression, an anxiety, that presages an earthquake."[12] In short, Johannes is aware of a movement within him. Judge William interprets it as an indication of sensitivity, potentiality for the spiritual.

JOHANNES' AWARENESS

Johannes is aware of the energy and of the turbulence which it effects in his personality. He is aware of the present dispersion which he is

[10] *EO* 1, p. 20. Danish text reads: "Mit Tungsind er den trofastene Elskerinde jeg har kjendt, hvad Under da, at jeg elsker igjen." *S.V.*, I, 5.

[11] *EO* 1, p. 23. Danish text reads: "Hvad er alle saadanne Fiender tilsammentagne imod de blege, blødlose, seiglivede, natlige Skikkelser, hvilke jeg kjæmper med og som jeg selv giver Liv og Tilvær." *S.V.* I, 8.

[12] *EO* 1, p. 28. Danish text reads: "Over mit indre Væsen ruger en Beklemmelse, en Angst, der ahner et Jordskjælv." *S.V.* I, 13.

114   THE MOODS AND SUBJECTIVITY OF JOHANNES

suffering and he is aware too of a mounting crisis. And he is aware of the presence of melancholy. However, as is confirmed by the analysis of Judge William, he does not see, in this dispersed state before melancholy has been essentially overcome, that the same melancholy is at the root of his suffering, and that the stirring of the eternal within him is at the root of his melancholy. He is not aware that his suffering and its gradual increase are the measure of his refusal to will the birth of the eternal, of his spiritual dimension in a "repetition."

JOHANNES' TUNGSIND

Johannes properly labels his melancholy *Tungsind*. For his is not the sweet suffering of the poet, in *Melancholi*. His is already a sickness in an advanced state. The crisis phase has already been reached, as his incessant laments and groans indicate throughout the "Diapsalmata." There he semi-consciously experiences the insufficiency of the aesthetic life and its clash with the dynamism operating in his depths. And so, Johannes, who has been trying to think his way through existence, cries out, "My soul is so heavy that thought can no more sustain it …."[13]

Everything to which he would cling fails him: friends, outward position, love. Now even his intellect is forced to acknowledge its limits in the face of a crisis which goes much deeper. In an insight which goes part way in the direction of the only solution, he yearns for the return of the sense of potential.[14]

His reflections testify to the development of reflection within him. The first immediacy has been broken, although the break is not yet complete and he continues to lash himself with its chains. He has already lost the aesthetic moment. He has drained each to his best ability. But, as reflection grows and his consciousness develops, he becomes more aware of the barren moments between the aesthetically rich ones. By degrees he experiences the barren moments more acutely, until at last the experience and consciousness of barrenness displace the fleeting ecstasy of pleasure. This is depicted in the world- and self-hatred expressed in the "Diapsalmata" in which he says "My life is an eternal night"; "My life is absolutely meaningless."[15] The sense of meaninglessness is connected on deeper levels with the demand for a deeper meaning to life which arises as his consciousness develops. His former philosophy of life collapses as his real essence comes to the surface in the stirrings of the eternal.

NEED FOR RESOLUTION

Johannes is at the point where a resolution of *Tungsind* is demanded. It is more than a malady; it is a sin so long as he allows it to go on and

[13] *EO* 1, p. 28. Danish text reads: "Min Sjæl er saa tung, at ingen Tanke mere kan bære den…" *S.V.* I, 13.

[14] *EO* 1, p. 40; *S.V.*, I, 25.

[15] *EO* 1, p. 35; *S.V.*, I, 20.
  "Mit Liv er som en evig Nat…
  Mit Liv er meningsløst…

THE MOODS AND SUBJECTIVITY OF JOHANNES   115

to wreak havoc within him. As Judge William points out, what Johannes needs to do is to will: with all his energy to choose the self (the first act of despair). But willing is exactly what Johannes will not do. Although he suffers tortured in the moods which assail him, he does not yet connect his suffering with his refusal to will. According to William, he checks the movement of spirit by refusing to affirm it in an act of the will, and so he plunges himself into a deep melancholy in which he suffers dispersion.

The result of his refusal is to block, to misdirect, the great energy of the growth dynamism within him. Thus his unresolved melancholy leaves him the victim of moods,[16] of erratic desires and momentary passions.[17] "I seem destined to have to suffer every possible mood, to acquire experience in every direction."[18] He who seeks mastery over the world can no longer control himself, and has never been able to. Life becomes a bitter medicine; he spits into his own face.[19] "Time stands still, and I with it. All the plans I make fly right back upon myself . . ."[20]

He feels shrunken, closed-in entirely within himself and increasingly isolated from people. He condemns himself to an existence in which he ironically experiences even his feeble attempts to escape as only another moment in a poet's existence. He suffers a misrelationship to time, in which he is cut off from the future, no matter how poetically gifted he may be in speaking about hope. For the only relation to the future which is open to him in his crisis depends upon his opening his own consciousness and personality to the natural course of development it seeks to take. The crucial transition point in this movement toward the higher plane of the future remains the act of the will which he refuses to make.

Vainly I strive against it. My foot slips. My life is still a poet's existence. What could be more unhappy? I am predestined; fate laughs at me when suddenly it shows me how everything I do to resist becomes a moment in such an existence [Tilværelse]. I can describe hope so vividly that every hoping individual will acknowledge my description; and yet it is a deception, for while I picture hope, I think of memory.[21]

The "Diapsalmata" are a study in a melancholy which refuses to resolve itself. Johannes is a personality impregnated with the spiritual

[16] *EO* 1, p. 25; *S.V.*, I, 9–10.

[17] *EO* 1, p. 26; *S.V.*, I, 11.

[18] *EO* 1, p. 31. Danish text reads: "Jeg synes bestemt til at skulle gjennemilde alle mulige Stemninger, at skulle gjøre Erfaring i alle Retninger." *S.V.*, I, 16.

[19] *EO* 1, p. 25; *S.V.*, I, 10.

[20] *Ibid.* Danish text reads: ". . . Tider staaer stille og jeg med. Alle de Planer, jeg udkaster, flyve lige tilbage paa mig selv . . ."

[21] *EO* 1, p. 35. Danish text reads: "Forgjeves strider jeg imod. Min Fod glider. Mit Liv bliver god en Digter-Existents. Kan der tænkes noget Ulykkeligere? Jeg er udseet; Skjebnen leer ad mig, naar den pludselig viser mig, hvorledes Alt hvad jeg gjør imod bliver Moment i en saadan Tilværelse. Jeg kan skildre Haabet saa levende, at enhver haabende Individualitet vil vedkjende sig min Skildring; og dog er den et Falsum, thi medens jeg skildrer det, tænker jeg paa Erindringen." *S.V.* I, 20.

116 THE MOODS AND SUBJECTIVITY OF JOHANNES

but which refuses to bring it forth. Because of his poetic gifts, which are at the same time a measure of his sensitivity and his potentiality for spiritual development, he is condemned to suffer all the more. He is aware of a crisis, aware of a storm energy, and aware of a melancholy. There he stays and there we leave him, in a consciousness battling against itself as it refuses to move in a natural process toward higher consciousness.

But because we have seen the fuller scope of *Tungsind* and the dialectic of which it takes part, we know also that Johannes' critical melancholy can only be relieved by the religious. For, as we have seen, *Tungsind* requires a religious solution – the same solution required by the state of despair.

D. HIS DESPAIR

The despair of Johannes exhibits and taxes the categories defined in Chapter Four. When we speak of the despair of Johannes here, we mean the state and structure of despair. For he flees the experience of despair in his refusal to choose. Judge William has called the life of Johannes despair and has also counselled him to despair, thus employing two senses of the term. But Johannes stands back and will not will in the first act of despair. Thus in considering him, at the precipice of the aesthetic life, we consider only his state of despair and refusal to go further.

Fundamentally, Johannes' is the despair of all aesthetic existence. However, as an existing individual, his despair will have its own individual form. His is a poetic existence, but a developed one. For while he remains despairingly and defiantly within the aesthetic, he has already lost the immediacy which characterizes the majority of men who stay within aesthetic categories.

JOHANNES' DISEQUILIBRIUM

By definition, the way of life and every moment of refused choice is sin. Like all poetic existences, that of Johannes is characterized by an imbalance of imagination (despair of infinitude) which tends to lead him off into the realms of the fantastic. At the same time, he experiences a disequilibrium under the possibility-necessity aspects of the synthesis. He is neither exclusively in the one form of disequilibrium nor in the other; it is as if the scales are so out of control that they alternately tip one way and then the other. In the sense that he is carried away with the infinite range of abstract possibilities of a self, he is the victim of the despair of possibility, in that he lacks the balancing sense of necessity representing a true self-understanding. But, paradoxically, he does have an understanding of himself. He is not the average man under aesthetic categories who lives in self-ignorance, nor is he the eternal aesthete who is the poet entirely off in the realm of the imaginary. No, Johannes does

THE MOODS AND SUBJECTIVITY OF JOHANNES 117

understand himself and his existence. For this reason his irony is positive, as contrasted with the negative irony of the Romantics. For this reason he despairingly sinks under the weight of his own self-knowledge and in the despair of necessity cries out for the sense of possibility.

HIS STANCE: CONSCIOUS DESPAIR

Johannes' despair is further distinguished from the majority who live under aesthetic categories by his higher level of consciousness. His despair is conscious because of some degree of awareness of the eternal self. As drawn by Kierkegaard, the character Johannes' exact level of consciousness is difficult to determine and this is thus a matter open to various interpretations.

Johannes' despair is defiant as well as conscious. He is aware of the eternal and he refuses it, not out of weakness but out of pride. The pitiful Johannes of the "Diapsalmata" is a victim of his own pride, for he will accept no limits nor will he cooperate in a situation in which he is not entirely master. To confirm this, one need only witness the "Diary" and the total desire there to manipulate all, including himself. Johannes proudly refuses the eternal which, he is at least vaguely aware, is the sole solution for him in his crisis.

He operates with at least a vague intuition of the self, and his stance is avoidance of a seemingly inevitable choice. Even if Johannes is not entirely clear about his problem, he knows whence his problem stems and the basic direction wherein the solution lies.

Because of his melancholy *(Tungsind)*, his being is already called to a solution higher than the first act of despair which William counsels. And the aesthete himself is aware of the fact that his experience of life has not only taken him beyond the cool reflective ironist but also beyond the balanced reflective ethicist. He requires a higher and more passionate solution. But he will not accept it, for it is not he who creates the solution and controls the process. The despair of the aesthete is his sin, and his sin lies clearly grounded in his will. It is not ignorance which keeps him in despair but the will which succumbed to sin and will not now rise above it, despite a felt imperative to do so.

E. THE DIALECTIC OF MOODS IN JOHANNES

In the existing individuality portrayed in the pseudonymous character-author Johannes, we see clearly that the principle moods which we have been discussing cannot be separated from one another. The four in concert call for a higher solution to the problem of the self. In Johannes, we see them existing as spheres, rather than as stages. For they all exist at the same time and they overlap. However, they do not all appear at the same time. The fact that all four are found in Johannes, and that he moves from one to the other in his passing moods, is an indication of the

118   THE MOODS AND SUBJECTIVITY OF JOHANNES

level of development which he has achieved. We have already indicated that Johannes is not the typical aesthete. He is not the average man who lives unconsciously under aesthetic categories. Nor is he the self-glorified poet aesthete. While he remains in the aesthetic, he is at the very brink of it. To get there, of course, he has passed through all that the aesthetic means for an existence. And for this reason is he depicted as barren and desperate. Because he has passed through the aesthetic in its entirety, it is only natural to find in him the four moods which characterize the total span – and collapse – of the attempt to live under aesthetic categories.

Johannes is, of course, *melancholsk*: he has the natural sensitivity of the poet; he is a sensitive and developed individual with a capacity for personal development in an inward sense. He is also ironic. He has come to irony through experience. Thus he uses his ironic consciousness to spurn the aesthetic existence which he has lived out. But his irony is also positive: it orients him toward the search for a new life-view (although we know that he will not go through the transitional stages of an accepted anxiety and of the act of despair so that he can come toward the new, positive life-view, viz. Christianity).

He is in anxiety, and profoundly so. He is shaken with the tremors of the experience of possibility which he at the same time refuses. But the experience is there: an involuntary thrust toward the realm of possibility in which the new positivity is to be found, if it is to be found at all.

At the same time, another mood thrusts Johannes further in the direction of specific possibility, and of a specific solution for his unhappiness in a collapsed life-view. He experiences the stirring within him which is *Tungsind*, "religious melancholy." He is depicted with a capacity for some vague development; and he is depicted with a capacity for the religious. And not merely capacity, but with an inner dynamism which naturally functions to impel him in that direction. Because he refuses and resists that impulsion coming from the depths of his being, he is characterized by the gloom of the darkly melancholic personality. This gloom is witness to the fact that he is in a crisis situation, in which personal growth is no idle matter but one of urgency.

Although Johannes refuses the choice of the eternal self – which would take him concretely toward a new positivity, which would creatively channel the experience of possibility, and which would resolve the melancholy which presses him in the direction of a specific possibility – he is totally in despair, in the sense that he is and remains in sin. But because he has passed through the other moods stadially (and he remains in them all simultaneously), his is a conscious despair which has an intuition of the specific possibility to which he is called: the becoming of the higher self restored and grounded in a relation to the Constituting Power. Johannes is still far from the sin-consciousness of the Christian before the restoration effected by the grace of forgiveness, but he is aware of the mis-relation within himself and aware too of the possibility of the higher self. He has not experienced the most intense and highest

THE MOODS AND SUBJECTIVITY OF JOHANNES   119

aspect of despair which is the experience of specific possibility. But he has certainly experienced possibility, and he has also experienced the need for a religious solution (i.e. the need for the concretizing of the religious possibility). But he will not will. Herein lies the tragic block and the root of the sin which his despair is.

Despite the sensitivity his nature has and its potentiality for the religious and despite the development of consciousness he has experienced as each of the moods has stadially made its appearance in emotional and psychic life, his will remains defiantly and consciously opposed to the direction in which the natural dynamic of spiritual growth guides and impels him.

Here therefore is a subjectivity ready to break forth from the mass of the unconscious and from the futile elite of Romantics. But his subjectivity is incomplete, however clear the outlines of its specific potential. It is incomplete and remains such. For Johannes will not heed the self-revelation of his moods, despite the upheaval of their individual appearances and the suffering entailed by their recurrence. *Johannes will not will.* Here is the key to the spiritual transformation process, the birth of religious subjectivity, which he adamantly rejects. But in rejection, he teaches us negatively about moods and subjectivity all the same. The lesson is momentarily captivating and ultimately tragic. Yet in the course of it we begin to perceive both the limits of subjectivity and the freedom essential to it, in a tragically flawed religious personality.

CHAPTER VI

THE DIALECTIC OF MOODS

He who can view things in their connection is a dialectician.

– Plato, *Republic*, VII, 537C.

But enough of this. I can say with the emphasis of truth, "To whom am I talking?" Who will bother about such psychological investigations carried to the nth power.

– Anti-Climacus, *Sickness*, pp. 209–210; *S.V.*, XI, 190–191.

In examining the four critical moods of the aesthetic life, if we have found Kierkegaard and his pseudonyms abstract, we have perhaps been even more so. For we have abstracted the moods from the writings in general and from specific treatises. We have seen both that the moods are underlying structures which, after their initial manifestation, can lie dormant, and that the moods are crises in the growth of the personality. The moods well up from subliminal structures of the psyche to confront the individual with the prospect of higher self-understanding to be effected by willingly passing through the mood and thus beyond it.

In examining the four principal moods of the aesthetic life, our attention has been drawn time and again to the inter-relationships which exist between the several key moods. In the moods, we have isolated two aspects: the structure and a crisis state, except in the mood of irony in which the crisis-state and the structure are identical and simultaneous. When one looks closer, one notes that not only are the structures overlapping, but that the crises-states follow a discernible sequential order. The sequence has already been reflected by the order followed in this study in presenting the discussion of the individual moods.

In sketching the order of the crises, one notes a steady progression, as each crisis phase brings the personality and each mood to the point of preparation for crisis in the next.

To speak of a progression of mood phases is not to suggest, however, that this progression is found in every existing individual. The complete "dialectic of moods," as we shall term the progression and interrelationship of the four moods, is found only in the individual who accepts each mood and passes through it. The process seems to take place only in the religiously sensitive personality, and never is there the promise of going the whole way. This is unmistakably clear in the presentation of the aesthetic characters themselves who represent different phases. Both the young man of the *Repetition* and the young aesthete of *Either/Or* are in a crisis of *Tungsind*. However, we have no evidence that they ever go on into the initial movement of despair and toward the "repetition". In the case of Johannes, it is rather clear that he will not go on.

THE DIALECTIC OF MOODS

Thus the dialectic of moods is a potential dialectic; it is the dialectic that will develop if one pursues the path of religious awakening, responding to one's inner promptings and the stirrings of spirit. In schematizing this dialectic, therefore, we sketch the path of psychic reintegration and evolution, with its marked religious character and direction. It provides us, in effect, with a chart by which we can later measure the progress or stand-point of any existing individuality in the advance toward the religious. The dialectic begins in the aesthetic. But even with irony, we are already at an advanced point within the aesthetic. Irony is already in the process of breaking with the aesthetic; it does not represent unconscious immersion in aesthetic categories. The Romantics and all poet-existences, who are Kierkegaard's chief objects of criticism, are already active, highly sensitive existences who are quite capable of over-coming the aesthetic and moving into redeeming religious categories. It is because this possibility is squandered by these prodigal poets, in directionlessness and in the glorification of sensitivity and mood, that Kierkegaard launches his critique to show the function of mood and to suggest its proper channeling toward the religious.

With the first act of despair, one leaves aesthetic categories. Although our principal realm of exploration is the aesthetic, we follow briefly, even as far as the threshold of the religious in the second act of despair (the assuming of sin-consciousness). However, we do not complete the movement in resignation, for resignation is firmly in the realm of the religious and tied to the supernatural action of grace. Our study remains rather within the category of the aesthetic itself, as it watches the progression and transformation, but never itself leaves the purely human level of observation, psychological and otherwise, for the promised realm of grace. Kierkegaard himself in his literary and philosophical writings never observes psychologically the details of the final reintegration and transformation by grace. For us to do so would be to introduce material and observations not grounded in what Kierkegaard and the pseudonyms provide.

We have ordered Chapters One to Four according to the order of the crises in the moods. Since the moods overlap, no strict separation is ever possible in any complete sense, and thus reference has been made in the course of each chapter to the relationships of certain phases of a mood to one or other moods. There are several possible orderings and, for example, we might have followed Kierkegaard's order of publication in presenting them (viz. *Concept of Irony, Either/Or, Concept of Anxiety,* and *Sickness Unto Death*), but this would not have added to their understanding. The order which we have chosen emphasizes the crisis aspect of each mood and the sequence of the crises, since it is these which are most essential both to the critique of the aesthetic life, to the heightened self-understanding which allows one to move beyond it, and to the emergence of religious subjectivity.

We here propose to review in more detail the conscious, crisis aspect of each mood and then to offer several observations upon the interrela-

122 THE DIALECTIC OF MOODS

tionships of the moods and their thrust. This is preliminary to the study in Chapter Seven which will attempt to show the function of mood in creating a new life-view, on the basis of the deepened self-understanding which comes from allowing oneself, and willing, to pass through the natural movement of the moods. It will be shown 1) that the sweep of the moods are the passageway from the aesthetic to the ethico-religious, 2) that the moods are natural and essential to the growth of the personality and 3) that they also serve in the redemption of philosophy from the abstract and speculative for the service of man in the articulation of a dynamic life-view grounded in the existential realities of man's being.

A. DEFINING "MOOD."

Up to the present, our discussion has followed the lines of Kierkegaard's own presentation in which he describes the functions of four cardinal moods in the emergence of religious subjectivity. In the process, we have schematized and edited treatises and novels where each individual mood is described but also sometimes obscured by the author's over-abundance of purposes. We have simply used the term "mood" as it is found, and have not stopped to define it. But some definition is called for, and here we wish to engage that task.

Kierkegaard himself does not define mood, nor did he ever write a treatise on moods. Rather he set forth descriptions of potential religious subjects and the outlines of religious subjectivity, in character portrayals and abstract treatises, in which the role and prominence of four particular moods is constant and inescapable. As for mood itself, his silence may be either simple or subtle. We tend to think that here the former is the case. But we approach the task of definition with caution nonetheless. For the definition is not simple or beyond debate in our own times. In addition, Kierkegaard has been made into a proto-existentialist, proto-phenomenologist, etc., and the list is far from complete. We do not wish to make him here into a proto-depth-psychologist or a proto-Heideggerian. The function of the moods which Kierkegaard describes does not in essence contradict the interpretation of either; it may even support them. But that is its own venture of interpretation more appropriate to its own extended consideration elsewhere.

Kierkegaard does, however, give some sense of what a mood is, and this is a contribution to subsequent thinking about moods. These descriptions are not incongruent with this later thinking. In 1929, Heidegger wrote in *Being and Time*[1] that the psychology of moods is "a field which in any case still lies fallow ..." The assessment is all too true, in 1929 and in our own times as well. But Kierkegaard has ploughed the field deep

[1] Pages 172–173.

THE DIALECTIC OF MOODS
123

and well, as we have already seen. Others have made advances too in description of moods, such as Heidegger and Sartre, with debts to Kierkegaard, and in our talk of moods, such as Wittgenstein and Ryle. Moreover, it is not inappropriate to introduce them here with the proper *caveat.*

DISTINCTIONS. When we speak of moods and emotions, we are not entirely in the vague and imprecise area that some might suppose. Emotions are not irrational eruptions, nor are moods, when their deeper meaning is probed. There is precise emotion as well as vague emotion.[2] Emotions belong as essentially to a person as does reason, and they explain themselves when probed. Emotional life like intellectual life is subject to greater refinement. Types of emotions and sub-divisions into feelings, moods, agitations, etc., can be distinguished. Analysis of the full emotional life can be shallow and superficial, or deep and pervasive, as can the analysis of ideas. On this subject, there can be little doubt that Kierkegaard makes one of the most profound analyses of the emotional life and its role in the life of the whole man since Augustine in the 4th Century.

Gilbert Ryle, in *The Concept of Mind,* attempts to define moods within the larger context of the emotional life. The term "emotions," he writes, is used to designate "inclinations," "moods," "agitations" ("commotions") and "feelings." Of these, only feelings are occurrences as such; the others are not.[3]

"Moods," he writes, "or frames of mind are . . . temporary conditions which in a certain way *collect* occurrences, but they are not themselves extra occurrences."[4] They are propensities, not acts or states. And they are short-term conditions, although Ryle does allow for an individual's chronic susceptibility to a particular mood, which would then be a character trait.[5]

In saying that he is in a certain mood we are saying something fairly general; not that he is all the time or frequently doing one unique thing, or having one unique feeling, but that he is in the frame of mind to say, do and feel a wide variety of loosely affiliated things.[6]

Moods monopolise, he adds. "To be in the mood to act and react in certain ways is also not to be in the mood to act or react in a lot of other ways."[7]

Insofar as this indicates that a mood colors a person's actions and reactions, we can agree for Kierkegaard. But the four moods which we

---

[2] Paul Holmer, "Theology and the Emotions" (Unpublished Essay), p. 5. In the entire discussion of mood language here, I am much indebted to Professor Holmer for several discussions and many suggestions.

[3] New York: Barnes and Noble, p. 83.

[4] *Ibid.*

[5] Page 96.

[6] Page 99.

[7] *Ibid.*

124 THE DIALECTIC OF MOODS

have examined in detail are not exclusive moods, not of each other certainly. Rather, the four are *allied* moods which overlap and are sometimes present together. One can be ironic and melancholic simultaneously. There are individual colorations which combine to produce a dark moodiness pressing for a decisive resolution in the religious, as we have witnessed in the analysis of the young aesthete. Ryle is correct that one cannot be joyous and anxious simultaneously. Some moods then do exclude, but not all. Some alternate with remarkable rapidity, as we have seen in the "Diapsalmata" of *Either/Or*. But this is more a reflection on the underlying state of the individual than an insight into mood itself.

Paul Holmer, who is influenced by both Wittgenstein and Ryle on the subject of moods and emotions, has written, "Emotions that are unrelated become moods and then they are as irrelevant and damaging as are thoughts that float aimlessly."[8] In the moods which we have examined in Kierkegaard's authorship, emotional disequilibrium, due to a more basic disequilibrium in the self, brings about moods or susceptibility to them. But the four moods which we have examined are clearly and importantly related one to the other, in a dialectic of moods. They can be aimless and damaging, as Holmer suggests and as the young aesthete evidences, if they are not related back to the deeper process of transformation and cohesion in the self, through the decisive act of the will which Kierkegaard has his pseudonyms call for.

The term mood in Danish, *Stemning* (German: *Stimmung*), suggests "attunement." One is always "attuned," and thus always in a mood. One is always in a "frame of mind" which influences the entire emotional and psychological life, the extent of the influence depending upon the intensity of the particular mood.

But this "attunement" asks the question of "attunement to what?" And in attempting to answer, one can easily get pulled into ontological language such as Heidegger's. Heidegger is himself insightful and very profound on the subject of moods, but Ryle and Wittgenstein here are good gadflies who make us hesitate before the tempting ontological leap.

Heidegger has the category of *Befindlichkeit* (state-of-mind), in *Being and Time*, as the ontological structure of moods. One is attuned; one finds oneself attuned to one's "being-in-the-world." It is the quality or nature of one's particular being-in-the-world which is responsible for the moods which come forth. Ryle more than winces at the language which suggests moods from "down there," where structures must be. But the language of Heidegger is suggestive nonetheless, and Kierkegaard is already some way in the direction of Heidegger, although he cannot be said to have an ontology of moods,

Nonetheless, for Kierkegaard, the moods of irony, anxiety, melancholy and despair arise and return because of a deeper underlying

---

[8] *Op. cit.*, p. 5.

THE DIALECTIC OF MOODS

125

situation, which is metaphysically described in *Sickness Unto Death.* Moods come due to some external catalyst; but they can only come because the individual is susceptible to them so long as the problem and task of the self remain.

The basis for the four moods we have analyzed is the fact of the individual's not being the self. An agent-catalyst brings about a mood which then presses the individual towards the transformation and restoration of the self, as the resolution of an immediate emotional crisis but also of a larger problem which has become clear as such.

Moods do not endure in time. They come and go, as is witnessed by the "Diapsalmata." In a strict sense, they do not have structures which endure, except to the extent that they share one common enduring structure, or state: the fact that one is not (yet) the (religious) self. This language of *Sickness Unto Death* begins to resemble in advance that of the later Heidegger. But any ontology here would be one imposed on Kierkegaard. There is metaphysical language, arising from metaphysical conceptions, but no explicit, worked out ontology of moods. Moreover, the one state which Kierkegaard connects with moods is already narrower in scope than the "being-in-the-world" which Heidegger posits.

For Heidegger, one always has mood.[9] Moreover, "A mood makes manifest 'how one is, and how one is faring'."[10] What one must do, according to Heidegger, is to "give in" to mood. He writes that it is an everyday matter for the individual (*Dasein*) not to give in to moods, and thus not to follow up their disclosure. "*Dasein* can, should, and must, through knowledge and will, become master of its moods."[11] He continues, "When we master a mood, we do not do so by a counter mood."[12] Here Heidegger is in perfect accord with Kierkegaard. For this is exactly what Kierkegaard calls for: (1) mastery of mood, by making an act of the will and passing into and through mood, in order to come to the disclosure mood brings about the self, and (2) higher consciousness.

For Heidegger, as for Kierkegaard, mood has as its basic character to bring one back to something.[13] This is the "repetition" of which Kierkegaard speaks: coming back to the self grounded in relation to its Constituting Power.

THE FOUR MOODS OF THE SELF

The four moods which we have analyzed are deeply inter-related. They have a common source which creates susceptibility to them in the individual, viz. the shattered self requiring restoration and completion.

We have observed four individual moods and their decisive function at a particular threshold of new consciousness and higher integration.

[9] *Being and Time*, p. 173 and p. 395.
[10] *Ibid.*, p. 173.
[11] Page 175.
[12] *Ibid.*
[13] Page 390.

126 THE DIALECTIC OF MOODS

They have the quality, as *Stemning*, of tonality. "Tonality" is suggestive in that it connotes a quality which pervades the personality, a quality not strictly localized. It further suggests a coloring of perceptions, rather like a filter which intensifies, minimizes or maximizes, alters percepta so that the "objective world" is experienced through this filter and "less than objectively." But this filter is really a form of intensified subjectivity.

The moods make their appearance in the emotional life and announce "something" going on which must be explored and each mood willingly gone through in order for it to be understood. What is transpiring is eventually seen to have deeper roots in the personality. It is not a matter of something external momentarily coloring, like a passing cloud, the emotional life, but rather something deeper and essential to the individual, whose meaning will be found only by exploring the movement.

While some external factor may be, and normally is, the agent-catalyst for the appearance of a mood in the personality (i.e. appearing as an emotional coloring of the personality for a period of time), the external cause is not essential to mood. The essential cause of mood is rather seen to lie on the one hand in the state of non-integration and on the other in stirrings of spirit which press in the direction of integration.

Since mood is prominent in the emotional life, in normal social involvements others are bound to be involved. But in their essence, moods essentially have little to do with others, and it is a mistake to think that they do. While others may indeed be the external cause which brings a mood to the surface, the moods are essentially about the self. Something about oneself, one's self-perception and one's self-understanding is at issue in the moods.

Love and hatred and anger and other powerful emotions relate a subject and an object. In the moods, properly understood, there is no object. In neither irony; melancholy, anxiety, nor despair is any subject made the object. Melancholy is passive, pained longing for an impossible ideal object, and even when the longing becomes properly directed toward God, this is not properly speaking an "object." Irony is a movement of rejection which relates positively to no object. Anxiety revolves around the problem of "nothing" and its intensification in despair points back to oneself who cannot be an object for oneself.

In mood, the subject comes to the fore both by an intensification of feeling, which makes one more aware of oneself, and by the absence of any object. In normal emotional life, it is the object of the emotion which is emphasized and in extreme forms of love, for example, it is often said that the subject forgets himself and concentrates on the object of love (or hatred, etc.). In the moods, however, the subject is intensified not only in feelings but in consciousness. Thus, in melancholy, for example, it is oneself and one's presence to oneself that is intensified by a yearning that cannot find an object. In irony, the rejection of all finitude emphasizes oneself in the sensation of freedom in rejection. In anxiety and despair, one experiences oneself as the problem. Thus in the moods subjectivity is intensified by the individuation produced by a

THE DIALECTIC OF MOODS 127

mood and by the intensity of feeling in mood. By the very absence of object, mood additionally heightens the sense of subject. It forces a subject to confront his own subjectivity and presses him to probe its meaning.

The moods represent a clash, and the result of a clash, between one's being as man and the way he is attempting to live out his human being. In effect, the clash is constituted by the conflict between a lived-out philosophy of life which posits man as a static being and the deeper reality of man's being, which, when correctly understood, reveals man as dynamic and evolving. Followed through, the moods lead to understanding oneself as a dynamic being and to the self-articulation of one's being in a new life-view.

Within any existing individual, once the moods have appeared and cast their shadow over the personality, they continue to exist spherically and simultaneously in a person until the one problem they all represent, viz. the reintegration of the self, is resolved. However, there is an aspect, or phase, when each mood rises to critical prominence and entails a widening of consciousness. In becoming conscious of the mood, one is on the threshold in each instance of higher consciousness about the self, provided one allows oneself to pass through the mood rather than merely waiting for it to subside. Thus potentially, each mood represents a deepening of inwardness and spiritual life. But the conscious aspect, or phase, of each mood comes stadially and in relation to the preceding mood. And it is concerning this stadial movement and interrelation of moods that we speak in the phrase "the dialectic of moods." The stadial progression, and then interrelationships, between the aspects of the four moods represent heightening crisis, the potential of higher consciousness, and the need for decision.

B. THE CRISES-SEQUENCE

The crisis aspect of the moods we have been considering occurs in the sequence: irony, anxiety, melancholy (*Tungsind*), despair. However, the ground-work is first set, as it were, by the initial *Melancholi*. For *Melancholi* is the result of the very first stirrings of spirit, the awakening process, in which yearning and longing first occur. As we have already noted, it represents an essential sensitivity and openness to the spiritual which will later be developed and more properly directed. In initial *Melancholi*, it is still undirected. But as the seed of mature religious consciousness, its importance cannot be stressed enough. It is the fundamental potentiality and predisposition toward spiritual evolution upon which the other moods work their effect in the personality.

IRONY. Irony as consciousness represents the rupture of the illusions of the phenomenal world. The illusions of finitude and temporality are shattered. One realizes that that which one seeks and yearns for is not

128 THE DIALECTIC OF MOODS

to be found in the finite and the temporal. One has lived the finite and the temporal and found them incapable of making good on illusory promise. Finally one perceives the obstacle posed by finitude and temporality as such and sees the need to move beyond them.

The move beyond first takes the form of passionate rejection of all finitude and all that is involved with finitude – thus the phrase "infinite negativity" of irony. One rejects, and puts behind, one's illusions, but equally importantly one breaks with the society of men who have shared and reinforced those illusions and who continue in them. The world, world-view and society of men who constitute finitude's kingdom of illusions are emphatically rejected, and one seeks to soar in freedom in search of a possible worthy object of desire.

The stirring of spirit has set into motion the dynamism of movement and growth in the psyche and will continue now more strongly. The ironic consciousness represents seeing through illusory direction and passionately rejecting it. However, the break is not complete, and here lie the dangers of irony. One remains a man among men, rooted in the material world even if one can no longer feel part of them. Their intellectual and emotional holds have been broken, but the physical facts cannot be. The danger is that one then turn to imagination and seek expansion and fulfillment there, that one attempt to deny, in rejecting the illusions of finitude, one's finite humanity. Mastered irony, which overcomes the dangers of the ironic consciousness, emerges only after a subject has transcended aesthetic categories, and when irony has negated itself.

Positively considered, the new ironist is poised for higher development. He has taken up higher consciousness both about his world and about himself, although that consciousness is yet defined only negatively. He has broken with the past, but only negatively posited the future toward which he seeks to move. With irony alone, no matter the force of its passion, he cannot move there. He stands on the threshold of possibility, awaiting further movement. He no longer defines himself in externals, and he knows that they will not suffice, but the movement of spirit will have to raise another mood up to the surface before he knows that it is in the internal, rather than in imagination and the imaginary, that he must discover and actualize the self.

ANXIETY. Anxiety marks the beginning of positive movement. It represents first of all a purification experience in which the last vestiges of finitude are purged by the inner torment of confrontation with one's own nothingness. Anxiety's first offering is consciousness of the nothingness which is at the core of one's being. Yet at the same time it poises one on the threshold of positivity. For anxiety also brings the experience of possibility: that as a human being one has a vast scope of possibilities.

Anxiety marks a great advance in consciousness. For, by allowing oneself to pass through the experience of anxiety with the wrenching

THE DIALECTIC OF MOODS 129

experience of nothingness, one comes to understand that the nothingness which one is is an as-yet-unactualized scope of possibles. Thus one
discovers that one has possibles, that one's positive identity consists in
the actualization of possibilities. In this, one comes to a fundamental
self-understanding as human being: that becoming is an essential aspect
of one's being.

With the experience and consciousness of possibility, an invigorating
sense of potentiality returns to the personality, as well as a sober sense
of responsibility. Having rejected the old in irony, one now is ready for
actualization of the new. And with anxiety comes the heightened
inwardness which will later lead to resolving the religious problem of the
personality in a more focused set of possibles.

TUNGSIND. *Tungsind* represents an aggravation of the condition of
pained longing sensitivity which is *Melancholi*. As the image of the word
suggests, it is indeed a becoming-heavier, -darker, even -gloomy, of the
personality as it remains open to the possibility of growth but does not
yet move actively toward the affirmation of a definite direction and then
concrete actualization.

As an experience, it is a religious crisis which succeeds the jarring
experience of possibility in anxiety. Only upon reaching the destiny in
which it presses, and thus only in retrospect, does one see that it
requires the religious for its resolution.

Tungsind announces the imminent need for decision and resolution of
an enduring problem. Negatively, it suggests the religious, for *Tungsind*
is the heavy emptiness of longing continually frustrated by the finite and
non-religious. One might imagine a *Tungsind* growing progressively
heavier and darker with each attempt at a non-religious solution.

Thus negatively (i.e., by simple process of elimination), it suggests a
new and positive direction for the actualization of possibility. Its very
pain testifies to the failure of all else: all abstract and finite possibles. So
long as sensitivity continues and is not extinguished in the personality,
Tungsind grows heavier and more critical. This is basically the predicament of Johannes who has rejected all finite possibles, remains sensitive
and full of religious longing, but who steadfastly refuses to move beyond
the imaginary possibles of his mind's creation.

Tungsind brings one to consciousness of genuine crisis within the
personality and the need for imminent resolution. The proper direction
it suggests negatively and by elimination of all else. It prepares the
evolving religious personality to accept the higher consciousness and
more specific direction to come through the intensification of anxiety in
despair.

DESPAIR. Despair as a crisis experience occurs at a conscious level
only after the preceding moods have been gone through. For it is the
passageway for the departure from aesthetic categories into the ethico-
religious. It is the result of the ever-stronger stirring of spirit within the
psyche and of a greater awakening of spirit to the point where the

130   THE DIALECTIC OF MOODS

individual begins to recognize more clearly Spirit and the eternal. The first act of despair is choice of oneself as spirit in relationship with Spirit and the eternal and affirmation of the spiritual growth process.

But the consciousness brought in despair is much more. It is the fuller realization that one has fallen away from an original openness to possibility, through sinning, into an unnatural state, viz. continuity in sin. One has been struggling to break the limits, first in the negative passion of irony and then in the purgation of anxiety, but one cannot (yet) do so.

Before the first act of despair, one has come to the point of recognizing the need for reintegration of the personality by some decisive action which will recover one from the dispersion for which one oneself is responsible. In the higher consciousness before the second and decisive despair which consists in taking on sin-consciousness, one is more clearly aware of the sole specific source of resolution. This comes with a new level of self-understanding in which one comes to appreciate painfully, first, the nature of the relationship to the Constituting Power which is essential to the synthesis man is and, second, the consequences of the rupture.

In the higher despair, one comes to a final agonizing realization of one's inability to win through to one's essential freedom possibility which is relationship to the eternal and the infinite. Having discovered the significance of the spirit dimension of one's being and the disequilibrium due to rupture with Spirit, one finds oneself helpless to actualize that which one now knows to be the sole possibility which can reintegrate and marshal the dynamism of spirit in the direction in which it presses.

Having understood the nature of the self, the need to affirm the self, its dynamism, and destiny in an act of the will is now the pre-condition for reintegration. First guilt-consciousness and then sin-consciousness become the essential conditions for the enhanced restoration of man's essential spiritual possibility. These levels of consciousness come about with the progressive deepening of self-understanding and the affirmation of that understanding in acts of the will.

By movement into and through the profound experience of despair, one transforms oneself finally into a helpless conscious sinner. But in so doing, the stage is set for the restoration which Revelation promises (although this relieves none of the anguish of the transformation process). At the extreme of helplessness in which the gravity of the disequilibrium is recognized and the rupture sensed most painfully, a mysterious fusion takes place in which there is an *Aufhebung* in the fullest sense: the hold of finitude, temporality and necessity are annulled while at the same time they are preserved in a higher synthesis prepared by man's uncovering infinitude, the eternal, and freedom and then by their grounding in the Constituting Power who restores the rupture and synthesizes the elements. This, according to Kierkegaard-Anti-Climacus, he does by his grace of forgiveness.

THE DIALECTIC OF MOODS 131

C. INTERRELATIONSHIPS

The four moods which we have discussed are interrelated in the highest degree. Their structures endure simultaneously and together, after each has come into being singly. The structures have their own sequence: primal anxiety, despair as sin, *Melancholi*, and irony. But each presumes the anterior. Irony is a breakthrough in the sensitive longing for that which one has not. Sensitive longing (*Melancholi*) is awakened by and results from rupture with the fulfilling and longed-for object – a state which constitutes despair and which in turn depends on the fact that one is a being with possibility and in the first dizzying experience of possibility, which is primal anxiety, one has fallen.

In terms of the crises-sequence, the interrelationships are of a different kind and of a different order. In each instance, the way is open to higher crisis by an act of will affirming the process and thus allowing it.

Melancholi and irony are basically negative in function and content. *Melancholi* is longing for that which one has not and for that which one cannot attain. Irony is realization of the unattainability of the desired on the plane of the finite. Both represent together the first convulsions against the aesthetic life which implicitly promises that which experience teaches it cannot deliver.

Anxiety, *Tungsind* and despair are basically positive, not in the sense that they deliver the required content for fulfilled existence but rather in the sense that they are preparation by moving in the direction of true positive content and represent potentially a final overcoming of the finite. Anxiety is the discovery of possibility, the discovery that one is an evolving being with spiritual possibility. In *Tungsind* comes the clearer realization of the religious nature of the desired and realization of the religious as the end solution for the soul's longing. In despair, one realizes that choice of the eternal, and of the self in relationship with the eternal, begins the process of healing and growth, and finally that consciousness of one's sinfulness and helplessness before the Constituting Power brings one to the final point of preparation for a higher life.

Underlying all the moods and constituting the common ground for their interrelationships is the stirring of spirit out of which each mood issues. Spirit stirs in the unformed religious depths of the soul. (The mythological metaphor too springs from Romanticism.) The moods issue from the interrelationship and conflict between the growing spiritual dimension of the personality and a way of life which contradicts and blocks that reality. The growing assertion of spirit posits man as an evolving, future-oriented, dynamic being, and this existential fact clashes with increasing force and violence against a way of life which posits and attempts to keep man static in a life consisting of nothing more than the endless repetition of past moments. Spirit will not let itself be mocked, and the result is a series of moods which punish and chastise, then potentially purify and raise one's awareness to the inner reality. The

132 THE DIALECTIC OF MOODS

critical moods command and call one back, not in the coolness of reasoned argument but in the passion of emotions which seize and fill one and cannot be ignored. And they re-emerge until their revelation is finally heeded and internalized.

D. FUNCTION OF MOODS IN EMERGING RELIGIOUS SUBJECTIVITY

Each mood as it rises to consciousness commences a process of revelation, negative and positive, which is extended in content and urgency with each succeeding mood. Each reveals in an ever-deeper sense the bankruptcy and inadequacy of the aesthetic life. This happens existentially, in the sense that the passion and pain of the moods reveal the inability of aesthetic categories to bring the happiness and peace the soul craves. Each mood, to the extent that one masters it and reaches new self-understanding, also reveals the inadequacy of the aesthetic intellectually, as one contrasts new self understanding to that which the aesthetic posited. Each mood declares in an ever deeper way: "This life has been inadequate; this life is despair."

To the extent that one passes through each mood, one penetrates to its positive meaning to understand more clearly one's nature as creature but also one's final spiritual destiny.

The revelation constitutes a progressive self understanding, as one penetrates to an awareness of oneself as spiritually qualified being and to discernment of the spiritual process out of which moods issue. In experiencing fully the purgation and revelation of each mood, one learns something universal, one comes to an understanding of man; but more important is the self-understanding which has immediate practical application. This self-understanding counters the aesthetic with its lie about the nature of the self and it sets the stage for the construction of a new, lived out life-view which will solidify and articulate the dynamism of growth in the spiritual. For the dialectic of moods is also relative: a process between points; a transition, by way of inner transformation, from the aesthetic to the religious. A coherent life-view based on the realities of man's being and the world he lives in remains to be worked out and articulated after the dialectic of moods has performed its task.

In the ironic consciousness first one sees through illusion and rejects it in negative passion. Anxiety, *Tungsind*, and despair then take one in the direction in which irony would soar, in the discovery of the infinite and the eternal. But by this discovery comes a redemption of the finite and the temporal. Limits of the aesthetic are seen, but also the limits of the self, so that finally one is forced to recognize one's limitations, as well as possibilities, as creature. This constitutes the process of "undoing the spell," the mythological metaphor for recovering the self from despair. However, one cannot complete the process alone; one is left finally before God awaiting the grace which brings about the final fusion of the elements of the synthesis. The moods have set one in right relationship

THE DIALECTIC OF MOODS 133

with the elements of the synthesis, within the limits of human possibility. The reality and limitations of the finite and the infinite, and of the temporal and the eternal, of possibility and necessity, are perceived; and grace is awaited.

The many revelations of the moods, as the undoing of the mythological spell which keeps one captive, constitute the rediscovery of the lost path. For what is revealed in the self-understanding of the moods is not only that there is a path, but that there always was a path and that this path had been lost, obscured to the self fragmented by sin. And while the path had been lost, it is eventually recovered because of the surviving spiritual instinct within the personality. Feeble and handicapped, the spiritual instinct endures and eventually provides the basis of self-recovery. Furthermore, by the paradox of the *felix culpa*, fall into sin provides the basis for the spiritual instinct's becoming conscious, as spirit moves after sin from dreaming state to gradual awakening. Spirit awakens and by degrees is reintegrated into the personality in a gradual opening to the religious.

But the true significance of the sequence of moods is preparation for transformation and for synthesis. The moods too are but the phase of a higher process. Man's being seeks fusion of the synthesis and total reintegration of spirit. And this movement the moods, neither individually nor in their dialectic, can bring about. They merely prepare the stage, through fulfillment of the natural human, for the decisive action of the super-natural. The anguish of the consciousness of despair is that one cannot recover oneself from the dispersion of sin, that one cannot reach the Transcendent God whose immanent presence has been discovered in the spirit of man.

This fact is mirrored in Kierkegaard's authorship by the scope of the two stages beyond the aesthetic. Considered either as the ethico-religious or as the ethical and the religious, that which is beyond the aesthetic relativizes it significantly and places it within a much larger perspective. *The meaning of moods is the religious,* but that meaning is discovered entirely on the natural plane. The moods have taken us as far as they can, and our study goes no further in this respect. It declines to enter the "promised land," the realm touched by the super-natural. Instead, we content ourselves to stay on this side of the crossing as we philosophically survey the process of advance to the water's edge.

E. MOODS AND LIFE-VIEWS

Life-view is a key term and a key notion in Kierkegaard's authorship. And its relationship to moods is quite essential. (It will be discussed at length in Chapter Seven.) Seen in the proper perspective the moods are but a transition between life-views.

The four critical moods uncover the existential inadequacies of the aesthetic life-view. They thus constitute a more powerful critique than any

134 THE DIALECTIC OF MOODS

intellectual analysis and serve as the necessary prerequisite to the construction of a new life-view. They are as such an initiation into the spiritual which provides the perspective for a realistic and workable life-view: one which does not collapse in the living-out, but rather strengthens and is strengthened.

The moods show that aesthetic categories do not hold when put to the test in a concrete existence. For the moods reveal conflict and thus the contradiction of the harmony which life-view should bring about. The aesthetic life-view is always synonymous in Kierkegaard's writings with Romanticism and its intellectual off-shoot Idealism. Kierkegaard was stirred by the High Culture advocacy of a false life-view in his times. This consisted in part in the enticing moods of melancholy and irony prominent in the writings of the Romantics. Kierkegaard concedes that the Romantics are on the threshold of something, but that they do not know it. Thus their irony is futile, as is the sweet pain of their melancholy. They are trapped in ignorance, because they do not realize that what is needed is a breakthrough, a passing through and beyond the moods to something higher, and that this can only come about by an act of the will and the shift to new understanding and way of life.

Kierkegaard's concern is to redeem the understanding of moods and then to place them in a larger perspective, so that their purpose be seen. This involves relativizing them, so that they no longer are viewed as final ends as are irony and melancholy among the Romantics, but part of a larger, transcending process. Providing perspective, for Kierkegaard, involves showing the function of moods as a negative index of the viability of the aesthetic life-view, and hence rejection of it and of its proponents, the Romantics. Thus the analysis of moods in Kierkegaard's writings has the ironic purpose of rescuing the significance of moods from the Romantic's limited understanding, of showing how the same moods discredit the Romantic's life-view, and then finally of indicating moods' purpose in the construction of a new, higher life-view.

For if Kierkegaard is passionate against Romanticism's flaws and the aesthetic life-view, it is only because he sees them as a deception and a distraction from a positive possibility. Rejection of the aesthetic is not merely ironic, in the sense of being fueled merely by the negative passion of rejection. It is equally based on the vision of a positive, viable life-view which will indeed provide all which the aesthetic claims but cannot do. The new life-view is within the religious. It is further defined as the Christian life-view, a life-view based on the highest aspect of the religious. But such a life-view is not the total rejection of aesthetic categories. In this sense, the image of "spheres" is more apt than that of "stages." Much of the aesthetic remains, contained within the religious sphere. For the Christian religious is in a dialectical relationship with the aesthetic, is permeated with the aesthetic, indeed consists in the redemption of the aesthetic by the rejection of stadial aspects which need to be overcome and left behind and below, as one ascends.

CHAPTER VII

FROM VICTIM TO MASTER OF MOODS: TOWARDS THE CHRISTIAN LIFE-VIEW

> If there should ever by such a thing as Danish philosophy, it will differ from the German in not beginning with Nothing. Neither will it be presuppositionless, nor explain everything by Mediation. Let it rather begin with the sentence, 'There are many things in heaven and earth which no philosopher has explained'.
>
> – Papirer V A 46 (1844)

Having witnessed in the preceding chapters the inner drama described by the moods and their dialectic, it may seem anti-climactic to introduce a discussion of life-view at this point. However, to fail to do so would be to miss an essential element in the spiritual transformation and emerging religious self which the moods reveal and effect.

"Life-view" is an undramatic term, but that is not to suggest that the formation of a life-view is an undramatic process. On the contrary, the formation of a life-view requires vigilance and struggle. Unlike the moods, it represents an end product rather than a process. And it is an essential category in Kierkegaard's thought. It is the Romantic's illusory beginning and the genuine Christian's enlightened end in articulating the meaning of his own existence.

Most men "begin" with a life-view – begin with the illusion of having a philosophy of life but which can only properly come after having lived long and intensely. Thus, much of Kierkegaard's effort will be devoted to dispelling illusory life-views and illusory understandings of how one goes about forming a life-view. In the end, and strictly speaking, there is only one life-view and only one way of coming to it. In retrospect, we will see that life-view is a rather clear concept which in itself does not require extended explanation, once *false* views have been dispelled. We trace Kierkegaard's treatment of it in order to show how he deals with different facets of it, to demonstrate its underlying importance through-out the authorship, and to show that the one viable life-view is the inevitable goal toward which the moods move the soul of man. In addition, this life-view represents a decisive transformation from victim to master of moods.

The issue of a life-view involves much more as well. It goes to the heart of Kierkegaard's existential philosophy. Life-view emphasizes the duty and importance of the individual to understand himself, both his "premises" and his "conclusions", his conditionality and his freedom. Each man must answer for himself about the meaning of life, and thus he cannot take his cue from the spirit of the age which will all too readily answer on his behalf. In addition, life-view, as philosophy of life, challenges established, academic philosophy which proceeds exclusively

136 TOWARDS THE CHRISTIAN LIFE-VIEW

from thought. The new philosophy which Kierkegaard suggests by his emphasis on life-view and his definition of it is no longer detached thought but reflection upon the meaning of experience and then its articulation in a coherent view. Life-view is not be to the sole aspect of new philosophizing, but will instead properly take its place at the center of the search for wisdom, which philosophy once claimed to be.

A. PRELIMINARY CONSIDERATIONS

THE TERM "LIFE-VIEW"

Kierkegaard's term does not translate into everyday English. He speaks of a *Livs-Anskuelse*, an outlook on life, a *life-view*. This parallels the German term *Lebensanschauung* (also *Lebensbegriff*). Unfortunately for the clarity we would like, Kierkegaard does not contrast "life-view" and "world-view" (*Weltanschauung*) as terms. He does however, contrast life-view to a view provided by the spirit of the age, and this latter is Hegel's use of the term "world-view". Kierkegaard makes the contrast, but not in the contrasting terms. In fact, at times he uses "life-view" (*Livs-Anskuelse*) and "world-view" (*Verdens-Anskuelse*) synonymously (as in *Papirer* VII[2] B 235).

For Hegel, *Weltanschauung* means the world-view of a certain nation, in a certain time: a shared view in which the poet participates.[1] Thus a world-view is a general, shared view which one acquires automatically by participation in the times and society which one forms with one's fellows. For Kierkegaard a life-view is the very opposite. It is personal and acquired only by effort in one's individual life. In life-view as a term, the emphasis in Kierkegaard is always on the individual, on the interior life, and on active effort in the exterior life. For only by reflection upon important inner happenings does one come to the essential self-understanding which is a life-view. World-view, à la Hegel, is the understanding from apprehending the unfolding of Spirit in the exterior world. Life-view depends upon understanding the inner life of Spirit, i.e. within the individual. Hegelian world-view revolves around the necessary, while life-view, for Kierkegaard, discerns the possible and holds it up before one.

References to the importance of a life-view, its nature and its function in existence are numerous in Kierkegaard's authorship. We will proceed in the following pages to survey and gather together discussions of this category with the goal of (1) defining it, (2) seeing its integral connection with the function of moods, and (3) seeing the interaction of moods and the category of life-view as pointing to the inevitability of the Christian life-view for one who continues to grow in the spirit and, more exclusively, pointing to the Christian as the sole sphere with a claim to the predicate "life-view".

---

[1] Emanuel Hirsch, *Kierkegaard-Studien* (Gutersloh, 1933), p. 20.

TOWARDS THE CHRISTIAN LIFE-VIEW

BIOGRAPHICAL PRELUDE

In the summer of 1835, at the age of 22 and with the encouragement and financial support of his aged father, the young Kierkegaard set off for the north Sjælland fishing town of Gilleleje. There he began to think through the impasse which he was experiencing in seeking inner equilibrium. The journal entry of August 1st of that year represents a crystallization of reflections about this problem and initially articulates themes which reappear in the subsequent authorship.

The entire entry is lengthy and oft-cited. In it, Kierkegaard reflects that he now realizes that a philosophical system, a political theory or an exposition of Christianity amounts to nothing if it has no deeper meaning for oneself and for one's life. For himself, he recognizes that the imperative of understanding is strong, but he recognizes too that the search for understanding must be included within the larger perspective of his life. He hopes that understanding *himself*, and not merely intellectual problems, will provide the anchorage which he has been able to find neither in the boundless sea of pleasure (the aesthetic in general) nor in objective understanding (philosophy). He is searching for something which will allow him to live a whole human life, and even while he describes this aim in still-abstract terms, he sees that it must be real and connected to his own individual existence. He writes,

What I really need is to get clear in my mind what I am to do, not what I am to understand, except insofar as an understanding must precede every action. The thing is to understand my destiny, to see what the deity really wishes me to do; that means finding a truth which is truth for me, finding the idea for which I can live and die.[2]

The "idea" which will ultimately satisfy these conditions is the Christian life with which the young Kierkegaard gradually reaches *rapprochement*. The relation here between understanding and acting is significant. He sees that he must act and that understanding, rather than being an end in itself as it may be in philosophy, is a guide to action, the action of becoming himself. His destiny is ultimately Christianity as the truth which is truth for himself (and for others, he will add) and the action he is called to is the theme of the latter part of the authorship: "becoming a Christian."

One must first learn to know himself, before one knows something else (γνῶθι σεαμτὸν). When a person has thus understood himself inwardly and now sees the path of his journey, then does his life acquire peace and meaning, then does he become free from that troublesome, ominous fellow-traveller – that life-irony which shows itself in the sphere of understanding and bids true understanding

---

[2] *Papirer* I A 75, p. 53. (My translation.) Danish text reads: "Det, der egentlig mangler mig, er at komme paa det Rene med mig selv om, hvad jeg skal gjøre, ikke om hvad jeg skal erkjende, uden forsaavidt en Erkjenden maa gaae forud for enhver Handlen. Det kommer an paa at forstaae min Bestemmelse, at see, hvad Guddommen egentlig vil, at jeg skal gjøre; det gjælder om at finde en Sandhed; som er Sandhed for mig, at finde den Idee, for hvilken jeg vil leve og døe."

138 TOWARDS THE CHRISTIAN LIFE-VIEW

begin with not understanding (Socrates), just as God created the world from nothing.[3]

The way to inner peace consists of understanding the structures of one's being as created by God. Thus this understanding does not begin with imaginative self-description through speculation, as creation *ex nihilo*, but consists rather in an exploration of the self which God has created. Such understanding surpasses the ironic stance of Socrates which is negative and surpasses too the Platonic Socrates who represents Platonic Idealism by restoring understanding to existence as the sphere to which it properly belongs.

PHILOSOPHY

The soul-searching which the young Kierkegaard began in earnest in 1835 led him more and more to question the meaning and importance of philosophy. Something of the "love of wisdom" appealed to him, while at the same time he came to see that what the professional philosophers were doing was quite different. Whether it were sophistry or philodoxy, it had little application on the personal level.[4]

One must keep in mind the cultural world in which Kierkegaard lived in order to appreciate the questions he is about to raise. Humanists on our own shores, academicians or not, would probably not view academic philosophy as such an obstacle to the raising of humanistic questions, for they would nowadays not be likely to choose philosophy at all as the course of preparation for raising such questions. But Kierkegaard's times and intellectual world were quite different. Philosophy on the Continent had apparently just reached its fulfillment in the System of Hegel, in the context of a culture which encouraged its best minds to take up the study of philosophy. Philosophy was a noble calling. Philosophical issues were the talk of the educated and the cultured. The German philosophical tradition, self-conscious of its accomplishments, had begun to compare itself to the Greek experience in philosophy.[5]

The "latest" in philosophy, viz. Hegelianism, had been recently

[3] *Papirer* I A 75, pp. 56–57. (My translation.) Danish text reads: "Man maa først lære at kjende sig selv, inden man kjender noget Andet (γνῶθι σεαμτὸν). Først naar Mennesket saaledes inderlig har forstaaet sig selv og nu seer sin Gang hen af sin Bane, først da faaer hans Liv Ro og Betydning, først da bliver han fri for hiin besærlige, unheldsvangre Reisekammerat – hiin Livs-Ironi, der viser sig i Erkjendelsens Sphære og byder den sande Erkjenden at begynde med en Ikke-Erkjenden (Socrates), ligesom Gud skabte Verden af Intet."

[4] For Socrates, the Sophists represented false wisdom, since it depended on technique and could be sold. Socrates also refers to "philodoxers." who are lovers of opinion (φίλοσ/δόξα) rather than lovers of wisdom (φίλοσ/σοφία).

[5] The comparison of itself to the Greek experience was characteristic not only of German philosophy, but of German Romanticism in general, into which Kierkegaard subsumes German Idealism. The theme of attending the rebirth of philosophy continues long after Hegel, until so recent a figure as Heidegger who compares his philosophy implicitly with the pre-Socratics.

TOWARDS THE CHRISTIAN LIFE-VIEW

introduced even into tiny Denmark, that outpost of Germanic culture, by Copenhagen's Professor Martensen and was taking hold there even as the philosophical fashion was already changing in Berlin. Against this intellectual backdrop, Kierkegaard begins to formulate the questions: What is philosophy?, What is the philosophic life?

In his own philosophical masterwork entitled *Philosophical Fragments*, Kierkegaard proceeds from a distinction made by Leibniz between the truths of experience and the truths of thought.[6] Kierkegaard clearly saw that philosophy proceeded to develop the truths of thought, but unfortunately did not stop there. In its claim to be all encompassing, Idealism subsumed the truths of experience, in Hegel's System. In addition, it went on to declare the content of Christianity and philosophy identical. Such a claim, while undisturbing and even encouraging to those theologians awed by the progress of philosophy and seeking fashionable intellectual buttressing, deeply disturbed Kierkegaard who saw in Christianity a truth of experience which could not be subsumed by thought, a truth which was in fact a scandal to thought (the theme of *Training in Christianity*), and a truth of history (the Christ-event) which could never be reduced to merely one more necessary event in the unfolding of Spirit in history. This third point Kierkegaard specifically engages in the *Fragments*.

"Philosophy" for Kierkegaard always means academic philosophy: Idealism in both its Greek and German forms. Less explicitly than the later Heidegger, Kierkegaard suggests that philosophy went astray as early as Plato. To be sure, the man Socrates remains a hero worthy of imitation, but there is a distinction to be made between the historical Socrates and and the Platonic Socrates of the *Dialogues*. Plato has given to world literature both the historical figure and the mouthpiece of Platonic philosophy. Historically and symbolically, Socrates represents for Kierkegaard the culmination of the "love of wisdom" in an authentic human existence grounded in reflection and the desire to understand oneself. This Socrates he affirms and admires. But the Platonic Socrates he debates, socratically, and nowhere more clearly than in the *Fragments* where the Platonic Socrates in effect is challenged by Christ (Socratic humanism challenged by the Christian position of faith.)[7]

Again and again, Kierkegaard raises the question: What is philosophy? – an age-old question which philosophy has always been asking itself. Kierkegaard had been stung by philosophy and could never entirely reject it, but at the same time he could not accept its pretensions and *hubris*, especially as represented by Idealism. He was equally stung by, and convinced of the importance of, Christianity. Thus Idealism's claim to be identical with the content of Christianity, and Christianity's seeming acceptance of this, enraged him. The *Fragments* sets out

[6] Cf. Niels Thulstrup, Introduction to *Philosophical Fragments*, 2nd edition (Princeton, 1962), trans. by Howard V. Hong, xlvii.

[7] For a more complete treatment of Kierkegaard on Socrates, cf. Jens Himmelstrup, *Søren Kierkegaards Opfattelse af Sokrates* (Copenhagen, 1924).

140   TOWARDS THE CHRISTIAN LIFE-VIEW

to show the irreconcilability of Idealism and Christianity at the most important level by showing that Christianity depends essentially on the individual's acceptance, in faith, of a non-necessary historical event upon which his eternal happiness depends.

He continues the argument of irreconcilability by emphasizing the subjective aspect of Christianity as over against the objective claims of philosophy. The emphasis on the subjective, which is most pronounced in the *Postcript*, applies however both to the essential in Christianity and also in the relevance which philosophy might have in life. For a philosophy of life holds a high value for Kierkegaard, and ultimately philosophy of life (life-view) and Christianity become identified as Kierkegaard more and more clearly suggests Christianity as both the "new" and only truly possible philosophy of life.

The religious humanist Johannes Climacus, pseudonymous author of the *Fragments* and the *Postscript*, makes an earlier appearance as a young man not yet mature about life in the unpublished *De Omnibus Dubitandum Est* of 1842–3, in which he sets out to lead the philosophic life, as he proceeds from doubt (in imitation of modern philosophy) and applies it with passion to all of existence. The young Johannes Climacus is a melancholy youth in love with thought.[8] By degrees, he realizes that the philosophic life which is led in thought and in love with thought is really Romanticism.[9]

The incomplete and unpublished *De Omnibus Dubitandum Est* leaves unanswered the question whether there is an authentic and viable philosophic life. But it shows that such a life cannot begin with the intellectual doubting which sets modern philosophy into motion. A philosophic life is ultimately possible, but only if it is led not in the service of thought but of existence. Such a life seeks in seriousness to understand itself and its dynamic nature and then to articulate that understanding. It will then provide coherence and equilibrium in life, while reinforcing the direction of one's life. If a philosophic life can come about, it must begin not with doubt but with the wonder ($\theta\alpha\upsilon\mu\acute{\alpha}\zeta\epsilon\iota\nu$) which originally prompted Greek philosophy and with the despair which redeems existence.

B. LIFE-VIEW IN *FROM THE PAPERS OF ONE STILL LIVING*

BACKGROUND

From the Papers of One Still Living appeared in 1838 and represents Kierkegaard's first published work, although he does not include it in the list of his formal authorship. It is short, numbering about forty pages, and is probably best considered as an overgrown newspaper article. For *From the Papers of One Still Living* really belongs to the

[8] *DO*, p. 103.
[9] *DO*, p. 143.

TOWARDS THE CHRISTIAN LIFE-VIEW

period in which Kierkegaard published occasional articles in Copenhagen newspapers. Its style is pedantic and difficult, and its syntax is highly complex, being rather an imitation of German high literary style. After its publication, Hans Christian Andersen, the man against whom the polemical review was written, boasted that only two people in Copenhagen had ever read it, viz. himself and the author.[10]

The curious title of the work apparently has nothing to do with the content, which is a review of Andersen's novel *Only A Fiddler*, but reflects Kierkegaard's surprise at having survived his father. The elder Kierkegaard had instilled in his youngest son Søren the belief that his family was cursed and that he was destined to outlive all his children, in the manner of a biblical curse. But Michael Kierkegaard died suddenly in 1838, at the age of 82.[11] The death affected the young Kierkegaard in many ways. One was to turn him decisively toward the completion of his theological studies. But even as he did this, he made an effort in the area of literary criticism, one that was not to be his last.

THEORY OF LITERATURE

In his critical review of Andersen's *Only A Fiddler*, Kierkegaard is thoroughly polemical, despite his claim to write with "sympathetic ink." He sets forth his view of the three forms of poetry, viz. the lyric, the epic and the dramatic, which in turn correspond to feeling (the emotive), cognition (the cognitive) and will (the area of conflict-creation) respectively.[12]

The novelist is the epic poet and the "primary qualification of the epic poet is a solidly constructed philosophy of life as the background for his epic productions."[13] To Kierkegaard, Andersen is essentially a failure as an epic poet, and thus as a novelist, because at root he lacks the depth and maturity necessary for a life-view, and consequently for a mature work. Andersen thus remains a lyric poet who fails to bring the epic material into living, organic coherence.

Andersen is indeed the object of criticism in the work, but he also provides the opportunity for Kierkegaard to set forth his views about literature and the importance of a mature, serious life-view. What he demands of Andersen, he also demands of himself and of every writer: the forming of a mature life-view before any epic literary attempts. As Emanuel Hirsch notes,

---

[10] Hirsch, p. 52. Hirsch provides perhaps the best and certainly one of the very few studies of this first work of Kierkegaard. Some fifty pages of *Kierkegaard-Studien* are devoted to it, and it is thus longer than the work itself. Cf. pp. 10–60.

[11] The idea of a family curse was not dispelled by the death of his father. Kierkegaard still expected to die before the age of 33. And this expectation has not a little to do with the title of the work published at the age of 33, *The Concluding Unscientific Postscript*. After the *Postscript*, which did not represent a "concluding" of his life, the authorship took a new direction.

[12] Cf. Malantschuk, p. 183.

[13] *Ibid.*

142   TOWARDS THE CHRISTIAN LIFE-VIEW

Seine Härte gegen Andersen ist zuallertiefst Härte gegen sich selbst. Er hat selbst die Aufgabe übernommen, die er Andersen hier stellt: sich persönlich zu erwickeln, sich eine Lebensanschauung zu erringen. Er hat sie sogar unter besonders ungünstigen individuellen Lebensumständen übernommen.[14]

RELATION OF LIFE-VIEW TO THE NOVEL. Positively, a life-view gives a center of gravity to a novel, according to Kierkegaard, and provides the deeper unity which holds a work together. Negatively, it delivers a novel from arbitrariness or purposelessness. Kierkegaard thus points out that purpose is an immanent condition in a work of art, and that true literature must be characterized by an underlying seriousness. The lyric poet may describe, and even wallow in, moods, feelings, and other Romantic preoccupations, but let him not invade serious realms of literature. Life-view embodies the seriousness expected in serious, epic poetry.

Essentially a life-view plays the part of providence in the novel; it is the novel's deeper unity which provides it with an interior center of gravity; it frees the novel from becoming arbitrary or pointless, because the purpose is imminently present everywhere in the work of art.[15]

If a life-view is lacking however, then, says Kierkegaard, some theory will insinuate itself into the work, at the expense of poetry, or else the work will depend entirely too much upon the subjectivity – in this case immature subjectivity – of the author.

The lack of a life-view is precisely Kierkegaard's root criticism of Andersen's novel and of Andersen's attempt to be a novelist. Kierkegaard half-heartedly apologizes for demanding a life-view from such a young man as Andersen, but defends his demand when he claims that a life-view is a *conditio sine qua non* for a novel.[16] For Kierkegaard, the lack of life-view in the characters of Andersen's novel points back to the immaturity of the author who himself has none. Consequently, Andersen's novel exhibits no character development, since the immaturity of the author makes him incapable of such. The novel thus jumps across any developmental phase, in a work which evidences poetic talent which would be adequately suited for lyric poetry and short-stories but which fails before the larger and more serious demands of the novel.

Kierkegaard dismisses the notion that an idea, or recurring idea, can function as a life-view (and in a Journal entry he had firmly separated life-view from ideas).

[14] *Kierkegaard-Studien*, p. 27.

[15] Quoted in Malantschuk, *Kierkegaard's Thought*, p. 186. (Trans. by H. V. Hong.) Danish text reads: "En Livs-Anskuelse er egentlig Forsynet i Romanen, den er dens dybere Eenhed, der giver denne at have Tyngdepunkt i sig; den befrier denne fra at blive vilkaarlig eller hensigtsløs, idet Hensigten overalt er immanent tilstede i Konstværket." *S.V.*, XIII, 73.

[16] *S.V.*, XIII, 69.

TOWARDS THE CHRISTIAN LIFE-VIEW 143

...Perhaps one will go further and in so doing refer to the fact that there is however one idea which continually recurs in Andersen's novels, by which Andersen lays claim [to having] a life-view and by which he points out what I myself would have to concede, my inconsistency. To this I must reply (1) that I have never claimed that an idea as such (least of all a "smart idea") is to be considered a life-view and next (2) that in order to engage in examination I must know a little better the content of the idea. If the understanding now is that life is not a process of development of the great and distinguished that would arise, but a process of decline, then however I think I dare protest, perhaps rightly, against the use of "life-view" as a predicate here, to the extent that one will generally concede that I am correct that scepticism as such is not a theory of knowledge, or to stay with my point, that a mistrust of life might contain a truth to the extent that the mistrust leads to a [new] confidence (as e.g. when Solomon says that all is vanity), but it contains an untruth on the other hand at the same time as it makes a final decision about the question of life.[17]

In the above, Kierkegaard is saying that Andersen and other Romantics have a *de facto* negative life-view, at best, which consists in a single recurring idea. Because Kierkegaard affirms life is a development process (as we have seen in the meaning of the moods), he protests against the use of the term "life-view" for any single, negative idea or insight. For even though the negative asserts something true and can lead to finding new confidence in life (as may happen in irony), it quickly begins to make assertions about the meaning of life. In this case, it is untruth. Thus a life-view must contain positive assertions about life; negative wisdom does not quality for the predicate "life-view," even if offered by Solomon. For Kierkegaard, Andersen and the Romantics represent nothing more than negative insight.

---

[17] *S.V.*, XIII, 71. (My translation.) Danish text reads: "Maaskee vil man gaae videre, og idet man beraaber sig paa, at der jo dog er een Idee der idelig forekommer i Andersens Romaner, derved vindicere Andersen en Livs-Anskuelse, og forckaste mig, der jo selv indrømmer dette, min Inconsequents. Hertil maa jeg svare, at jeg aldrig har paastaaet, at en Idee som saadan (allermindst en fix Idee) er at ansee for en Livs-Anskuelse, og dernæst, at jeg, for at indlade mig paa denne Undersøgelse, mas vide lidt nærmere om denne Idees Indhold. Gaaer den nu ud paa, at Livet ikke er en Udviklings-Proces, men en Undergangs-Proces af det Store og Udmærkede, der vilde spire frem, saa troer jeg dog vel med Rette at turde protestere mod Prædikatet Livs-Anskuelses Anvendelse herpaa, forsaavidt man ellers vil give mig Ret i, at Skepsis som saadan ikke er en Erkjendelsens-Theorie, eller for at blive i mit Forehavende, at en saadan Mistillid til Livet vel indeholder en Sandhed, forsaavidt den leder til at finde en Tillid (f. Ex. naar Salomo siger, at Alt er forfængeligt), men derimod i samme Moment, som den determinerer sig til en endelig Afgjørelse af Livets Spørgsmaal, indeholder en Usandhed."
The footnote reads as follows:
"For at holde Spørgsmaalet saa reent som muligt, maa jeg erindre om, at jeg ikke søger at gjøre een Livs-Anskuelse gjældende, Andersen en anden; men at jeg søger uinteresseret for nogensomhelst bestemt Livs-Anskuelse, blot at bekjæmpe dette negative Standpunkt og dets Ret til at udgive sig for en Livs-Anskuelse."

144 TOWARDS THE CHRISTIAN LIFE-VIEW

In a telling footnote to the above-quoted passage, Kierkegaard writes:

For to keep the question as clear as possible, I must recall that it is not that I seek to make one life-view valid and Andersen another; but that I, uninterested as to any one definite life-view, seek merely to combat that negative point of view and its right to masquerade as a life-view.

The footnote is not true in claiming that the author has no particular life-view to advocate. For even in this early work, Kierkegaard suggests the contrast of human and Christian life-views; and in the formal authorship, the pseudonyms increasingly point, both negatively and positively, toward the Christian life-view as the only tenable one and the sole to have the positivity which is a prerequisite for the proper user of the term. The exposure of negative points of view masquerading as life-views is at least a true description of what he begins in *From the Papers of One Still Living*, and what he continues in the aesthetic writings which follow five years later.

FORMING A LIFE-VIEW

In the end, Kierkegaard would say that few arrive at forming a true life-view. The failures are many and take two principal forms. The first is what he terms "unsuccessful activity" in which one seeks to understand life, but eventually succumbs to the difficulties of life, amounting thus to what he terms a stance of "broken manliness." The second failure is what he terms "pristine passivity," an introspection that goes on with, and even enjoys, suffering and never seeks to understand or overcome it, thus amounting to what he terms a stance of "thorough womanliness."[18]

If we now ask how a life-view comes about, then we reply that for him who does not permit his life to fizzle out, but who tries insofar as possible to balance the individual events in life – that for him there must necessarily come a moment of unusual illumination about life, without his needing in any way to have understood all the possible particulars to the subsequent understanding of which he has in the meantime [come to have] the key: I say, there must come the moment when, as Daub observes, life is understood backwards through the Idea.[19]

[18] Modern readers may be offended by Kierkegaard's apparent male-chauvinism. In fairness to Kierkegaard, it must be pointed out that his attitude toward women's movements was generally positive. However, criticisms of women also abound. Perhaps the most pointed criticism against both man and woman is contained in the Banquet of *Stages* in which the character Ladies' Tailor asserts that woman is what man has made her.

[19] *S.V.*, XIII, 69. (My translation.) Danish text reads: "Spørge vi nu, hvorledes en saadan Livs-Anskuelse kommer istand, da svare vi, at for den der ikke tillader sit Liv altfor meget at futte ud, men saavidt som muligt søger at føre dets enkelte Yttringer tilbage i sig selv igjen, maa der nødvendigviis indtræde et Øieblik, i hvilket der udbreder sig et besynderligt Lys over Livet, uden at man derfor i fjerneste Maade behøver at have forstaaet alle mulige Enkeltheder, til hvis successive Forstaaelse man imidlertid nu har Nøglen, maa, siger jeg, indtræde det Øieblik, da, som Daub bemærker, Livet forstaaes baglænds gjennem Ideen."

TOWARDS THE CHRISTIAN LIFE-VIEW

Thus life-view represents a crystallization of understanding which comes as the result of constant effort to perceive the deeper meaning of one's life and of constant effort to maintain equilibrium. It is not a final articulation of the meaning of life; it is not an understanding of each particular. Life-view is rather an understanding of the outlines of the whole, an illumination – for which one long prepares oneself – as to the essential meaning and direction of human becoming.

Kierkegaard is careful to distinguish life-view, as the truth of experience, from ideas which are the truth of thought, and in this he emphasizes the radical difference between philosophy of life and academic philosophy as he viewed the latter in his day.

A life-view is more than a pure idea or a sum of propositions held fast in abstract neutrality; it is more than experience which as such is always atomistic, it is namely the transubstantiation of experience, it is an unshakable certainty in oneself which has been won by all [of one's] experience – either it has become familiar with all worldly relations (a mere human standpoint, e.g. Stoicism) which by doing this keeps itself out of contact with a deeper experience – or in its direction toward heaven (the religious), it has found therein what is crucial, both for its heavenly and its earthly existence, has won the true assurance 'that neither death, nor life, nor angels, nor Principalities, nor Powers, nor the present, nor the future, nor the heights, nor the depths nor anything of any sort shall be able to separate us from God's love in Christ Jesus our Lord.'[20]

In the above, we find a clear suggestion of the two alternative life-views: a limited human view, such as Stoicism, or the Christian view. The description of the Christian view already suggests its eventual emergence as the single possible life-view, as the authorship proceeds to expose the limitations of all purely human life-views and to show that the Christian alone contains the full understanding of the depths and destiny of the human person, since it understands man in relation to the eternal even in man's present earthly existence.

Perhaps most striking here is the phrase "transubstantiation of experience." For the true understanding of earthly existence – whether or not it yet has the perspective of the heavenly and the eternal – must involve an understanding of experience. The four cardinal moods, whose course

---

[20] *S. V.*, XIII, 68. (My translation.) Danish text reads: "En Livs-Anskuelse er nemlig mere end et Indbegreb eller en Sum af Sætninger, fastholdt i sin abstrakte Hverkenhed; den er mere end Erfaringen, der som saadan altid er atomistisk, den er nemlig Erfaringens Transsubstantiation, den er en tilkæmpt af al Empirie urokkelig Sikkerhed i sig selv, hvad enten den saa blot har orienteret sig i alle verdenslige Forhold (et blot humant Standpunkt, Stoicisme f. Ex.), der derved holder sig uden for Berøring med en dybere Empirie – eller den har i sin Retning mod Himlen (det Religieuse) deri fundet det Centrale, saavel for sin himmelske som sin jordiske Existents, har vundet den sande christelige Forvisning: at hverken Død, ei heller Liv, ei heller Engle, ei heller Fyrstendømmer, ei heller Magter, ei heller det Nærværende, ei heller det Tilkommende, ei heller det Høie, ei heller det Dybe, ei heller nogen anden Skabning skal kunne skille os fra Guds Kjærlighed i Christo Jesu vor Herre.'"

146 TOWARDS THE CHRISTIAN LIFE-VIEW

and emerging destiny we have traced in the preceding chapters, constitute transubstantiation of experience, since they direct one willingly to accepting the transformation process of the moods and to uncovering their meaning in religious subjectivity. In this process, the experience which each mood represents becomes something more, viz. revelation of a spiritual nature and of a natural dynamism moving in the direction of the spiritual. By the willing acceptance of the suffering of growth which the moods represent, one elevates suffering from apparent purposelessness to a spiritual end, viz. the transformation-reintegration into the higher religious self.

In summation then, we may view *From the Papers of One Still Living* as a work of polemical literary criticism in which Kierkegaard voices for the first time, in a publication, his concern with a mature, serious life-view not merely for the purpose of epic poetry but for the grasp of what is crucial for both heavenly and earthly existence. Mature reflection, seriousness and interiority combined with the will to live through the meaning of experience, rather than merely wallow in emotions, prepare one for the moment of illumination in which a life-view emerges. There is here as yet no suggestion of the details of the growth process, which we have seen in the preceding chapters' study of subsequent works of Kierkegaard. Nor is there yet a suggestion of grace which, in the end, brings about the crystallization for which one prepares oneself but cannot bring about of one's own power.

C. LIFE-VIEW IN *THE BOOK ON ADLER*

In discussing here *The Book on Adler*,[21] we depart momentarily from strict chronology. We do so because the Introduction to this unpublished work of 1846 continues themes begun in *From the Papers of One Still Living*.

The Book on Adler was prompted by the "phenomenon" of Adolph Peter Adler, a Magister Artium and a rural pastor of the Danish Church. In 1842, Magister Adler claimed to have had a "vision of light," a direct revelation from God (which turned him against Hegelianism, among other things). It appears that the man was deranged – a judgement supported by a reading of his works,[22] and also the grounds given for his suspension in 1844 by Bishop Mynster and for his being deposed in 1845. Adler continued to publish, however, and had already been the object of many theological attacks when Kierkegaard drafted his own work. Although he revised it many times, Kierkegaard finally refrained from publishing it and it is thus found among the "B" coded *Papirer*. Eventually the longest section of the

[21] Known in the present English translation as *On Authority and Revelation.*
[22] Walter Lowrie, Preface to *On Authority and Revelation* (New York: Harper Torchbooks, 1966), xlv. (Hereafter abbreviated as *AR*)

TOWARDS THE CHRISTIAN LIFE-VIEW

work was published in 1849, without reference to Adler, and was entitled "Two Minor Ethico-Religious Treatises" (of which we have in English translation the treatise entitled "Of the Difference Between a Genius and an Apostle").

Kierkegaard takes us to a discussion of life-view and its relation to literary production once again in the Introduction to this work, and thus it is with this Introduction that we concern ourselves here. Kierkegaard makes a fundamental distinction between a premise-author and an essential author in the work. A premise-author remains at the first stage of writing: he sets forth some material, he gives no indication of the conclusions to be drawn and thus he leaves it to the world to work them out. The essential author, on the other hand, has conclusions toward which he conducts the reader, even if he does not make them explicit.

According to Kierkegaard, Adler is a premise-author. (We might add that in his own writings Kjerkegaard fits the description of the essential author who leads toward conclusions without making them explicit.) He is such because he initially claimed to have had a revelation and then retreated steadily from his claim, leaving it up to the world to make sense out of it and indicating thereby that he himself understood neither his own claim, its implications, nor what a personal revelation would be. Kierkegaard rebukes Adler for taking a decisive and important stand before thinking it through. And this is the point which ties in with life-view and authorship.

For, claims Kierkegaard (making life-view and world-view synonymous here, but not using the Hegelian sense of the latter), ". . . After all, a world-view, a life-view is the only true condition for a literary production."[23] If a life-view is developed and stands out clear and coherent, the premise of a work is resolved and satisfied in the conclusion (which may or may not be explicit).[24] Without a life-view, however, in both a literary work and a human life, there is only stoppage rather than conclusion.[25] Thus what is at first said of writing applies equally to living.

Although he used the term world-view as well as life-view, Kierkegaard clearly opposes here the notion of a view provided by one's times and fellows, by the spirit of the age, and he is highly critical of instances when

Instead of having, each man for himself, a clear conception of what one will *in concreto* before one begins to express one's views, one has a superstitious notion about the utility of starting a discussion, one has the superstition that, while the individuals themselves do not know what they will, the spirit of the age should

---

[23] *On Authority and Revelation*, p. 4. Papirer VII^2 B 235, 6. Danish text reads: "Og en Verdens-Anskuelse, en Livs-Anskuelse er da den eneste sande Conclusion paa enhver Frembringelse."

[24] *Ibid.*

[25] *Ibid.*, 5.

148 TOWARDS THE CHRISTIAN LIFE-VIEW

be able by its dialectic to make clear what one really wills, so that by this
purposeful gentlemen may get to know what their purpose really is.[26]

The essential author waits until he has understood sufficiently; and he
writes only of what he himself has understood, rather than, in the
manner of the premise-author, waiting for something from outside to
appear suddenly and tell him what he meant by what he said.

The essential author... knows definitely what he is, what he wills; from first to
last he is attentive to understanding himself in his life-view.[27]

What is said of the essential author may be applied to the mature
person: he has a life-view which he has worked out for himself. No
outside source provides it for him, and thus too no outside source
provides the "conclusion," the goal toward which his life is directed.
The premise-author, who is basically the immature Romantic, is either
without a goal, in which case his life, like his work, merely halts abruptly
rather than reaching a resolution of its movement; or else his goal is
provided by the times or the crowd, which is to say that he is still
without a personal goal. For the point made in this Introduction and
repeatedly emphasized is that one must work through to one's conclusion oneself, in literary productions, in theological treatises (the specific
case of Adler) and in existence. If an individual has no life-view, the
spirit of the age may substitute one. But in allowing this, one loses one's
individuality and yet still cannot be said to move through to a resolution
of life's movement. For the resolution here is other than one's own; it is
a conclusion without a relationship to the premise. Life still halts
abruptly, but with conclusions artificially appended.

We now revert to the chronology of the authorship and turn once
again to *Either/Or* in which a premise-author (Johannes) is confronted
by an essential author (Judge William) who challenges the former's
illusory life-view.

D. LIFE-VIEW IN *EITHER/OR, STAGES* AND THE *POSTSCRIPT*

EITHER/OR. *Either/Or* (1843) is a richer source for the analysis of
life-views than it is for the idea of life-view itself. As the editor Victor
Eremita points out, A's papers contain a number of attempts at an
aesthetic life-view, while B's papers contain an ethical life-view.[28] Parts

[26] *AR*, p. 6. Danish test reads: "Istedenfor som Enkelt, Hver isaer, at blive enig med sig
selv om, hvad man vil in concreto, inden man begynder at yttre sig, har man en overtroisk
Forestilling om det Gavnlige i at foranledige en Discusssiion... Man har en overtroisk
Forestilling om, at Tidsaanden, medens Individerne hver for sig ikke veed hvad de ville,
skulde bed in Dialektik være istand til at gjøre aabenbart, hvad det er man egentligen vil,
saa Dhrr. Tendents-Haveere ved den kunne faae at vide, hvorhen de egentligen tendere."
VII² B 235, 9:9–12, 17–22.

[27] *AR*, p. 8. Danish text reads: "Den væsentlige Forfatter derimod veed med Bes-
timthed, hvo han er hvad han vil; han passer først og sidst paa at forstaae sig selv i sin
Livs-Anskuelse." VII² B 235, 12.

[28] *EO* 1, p. 13; *S.V.*, I, xv.

TOWARDS THE CHRISTIAN LIFE-VIEW 149

I and II, the papers of A and B respectively, contain opposing life-views, and the latter contains an analysis of the former view. (A fuller discussion of the content of the aesthetic life-view follows in section G.)

Much like Kierkegaard vis-à-vis Andersen, Judge William sees his role as unmasking apparent life-views which have no right to the name. And so he dismisses the view of A as an illusion.

Nevertheless you have no view of life. You have something which resembles a view, and this gives your life a certain composure, which must not be confused with a secure and refreshing confidence in life. You have composure only in contrast to one who is still pursuing the phantoms of pleasure.[29]

The quotation above begins the implicit definition of life-view which Part II of *Either/Or* contains. A life-view must originate in the interior; and this is the source of security, rather than of mere superficial external composure. In addition, a life-view must be positive: it must posit something about human existence. The view of A is merely negative, ironic. It represents a shattering of the illusions of sense pleasure, but nothing more. In emphasizing the necessary positive content of a life-view, William (or B) is *de facto* declaring that there is no life-view under strictly aesthetic categories. For in the schematization of the stages, irony serves as the transition between the aesthetic and the ethical. Irony is negative; it is infinite negativity. Irony posits nothing. Thus even he who has reached the borders of the aesthetic in irony still has no life-view, because his understanding of life as yet posits nothing.

Judge William becomes more explicit about the qualifications for a life-view in his emphasis upon choice. We have already seen in the discussion of moods the critical significance of choice as an absolute condition for moving through and beyond the moods toward new positivity. William declares the importance of

... the category of choice, which is my solution, the nerve of my life-view – and such [a thing as a life-view] I have, even though I do not by any means presume to have a system.[30]

Because of his ethical perspective, William perceives the absence of a life-view in most men and the significance of that absence as indicating a lack of responsibility toward self. He recognizes the rarity of a genuine life-view, as he allies life-view (representing seriousness, responsibility, and positivity) with the "task of life," an oft-occurring phrase in his letters. Without the ethical, he declares unequivocally, there simply is no life-view. Judge William's position is transcended by the religious sphere where a positive life-view is eventually to be formed. But the religious

---

[29] *EO* 2, p. 206 (with corrections). Danish text, *S.V.*, II, 182, reads: "Desuagtet har Du ingen Anskuelse af Livet. Du har Noget, der ligner en Anskuelse, og dette giver Dit Liv en vis Rolighed, som dog ikke maa forvexles med en tryg og vederqvægende Tillid til Livet. Rolighed har Du kun i Modsætning til Den, der endnu jager efter Nydelsens Gjøglebilleder..."

[30] *EO* 2, pp. 215. Danish text, *S. V.*, II, 190, reads: "... den Bestemmelse at vælge, der er mit Løsen, Nerven i min Livs-Anskuelse, og en saadan har jeg, om jeg end Ingensinde anmasser mig at have et System."

150 TOWARDS THE CHRISTIAN LIFE-VIEW

preserves the ethical which William rightly declares essential. And, it should be added, the religious will also preserve aspects of the aesthetic.

STAGES. (1845) The diary "Guilty?/Not Guilty?" of *Stages* represents an aesthetic view which has collapsed under the pressure of a religious crisis prompted by an impossible love. Thus Quidam marvels as his prior view simply collapses in the testing: "What I cannot get over is that my whole life-view, which is not pulled out of the air but is essential to my individuality, has failed."[31] He defines this view thus, "Let us see. My life-view was that in my closed-in-ness I concealed my *Tungsind*. It was my pride that I could do it, my resolution to proceed with all my might."[32]

Quidam realizes the importance of a life-view and indicates it repeatedly. He sees too that the collapse of his prior view leaves him insecure and emotionally unstable. He demands that everyone, including himself, be clear about the categories of his life.

This is what I *will*, and what I require also of everyone whom I admire, of everyone I am in any real sense to recognize, that by day he should think only of the categories of his life and dream of them by night.[33]

By degrees, Quidam realizes that a religious life-view must be constructed upon the ruins of his previous aesthetic view. This sentiment is clearly expressed in a draft of the diary, found in the *Papirer* VB 100, 20, which says,"... it is my life-view that demands a rebirth" as the clouds of an imminent religious struggle gather over him.

[The religious orator says] that everyone should prepare within himself the way of the Lord. This is of course the way one ought to speak, and upon this point one can construct a whole life-view. One understands that the individual has to do with himself essentially, and that the business of accomplishing something is accidental...[34]

The suggestion of the Christian nature of the new, religious life-view begins to emerge in this passage. Quidam-Taciturnus-Kierkegaard's emphasis here is on the interiority – and the religious nature of that interiority – which must be the basis for an enduring life-view.[35]

[31] *S.V.*, VI, 331. (My translation; cf. *SLW* p. 325) Danish text reads: "Det, jeg er strandet paa, er, at min hele Livs-Anskuelse, der ikke var greben ud af Luften, men netop væsentlig for min Individualitet, er rejiceret."

[32] *S.V.*, VI, 367. (My translation; cf. *SLW*, p. 359). Danish text reads: "Lad see! Min Livs-Anskuelse var, at jeg i min Indesluttethed gjemte mit Tungsind. Det var min Stolthed, at jeg kunde gjøre det, min Beslutning, af yderste Evne at fare for dermed."

[33] *SLW*, p. 282. Danish text reads: "Det er det, jeg vil, det, jeg fordrer af Enhver, jeg skal beundre, af Enhver, jeg egentligen skal anerkjende, at han om Dagen kun tænker paa sit Livs Kategori og drømmer om den i Natten." *S.V.*, VI, 285.

[34] *SLW*, p. 315. Danish text reads: "... at Enhver i sig selv bereder Herren Vei. Det er naturligviis, som der skal tales, og paa dette Punkt lader der sig lægge en Livs-Anskuelse an. Man forstaaer, at den Enkelte har med sig selv at gjøre væsentligen, at det at udrette er det Tilfældige..." *S.V.*, VI, 320.

[35] In spite of the reference to the accidental nature of accomplishing anything in the world, the above passage does partake of an ethical perspective. The point here is to leave it in God's hands whether or not one's efforts in the world ultimately bear fruit.

TOWARDS THE CHRISTIAN LIFE-VIEW

Equally applicable here is what is said in the essay "Observations About Marriage." For it posits a religious life-view as the solution to the collapse of the aesthetic.

The resolution is a religious life-view constructed upon ethical postulates, which is to prepare the path of love and secure it against every outward and inward danger.[36]

THE POSTSCRIPT. The *Postscript* has little to add by way of defining life-view, but does re-affirm its importance. Johannes Climacus allies life-view with the philosophizing about life which the early Greek philosophers did (until Idealism appeared). The author recognizes too that if one were to live today in the serious manner of the Greek philosophers, one would be regarded as a madman. For nowadays we already have the definitive understanding of life which the spirit of the age so generously provides! What need then to go further? Nonetheless, Climacus sees more than a little value in risking being thought mad for questioning, like Socrates, when others were comfortably certain. Thus he writes:

I am well aware that if someone were nowadays to live like the Greek philosophers, existentially expressing and existentially probing depths of what he must call his view of life, he would be regarded as a lunatic. Let it be so.[37]

Johannes Climacus would, in the end, say that such probing is essential to serious existence. Without it, one takes on the view of the spirit of the age. If the root "wisdom" in the word "philosophy" is to mean anything, it must surely mean personal searching, personal wisdom. "Objective wisdom" is a travesty of the on-going search which was once called the "love of wisdom" ($\phi \iota \lambda o \sigma / \sigma o \phi \iota a$). One may reach a shared wisdom (objective truth) but what is essential is that one reaches it oneself, acting in the main individually and subjectively.

In the *First and Last Declaration* which Kierkegaard appended to the work and in which he acknowledged his authorship of the entire pseudonymous production, he says that the pseudonymous characters express life-views in audible lines.[38] This comment applies in Judge Williams analysis of his fellow pseudonym's life-view. But it applies to Johannes Climacus as well who as a religious humanist has achieved the positivity of a life-view (even if it is not yet the Christian life-view) and who reflects this in the seriousness in which he explores existence and the meaning of truth, despite the spirit of the age which would provide him with all understanding in the System. The subjective stance and mature inwardness of Johannes Climacus, grounded as they are in

---

[36] *SLW*, p. 159. Danish text, *S. V.*, VI, 154, reads: "Beslutningen er en paa ethiske Forudsætninger construeret religieus Livs-Anskuelse, der ligesom skal bane Forelskelsen Veien og sikkre den mod enhver udvortes og indvortes Fare."

[37] *CUP*, p. 315. Danish text, *S. V.*, VII, 306, reads: "Jeg veed det vel, dersom Nogen nuomstunder vilde leve som en græsk Philosoph;ɔ: vilde existerende udtrykke, existerende fordybe sig i, hvad han maatte kalde sin Livs-Anskuelse, saa blev han anseet for gal. Faaer saa at være."

[38]*CUP*, p. 551; *S.V.*, VII, 545–546.

152   TOWARDS THE CHRISTIAN LIFE-VIEW

reflection and a consciousness of the eternal, form the basis of what he may rightly call his life-view.

E. LIFE-VIEW IN THE *PAPIRER*

In the *Papirer*, we hear echoes, restatements of and enlargements upon what we have heard in the works. The *Papirer* reveal a continuous concern with life-view during the entire course of the formal authorship, and before it as well, as is indicated in the entry of 1835 already quoted. Life-view remains an essential value in the authentic philosophic life, for Kierkegaard personally and in the message of his thought.

In an entry dated January 17, 1837, Kierkegaard rebuked those of his age who took their life-view from the times, i.e. had more of a world-view (in the Hegelian sense) than a proper life-view.

There are many people who reach their conclusions about life like schoolboys; they cheat their master by copying the answer out of a book without having worked out the sum for themselves.[39]

This is a rebuke to those who take on, rather than form, a life-view. For there are no objective answers that one can get from another. Life-view embodies subjective truth.

In the entry of 17 May 1839, Kierkegaard sets out the major outlines of what a life-view must be, with the continuing emphasis on the essential subjective.

Only when a life-view is no longer a thought-experiment among other thought-experiments, but rather an outlook which precisely by being this has a *drive* (an inner, immanental power) requiring actualization and because of this posits itself at every moment, only then does the true cleavage in man appear. Only then does one feel that he battles not with a volatile phantom but with a power, a body, a body of sin (Romans 7) which one must get torn out, whatever the cost; that it is a dying-away-from (which like every death occasions tears in the beginning, bitter because we must be separated from something in which we have lived and which we often have an unreasonable hard time to forget, but soon mild and quiet because we feel the Lord's consolation, soon tears of joy, when we see the end draw near); that it is a divine Kingdom, a *gegliedert* order of things that cannot be taken by force, in which we should be placed.[40]

---

[39] I A 322. Danish text reads: "Der er mange Mennesker, der komme til et Livs-Resultat ligesom Skoledrenge; de synde deres Lærer ved at skrive Facitet ud af Reg-nebogen uden selv at have regnet Stykket."

[40] *Journals and Papers* Vol. I (Bloomington, 1967), trans. by Howard and Edna Hong, No. 868. Danish text (II A 430) reads:

"Først da naar det ved Livets Opfattelse ikke længere er et Tankeexperiment ligeoverfor at andet Tankeexperiment, men en Anskuelse, der netop i Kraft af at være dette har en Drift (en indre, en immanent Magt) til at fordre sig realiseret, og desaarsag ogsaa ponerer sig i hvert Moment, først da intræder den sande Splid i Msk., først da føler man, at det ikke er et flygtigt Phantom man har at Kjæmpe med, men at det er en Magt, et Legeme, et Syndens Legeme (Rom: 7.) man skal udrives af, hvormeget det end Koster, at det er en Døen af fra (der som enhver Døen har sine Taarer i Begyndelsen bittre, fordi vi skulle adskilles fra Noget, som vi have levet i, og som ofte uforstandige nok have ondt ved at glemme, snart blide og stille, fordi vi føle Herrens Trøst, snart Glædestaarer, naar vi see det lakker mod Enden) at det er et Guds Rige, en gegliedert Tingenes Orden, som ikke lader sig tage med Vold, vi skulle indordnes i. –"

TOWARDS THE CHRISTIAN LIFE-VIEW 153

Three aspects of life-view emerge in the above entry. First, life-view is action rather than thought. And in moving toward the maturity of a life-view, one discovers the split which exists in man – the "two-ness" which exists in man by sin, i.e. his divided nature; this is reflected in the Danish word for despair employed by Kierkegaard to indicate this state, *For-TVIVL-else* (German: *Ver-ZWEI-flung*). Second, in this inner division which is sin, reintegration can only come from a purging struggle with one's sinful nature. But thirdly, and ultimately, the divine order toward which one is aiming (the City of God) cannot be reached by human effort alone. The life-view which represents this final point, the Christian life-view, can in the end be achieved only by the additional element of God's grace, for which man's own efforts are the necessary prerequisite.

In an undated entry of 1848, Kierkegaard discusses a test by which one may know if one's life-view has the full perspective which is necessary for a viable view.

Imagine a young man and how he would like to live – but let us make a test. Imagine a dying person, how he would like *to have lived* – and you will discover that you arrive at the very opposite result. Who then is right? Certainly the dying person. Because the young person desires for this life (these seventy years); the dying person desires for eternity or that he had lived for eternity.[41]

Thus eternity alone provides the complete perspective for understanding life. But one need not die or be at death's door physically in order to sense the eternal. One can "die to self" and in this dying attain the perspective of eternity.

Kierkegaard alludes time and again to two possible life-views: the aesthetic which lives for these seventy years and the (ethico-religious-) Christian which lives for eternity. With the latter, he associates dying, as is evidenced in an undated entry of 1854:

There are only two life-views which correspond to the duality that is man: animal and spirit.

According to the one the task is to live, to enjoy life and to put everything into this.

The other view is "the meaning of life is to die."[42]

But the aesthetic is merely an apparent life-view which ends in despair when one tries to live on the basis of it. For the aesthetic is really only

---

[41] *Journals and Papers*, Vol. 1, no. 841. Danish text (VIII[1] A 543) reads: "Tænk en Yngling, og hvorledes han nu kunde ønske at leve – men lad os saa gjøre Prøven. Tænk Dig en Døende, hvorledes han kunde ønske at have levet: og Du skal see Du kommer lige til det modsatte Resultat. Hvo har saa Ret? Dog vel den Døende. Thi Ynglingen ønsker for Livet (for disse 70 Aar), den Døende ønsker for Evigheden, eller at havde levet for Evigheden."

[42] *Journals and Papers*, Vol. 1, no. 1005. Danish text (XI[1] A 528) reads: "Det er kun to Livs-Anskuelser, svarende til det Dobbelte Mennesket er: Dyre-Skabning og Aand.

Ifølge den ene (er) Opgaven: at leve, at nyde Livet, og at sætte Alt ind herpaa.

Den anden Anskuelse er: 'Livets Betydning er at døe.'"

154 TOWARDS THE CHRISTIAN LIFE-1VIEW

an idea of man, the result of a thought-experiment rather than the transubstantiation of experience. The Christian view demands the transformation of the person, through symbolic death and rising. In an undated entry of 1850, Kierkegaard compares the life-view of old Christendom to the present one (*Den gamle Christendoms Livs-Anskuelse – den nu værende*):

In olden days one found it next to astounding that there were indeed in this life joyous days (so it is also expressed in one of the morning and evening prayers which is found in the evangelical Psalter) because one understood that life was ordained for suffering, and suffering for Christendom.

Now Christendom has become purely worldly, one enjoys oneself and holds fast to this life.[43]

Kierkegaard allies his notion of life-view to the idea of suffering, thus ever more welding life-view and the authentically Christian together.

Every man must ultimately decide about a life-view: either to accept the view which the spirit of the age will so readily provide or to form his own from out of his own experiences and sufferings. Every man must decide whether to live as "animal" or as "spirit." Kierkegaard makes this point in an especially sharp manner in an undated entry of 1854 in which he discusses a father's obligation to have a life-view, to have a mature and serious understanding of himself and his life, before he has children.

So must Christendom speak to a man who wishes to marry. In what capacity is it that you wish to propagate the race, is it *qua* animal-creature – or *qua* spirit-man? In the former capacity, the matter is indeed quite simple.

But is it so easy in the latter capacity? Do you not find that to be a father it is required of you that you have reached maturity, that you really possess a life-view for which you dare to answer, so that you dare pass it on to the child when it, with the right which comes from being a child, in owing you life, asks you about the meaning of life? . . .

. . . From a father the child has a right to demand a life-view, that his father really have such.[44]

---

[43] X[3] A 492 (My Translation). Danish text reads:
"I gamle Dage fandt man det næsten forunderligt, at der i dette Liv dog var nogle frydfulde Dage (saaledes er det ogsaa udtrykt i een af de Morgen-og Aftenbønner som findes i den evangeliske Psalmebog) fordi man forstod at dette Liv var indviet til Lidelse, ogsaa Lidelse for Christendommen.
Nu er det blevet Christendom jo mere man reent versligt fornøier sig og hænger fast ved dette Liv."

[44] XI[1] A 150 (My Translation). Danish text reads: "Saaledes maatte vel Christendommen tale til Menneske, der vil gifte sig. I hvilken Egenskab er det Du vil forplante Slægt, er det qua Dyre-Skabning – eller qua Aands-Menneske. I Egenskab af det første er jo Sagen kun altfor simpel.
Men er det i Egenskab af det andet saa bliv lidt. Synes Dig ikke, at til være Fader maa fordres, at Du have naaet den Modenhed, at Du virkelig eiede en Livs-Anskuelse, for hvilken Du turde indestaae, saa Du turde overgive til Dit Barn, naar det, med det, Berettigelse der liger i at være Barn, i at skylde Dig Livet, spurgte Dig om Livets Betydning? . . .
. . . Af en Fader har Barnet Ret at fordre: en Livs-Anskuelse, at Faderen virkelig har en saadan."

TOWARDS THE CHRISTIAN LIFE-VIEW

A child, the entry goes on to say, has as much right to expect the father to provide an understanding of life as he does to expect milk from his mother. (But this is not to suggest that the father provides a definitive life-view for his child, rather only that he is able to answer, from his own standpoint, about the meaning of life for himself and suggest an orientation for his child.)

Maturity and a mature sense of the meaning of life are key here. The Journal entry goes on to say that by the time a man reaches the maturity sufficient for a developed life-view, the inclination to propagate the species probably will have passed! But despite Pauline tendencies, what Kierkegaard really emphasizes is the true synthesis of body and spirit, by first allowing a maturing of spirit to take place. And this maturing is the evolution of a true life-view, grounded as it then is in self-understanding as spirit awakens, stirs, and emerges fully in religious subjectivity.

F. THE MEANING OF LIFE-VIEW

Having surveyed the published and unpublished works of Kierkegaard, we are prepared to ask now what the meaning of life-view is and how a life-view comes about. Our survey has indicated that life-view is a key term in the writings and that the works trace a course exposing false understandings of man and proceeding towards the construction and articulation of authentic understanding.

Simply stated, a life-view is coherent, authentic self-understanding. So many pages for so simple a definition! But, alas, simple wisdom is often deceptively complicated and arduous to reach. And this is Kierkegaard's point.

If the essence of life-view is a simple matter, the formation of a life-view is not. Above all, the formation of a life-view is an essential matter. For only he who has the understanding and vision of the higher self will carry through to the end the task of becoming the self. Reaching understanding and the moment of vision is already to have traveled well down the road.

Few attain a life-view, for few carry through with the task of understanding the self. Most accept a definition from others, or go a little way only to content themselves with the negative wisdom of uncovering the illusions of an apparent self (as in the ironic consciousness). The simple reward of composure, stability, and equanimity in having a life-view is only attained by constant vigilance, first, against the spirit of the times which, unasked, will provide a view and, second, against oneself who will shun the task or be tempted to abandon it.

To have a life-view means to have traveled a long road through one's own experience. On an emotional level it means experiencing the pain

156   TOWARDS THE CHRISTIAN LIFE-VIEW

of inner growth and, through an attitude of openness, discerning its deeper meaning and significance, thus by degrees discovering the essential spiritual dimension of the self and the goal of the relationship to eternal Spirit in faith.

Life-view represents a crystallization of understanding and a transubstantiation of experience, i.e. of the long process of spiritual opening and maturing. It is formed only by an individual for himself. It cannot be given by others, nor can it be attained by thought. The simple proof of this is that any exclusively poetic view (all of which are aesthetic views) collapses in the living out (as both the aesthete Johannes and young Johannes Climacus discover). Only that view may endure which is attained by the individual who with an attitude of seriousness wills and explores the meaning of the process of personal, inner growth. By going deeper into experience, one reaches maturity in finally coming to perceive the deeper meaning and direction of inner experience, viz. the becoming of the higher self.

Life-view is not so much having become the reintegrated self as having attained the vision of the reintegrated self and having begun the reintegration process. But we have seen that one does not do this solely by relying upon oneself. Although it seems to be a simple matter of "being oneself," there is a rift in the self caused by sin which man on his own is unable to undo. Consequently, one cannot alone attain either reintegration or full understanding of reintegration (repetition). One can will the transformation process beginning within and reach the limits of the human in the anguished consciousness of despair. Here one requires a Power which transcends the limits of the natural human. Illumination, the crystallization of understanding, the beginning of reintegration and the vision of the eternal self finally come only through the action of God experienced as a grace.

Life-view proceeds from that developing religious inwardness which sees the religious nature of the self and begins to sense that its destiny hinges upon the eternal. Life-view is the understanding which gives meaning to the isolated events behind one, now from within the perspective not only of present-to-past but of eternal-to-time. Moreover, the coherent articulation of self-understanding which is life-view provides inner strength on the road along which one has already come a decisive distance.

In the end, Kierkegaard will suggest, the sole view which meets all criteria is the Christian life-view as revealed by Christ, the God in time. All other views cannot bear the test of experience, and idle thought experiments prove barren. It is the dialectic of moods which exposes the illusory and brings one to this realization/revelation. The dialectic of moods brings one to the point where the new philosophy of life begins not with *Tvivl*, doubt rooted in thought, but with *Fortvivlelse*, despair as the doubt of the personality, which casts itself, in the experience of human finitude, before the expectation of grace.

G. THE AESTHETIC LIFE-VIEW EXPOSED

We have already suggested that the aesthetic life-view is really no life-view, that in the end it amounts to nothing more than an idea which has no application to life. Much of Kierkegaard's authorship aims to show that the aesthetic is but a collection of fragmentary conceptions and values – concerned in its highest form with living the poet's life: a life depicting the Beautiful. If we recall the three ideals of Greek culture, viz. the Beautiful, the True and the Good, we note that the poet concerns himself with the first. The philosopher goes a bit further, to Truth, but he too remains in the aesthetic. For the philosopher's Truth is intellectual knowledge, not the truth of experience. Thus Kierkegaard must mortally wound both stances in order to have his contemporaries see beyond them to the Good – the realm of practice, of ethics (in the manner of Socrates who in his ethics goes further than Plato who remained in the aesthetic). But the Good leads even further, to union with the Good itself in the religious life.

In either the poetic or philosophic life, the aesthetic life-view fails. The young aesthete Johannes illustrates this unmistakably for the poetic life, as does young Johannes Climacus of *De Omnibus Dubitandum Est* for the philosophic life. The aesthetic resembles a life-view and masquerades as one, until one asks the unmasking question: what should a life-view be? Above all, a life-view should have application to life. Personal misery is sure testimony to the inapplicability of any life-view to life, and this fact shows up in both the misery of Johannes and of Johannes Climacus, both of whom must move into the category of despair. For both characters are depicted as searching in the false paradise of the aesthetic, Johannes in love with pleasure, Johannes Climacus in love with thought. Neither love is able to bring inner equilibrium, nor able to surmount the melancholy which we have already seen suggests a religious problem and the requirement of a religious solution.

In *Either/Or* Part II, Judge William surveys a series of apparent life-views. The first which he examines is the view of enjoying life,[45] a view characterized by simplicity (in contrast to the view of pleasure which is complex). The view of enjoying life has two possibilities. In the first, the condition of enjoyment is in the individual, but not posited by him. This includes both health and beauty as the highest good, and also includes personality determined as talent – artistic, philosophical or practical.[46] In the second, the condition of enjoyment lies outside the individual: wealth, glory, prestige, or a lover. In each instance, it is one simple thing which is the source of enjoyment. Such a view makes that which confers satisfaction into the meaning of life.

[45] *EO* 2, p. 185 ff; *S.V.*, II, 164 ff.
[46] *EO* 2, p. 187; *S.V.*, II, 165.

158 TOWARDS THE CHRISTIAN LIFE-VIEW

In the second view, the life-view consists of searching for pleasure. Here some level of reflection is present, for the individual must determine what is pleasurable. The only obstacle to pleasure is control of a multiplicity of outward conditions. The difference between the views of enjoyment and pleasure is small. The first is child-like enjoyment of givens; the second is a more active, discerning search. Both are phases which are soon exhausted when the individual cannot discover a way to sustain either the enjoyment or pleasure.

In *Either/Or* Part I, Johannes has already lived out such a view, or attempted to do so, and we have witnessed his despair before we come to William's analysis. We have seen that his view of enjoyment and pleasure does not work out, because the view is not responsive to the total compass of his being. In enjoyment, he dwells on static being and ignores the movement of becoming which is then manifested in his explosive emotions.

Johannes is actually at the highest point within the aesthetic life-view. His view has begun to become conscious of its own nullity, and he is self-consciously in despair.[47] By degrees, he becomes intoxicated with despair and sees through the vanity of all. He recognizes that his life has neither continuity nor teleology. He is tempted to a new life-view of aesthetic sorrow and sadness, but his thought-despair sees through this in advance. But although he sees through the illusions of a life-view, we have seen that this does not imply that he will go further. We leave him as a character with a "negative life-view" and in the ether of irony from which he descends from time to time in order to immerse himself in some fleeting pleasure.[48]

In his despair, Johannes is actually at a higher point of development than the aesthete Johannes Climacus of *De Omnibus Dubitandum Est.*[49] For Climacus, whose talent is philosophic, proceeds to doubt and to apply doubt to everything. Thus he remains on an intellectual plane whose limits he perceives but above which he never rises (in this work). Climacus here represents modern philosophy briefly attempting to pose as a life-view. His view too collapses as soon as he tries to live it, for it relies on thought rather than on existence. Doubt, and the philosophy which begins with doubt, is reserved for the intellectually gifted and as such is doubly narrow. For it is for the few, and it is founded on the very narrow understanding of the human person as intellect. Despair is more inclusive: it is an expression of the whole personality and is open to all. Doubt tranquilizes thought, but only despair can tranquilize the personality.[50] But even when young Climacus sees this, he does not apply it to

[47] *EO* 2, p. 198; *S.V.*, II, 75.

[48] *EO* 2, p. 200; *S.V.*, II, 176–177.

[49] Climacus makes a rapid development to the religiousness of the *Fragments* of 1844, but he never represents Christian religiousness.

[50] *EO* 2, p. 217; *S.V.*, II, 191.

TOWARDS THE CHRISTIAN LIFE-VIEW 159

existence. Thus, for both Johannes, despair would be the true point of departure for a new and authentic philosophical life, which consists of touching the absolute in one's existence.[51] And despair is the true starting-point for the construction of life-view.

Judge William posits the ethical life-view as the alternative to the aesthetic. For the ethical view is constructed upon the essential human, not upon the arbitrary which is the base of the aesthetic.[52] The ethical view revolves around freedom, in contrast to necessity which is at the heart of the aesthetic. The ethical is that by which a man becomes what he becomes. The ethical man makes the universal concrete in himself as individual. William declares that to be one man and the universal man is the true art of living.[53] In his closing remarks about life-views, William points out that without place for the ethical, there is no life-view, (nor is there true friendship).[54] He is correct, but the ethical is but a brief pause in a process which should subsume the ethical too under larger – Christian – religious categories. The life-view which claims the fullest understanding of man, as individual and universal, according to Kierkegaard, is the Christian view which is ultimately reached by the dynamics of spiritual growth and the moment of grace. And it too must be tested finally in existence.

Kierkegaard never presents any Christian characters as pseudonyms (although Anti-Climacus is a Christian pseudonym, he is not a character), and the older Climacus of the *Fragments* and *Postscript* shies away from the characterization Christian. Rather Kierkegaard presents aesthetic characters who illustrate the bankruptcy of their own way of life, and who by degrees become conscious of it. This bankruptcy is in part illustrated by the spiritual growth process in the moods which the aesthetic works describe. The content of the Christian life is, in the main, taken up in the parallel religious discourses, and in such late works as *Training in Christianity*.

---

[51] *Ibid.*
[52] *EO* 2, p. 229; *S.V.*, II, 201.
[53] *EO* 2, p. 261; *S.V.*, II, 230.
[54] *EO* 2, p. 326; *S.V.*, II, 288.

CONCLUSION

We have explored the concept and importance of life-view as a term which surrounds the discussion of the moods and their meaning. The spiritual growth process which the four critical moods seek to set back on its natural course begins in a negative convulsion against an apparent life-view which defines man in various external terms that do not include his inner reality and the deeper movements beginning there. Here the moods are already present, and one is their victim. As spiritual growth takes place, and as the dialectic of moods unfolds corresponding to the awakening of spirit in the individual, the aesthetic view is denied both in the emotions which witness its impotence to supply equilibrium and stability and in the deeper revelations of the moods which suggest that man was meant for more than momentary pleasures. The moods indicate seriousness about human existence and becoming which demands incorporation in a deepened self-understanding which itself evolves as the moods are individually mastered.

The moods represent a maturing of spirit that will be satisfied only with a lived-out self-understanding responding to the reality of eternal spirit. In the path we have traced in this study, we have observed subjectivity awakening, victimized by a series of moods and challenged to master them and their deeper meaning. We have finally come to the dawning of the religious in the experience of the mood of despair. This is the true starting-point for the construction of a life-view, at the moment when grace intervenes and restores the rupture in the self. For at this point, experience is sufficient for, and grace is capable of, the "transubstantiation of experience" which is a life-view. The higher experience of despair is also the threshold of the positivity which grace then brings about.

As regards philosophy, the dialectic of moods represents a purgation which allows philosophy to take up once again its role of service to man's existence. The psychology which Kierkegaard develops in his presentation of and attention to moods calls philosophy to begin again with *thaumadzein,* with the wonder and awe which prompted Greek philosophy. Kierkegaard calls men to the philosophizing which once had its culmination in Socrates who searched for wisdom in human matters and sought to fulfill the Delphic prescription to Know Thyself. But for those of another era, the call for wisdom and for the articulation of wisdom in a life-view is a call beyond Socrates, not back to him. It is a

CONCLUSION   161

call to master irony and all the moods of religious subjectivity. Through
Revelation in history, according to Kierkegaard, we are beyond the
mastered irony and pagan ethico-religious humanism of Socrates. For
through the Christian Revelation, the road is open for the realization of
new positivity in new mastery. By a call to self-understanding in
mastering the four moods, Kierkegaard seeks to destroy the seduction of
the poetic and the false seriousness of academic philosophy, to ground
both poetry and philosophy in the depths of existence and to restore
them to authentic articulation of the realities of man's being, rather than
merely of the fancies of imagination. In the end, the new understanding
garnered from experience is thoroughly consonant with the Christian
Revelation about the meaning and destiny of human existence.

We have seen that the moods and the question of a life-view interact
throughout the course of Kierkegaard's writings: how the moods individually and in their dialectic first work to destroy the illusory life-view
which the aesthetic represents and then lead to the threshold of
positivity and to deepened self-understanding which are essential to an
authentic life-view.

We have traced the various lines and their point of convergence, viz.
authentic Christianity, as representing the religious solution provided
by the grace of an historical event and of personal forgiveness, resolving
the moods and positing the fullest understanding of man. This final point
of convergence, at which our study halts, is certainly not radically new.
On the contrary, Kierkegaard finally leads to an ancient view and
ancient wisdom. In the end, Kierkegaard is a Christian, and there is no
escaping the Christian perspective which suffuses his authorship and
marshals the direction of his analysis. Kierkegaard re-discovers ancient
Christian truth *for himself*, and, according to his wish, for his readers. In
the end, his analysis may be summarized in the ancient dictum of
Augustine, another psychologist of the soul, who said (*Confessiones* I, ii)
"Inquietum est cor nostrum, donec requiescat in te" ("Our hearts are
restless until they rest in Thee, [Lord]"). For this is indeed the meaning
of the unrest which the moods represent. Kierkegaard combines a very
contemporary understanding of human spiritual development with an
ancient notion of Christianity as decisive in one's life, against a background of a century which, perhaps like our own, was childishly fasci-
nated with the former, generally ignored the latter, and saw no connection between the two.

Our concern in these pages has, perhaps aesthetically, been not so
much the final discovery as the *path* of discovery and individual critical
points along that path. In this, we have emphasized directionality and
we have alluded to Kierkegaard's declaration of where the path inevita-
bly leads. Our study goes no further, confining itself to the wilderness of
the human spirit before it is touched by grace. Perhaps like Johannes
Climacus, who shied away from actually becoming a Christian, we
content ourselves to meditate upon the process and the preliminaries,
but with the inevitability of the Christian clearly placed before us.

SELECTED BIBLIOGRAPHY

I. WORKS OF KIERKEGAARD

A. *Danish Editions*

Samlede Værker. Udg. af A.N. Drachmann, J.L. Heiberg og H.O. Lange.
1 Udg. København, 1901–1906. 14 vol.
A second edition appeared from 1920–1936. 15 vol.
A third edition, revised by Peter P. Rohde, appeared from 1962–1964. 20 vol.

Søren Kierkegaards Papirer. Anden forøgede Udgave ved Niels Thulstrup. København, 1968. 20 vol.

B. *English Editions*

The Concept of Irony. Trans. by Lee Capel. Bloomington: Indiana University Press, 1968.

Either/Or. Part I trans. by David F. Swenson and Lillian M. Swenson, Part II trans. by Walter Lowrie. 2nd. ed. revised by Howard A. Johnson. Garden City: Doubleday, 1959.

Johannes Climacus, or *De Omnibus Dubitandum Est* and *A Sermon*. Trans, by T.H. Croxall. London: Adam and Charles Black, 1958.

Edifying Discourses. Vol. I–IV trans. by David F. Swenson and Lillian M. Swenson. Minneapolis: Augsburg Publishing House, 1943–1946.

Fear and Trembling and *The Sickness Unto Death*. Trans. by Walter Lowrie. Garden City: Doubleday, 1954.

Repetition. Trans. by Walter Lowrie. Princeton: Princeton University Press, 1941.

Philosophical Fragments. Trans. by David F. Swenson. 2nd revised edition by Howard Hong. Princeton: Princeton University Press, 1962.

The Concept of Dread. Trans. by Walter Lowrie. 2nd ed. Princeton: Princeton University Press, 1957.

SELECTED BIBLIOGRAPHY

Thoughts on Crucial Situations in Human Life. Trans. by David F. Swenson, edited by Lillian M. Swenson. Minneapolis: Augsburg Publishing House, 1941.

Stages on Life's Way. Trans. by Walter Lowrie. Princeton: Princeton University Press, 1940.

The Concluding Unscientific Postscript. Trans. by David F. Swenson and Walter Lowrie. Princeton: Princeton University Press, 1941.

The Present Age and *Two Minor Ethico-Religious Discourses.* Trans. by Alexander Dru and Walter Lowrie. London and New York: Oxford University Press, 1940.

On Authority and Revelation. Trans. by Walter Lowrie. Princeton: Princeton University Press, 1955.

Purity of Heart. Trans. by Douglas Steere. 2nd ed. New York, 1948.

The Gospel of Suffering. Trans. by David F. Swenson and Lillian M. Swenson. Minneapolis: Augsburg Publishing House, 1948.

The Works of Love. Trans. by Howard and Edna Hong. New York: Harper and Row, 1962.

Crisis in the Life of An Actress. Trans. by Stephen Crites. New York: Harper and Row, 1967.

Christian Discourses. Trans. by Walter Lowrie. London and New York: Oxford University Press, 1939.

"On the Difference Between a Genius and An Apostle," included in *The Present Age.* Trans. by Alexander Dru. New York: Harper and Row, 1962.

The Point of View for My Work as An Author. Trans. by Walter Lowrie. New York: Harper and Row, 1962.

Armed Neutrality and An Open Letter. Trans. by Howard and Edna Hong. Bloomington and London: Indiana University Press, 1968.

Training in Christianity. Trans. by Walter Lowrie. London and New York: Oxford University Press, 1941.

For Self-Examination and Judge For Yourself. Trans. by Walter Lowrie. Princeton: Princeton University Press, 1944.

The Attack Upon Christendom. Trans. by Walter Lowrie. Princeton: Princeton University Press, 1944.

Søren Kierkegaard's Journals and Papers. Trans. and edited by Howard V. Hong and Edna H. Hong. (Vols. I–V) Bloomington and London: Indiana University Press, 1967ff.

II. SECONDARY LITERATURE

A full bibliography of the literature about Kierkegaard already comprises more than two full volumes. Thus I shall here indicate the standard bibliographies. I

164   SELECTED BIBLIOGRAPHY

shall also list more recent works which have not yet been included among the Kierkegaard Bibliographies and shall include certain indispensable studies already mentioned in such bibliographies, as well as other works relevant to this study.

HIMMELSTRUP, Jens. *Søren Kierkegaard: International Bibliografi.* Copenhagen: Nyt Nordisk Forlag, 1962. A multi-language bibliography of works up to 1960.

JØRGENSEN, Aage. *Søren Kierkegaard-Litteratur* 1961–1970: *En Forelobig Bibliografi.* Aarhus: Akademisk Boghandel. A multi-language supplement to Himmelstrup's work, which includes works up to 1970.

THOMPSON, Josiah. "Bibliographical Supplement" in *Kierkegaard: A Collection of Critical Essays.* Edited by Josiah Thompson. Garden City: Anchor Books, 1972.

Other Works

CORNU, Michel. *Kierkegaard.* Lausanne: L'Age d'Homme, 1972.

DIEM, Hermann. *Kierkegaard's Dialectic of Existence.* Trans. by Harold Knight. Edinburgh and London: Oliver and Boyd, 1959.

ELROD, John. *Being and Existence in Kierkegaard's Pseudonymous Works.* Princeton: Princeton University Press, 1975.

FAVEN-BOUTONIER, Julliette. *L'Angoisse.* Paris: Presses Universitaires de France, 1963.

HEIDEGGER, Martin. *Being and Time.* Trans. by John Macquarrie and Edward Robinson. New York: Harper and Row, 1962.

HENRIKSEN, Aage. *Methods and Results of Kierkegaard Studies in Scandinavia.* Copenhagen: Ejnar Munksgaard, 1951.

HIRSCH, Emanuel. *Kierkegaard-Studien.* Gutersloh: Verlag C. Bertelsmann, 1933.

HOHLENBERG, Johannes, *Søren Kierkegaard.* Trans. by T. H. Croxall. New York: Pantheon, 1954.

HOLMER, Paul. "Theology and the Emotions." (Unpublished essay.)

JOHNSON, Ralph Henry. *The Concept of Existence in the Concluding Unscientific Postscript.* The Hague: Martinus Nijhoff, 1972.

McCARTHY, Vincent. "*Melancholy* and *Religious Melancholy* in Kierkegaard," *Kierkegaardiana,* Vol. X, Copenhagen, 1977.

McKINNON, Alistair, ed. *The Kierkegaard Indices to Kierkegaards Samlede Værker.* Leiden: E.J. Brill, 1970–1971.
 I. *Kierkegaard in Translation/ en traduction/ in Ubersetzuung,* 1970.
 II. *Konkordans til Kierkegaards Samlede Værker,* 1971.

MALANTSCHUK, Gregor. *Kierkegaard's Thought.* Trans. by Howard V. Hong and Edna H. Hong. Princeton: Princeton University Press, 1972.

SELECTED BIBLIOGRAPHY

——. *Frihedens Problem i Kierkegaards Bebrebet Angst*. København: Rosenkilde og Bagger, 1971.

RYLE, Gilbert. *The Concept of Mind*. New York: Barnes & Noble, 1949.

SCHMUELI, Adi. *Kierkegaard and Consciousness*. Trans. by Naomi Handelman. Princeton: Princeton University Press, 1971.

TAYLOR, Mark. *Kierkegaard's Pseudonymous Authorship*. Princeton: Princeton University Press, 1975.

THOMPSON, Josiah. *Kierkegaard*. New York: A. Knopf, 1973.

WAHL, Jean. *Etudes Kierkegaardiennes*. Paris: Librairie Philosophique J. Vrin, 1949.

WITTGENSTEIN, Ludwig. *Philosophical Investigations*. 3rd Edition. New York: Macmillan, 1968.

INDEX

Kierkegaardian pseudonyms are listed alphabetically by first name or title.

A, *see* Johannes
Abraham, 47
Absolute, the, 18, 65, 79–80
actuality, 7, 18
Adam, 37, 39(n13), 40–41
Adler, Adolph Peter, 146–148
aesthetic, the, 3, 8, 26–27, 29, 33, 42–43, 47(n29), 48, 50, 54, 57, 67, 75, 77, 81, 83, 87, 102–103, 106–108, 116, 120–121, 131–133, 137, 149–150, 153, 157, 159
Alcibiades, 15
Andersen, H. C., 28, 141–144, 149
Anti-Climacus, 4, 34, 37(n11), 47–48, 82–85, 87, 89–91, 93–99, 130
anxiety, 5, 29–30, 33–53, 103, 124, 126, 128–132;
—and despair, 82–84, 89, 98, 101;
—for the evil, 42–43, 50–51;
—for the good, 43–45, 50–51;
—of Johannes, 107, 111–113, 118
Aristophanes, 9, 109
Arvesynden (see also original sin), 37
Augustine, St., 5, 101

B, *see* Judge William
boredom, 24, 109

Chateaubriand, 67
Christ, 12, 39(n13), 156
Christendom (*see also* Christianity), 3, 154
Christianity (*see also* Christendom), 5, 8, 12, 25(n54), 29(n69), 38–39, 63, 88, 96, 134, 136–137, 139–140, 144–145, 150, 153, 155, 159, 161
Climacus, *see* Johannes Climacus
consciousness (*see also* guilt-consciousness, sin-consciousness), 7, 17, 19, 26, 28–31, 38, 42, 46–

48, 69, 83, 89, 95–96, 98–100, 103, 107, 125–130;
—of Johannes, 109, 114–116
Constantine Constantius, 4, 31, 72–74, 104, 107–109
Cornu, Michel, 10

demoniacal, the, 44, 113
demonic, the, 43, 47, 50, 62, 110
Descartes, 85
despair (*see also Fortvivlelse*), 5, 27, 34, 47–48, 53, 71, 80–105, 121, 124, 126, 129–132, 140, 153, 156–160;
—as choice of self, 83, 87;
—and doubt, 85;
—of weakness, 97–98;
—of defiance, 98–100;
—of Johannes, 107, 116–118
dialectic, 2, 88, 116, 120
Don Juan, 31–32, 58, 65, 106–108
doubt, 29, 140, 156, 158;
—and despair, 85
dread, *see* anxiety

either-or, 12
emotions, 2
eternal, the, 18, 21, 39, 43–45, 51, 67, 74, 79–80, 84, 89–90, 95–98, 100, 104, 112, 114, 117, 130–132, 145, 152–153, 156
ethical, the, 22, 26, 31, 33, 47, 67, 70(n50), 75, 77–78, 81, 111, 133, 149, 159
ethico-religious, the (*see also* the ethical, the religious), 22, 26–27, 48, 51, 83, 87, 96, 102, 104, 110, 122, 129, 133, 153
existence-spheres, 27, 33, 37, 51, 75, 77, 111

INDEX

existence-stance, 7–12, 16, 22, 29–31;
 —of Johannes, 108–111
existentialism, 2, 49, 122

faith, 38, 40, 43, 46–47. 88, 103, 139–140, 156
Favez-Boutonier, Juliette, 35, 49
felix culpa, 39–40
finitude, 14, 31–32, 88–90, 93, 111, 126–128, 130, 156;
 —despair of, 93, 103, 116
Frater Taciturnus, 4, 75–77, 150
freedom, 48–50, 159

Grimault, Marguerite, 54(*n*4)
Guardini, Romano, 79
genius, the, 38–39
God, 40, 42, 46–47, 49(*n*32), 95, 102, 126, 132–133, 138, 150(*n*35), 156
God-relationship, 49(*n*32), 51–52, 84–88, 93, 103
grace, 6, 29–30, 40, 42, 84, 98, 118, 121, 130–133, 146, 153, 156, 159–161
guilt-consciousness, 40, 42, 80, 130

Haufniensis, *see* Vigilius Haufniensis
Hegel, G. W. F., 8–11, 25, 40, 136, 138–139
Hegelianism (*see also* the System), 3, 11, 146
Heidegger, Martin, 35, 41(*n*15), 49, 66, 69(*n*44), 101(*n*41), 122–125, 138(*n*5), 139
Heine, Heinrich, 24
Hirsch, Emanuel, 141
Holmer, Paul L., 123(*n*2), 124
Horace, 108
humor, 12

Icarus, 21
Idea, the, 18
Idealism (*see also* Hegelianism), 8, 39, 45, 103–104, 134, 138(*n*5), 139–140, 151
Indesluttethed, 22(*n*40), 44, 58, 61–62, 76, 150;
 —of Johannes, 113, 115
infinitude, 21, 24, 27–28, 46–47, 64, 84, 88–90, 130;
 —despair of, 91–93, 103, 116
intentionality, 50
irony, 5, 7–32, 46–47, 51, 84, 121, 124, 126–132, 134, 143, 149, 158;

—of Johannes, 107–111, 113, 117–118
irrationalism, 2

Johannes (*A*), 4, 30, 32, 58–61, 75, 91, 103–104, 106–119, 120, 129, 148–149, 156–159
Johannes Climacus, 12, 17, 21, 23, 25–27, 40, 53, 57, 85, 140, 151, 156–159, 161
Judge William, 4, 31, 56, 58, 60–62, 66–73, 75, 78, 80, 83, 106–111, 113–117, 148–151, 157–159;
 —on despair, 86–87, 103–104
Juvenal, 108

Leibniz, 139
life-view, 2–3, 5, 28, 31, 52, 54, 58, 61, 68, 85, 107, 110, 112, 126, 132–160;
 —and despair, 103–105;
 —of Johannes, 107, 112–113, 118
Livsanskuelse, *see* life-view
logic, 2
Lowrie, Walter, 33(*n*1), 36, 55, 57, 106(*n*1)

Malantschuk, Gregor, 11, 82, 89
Martensen, 11, 139
mastered irony, 7, 16–17, 27–29, 111, 128, 161
May, Rollo, 35
Melancholi, 31, 33–34, 46, 55–56, 62–65, 69–70, 72–74, 79–80, 127, 129, 131;
 —of Johannes, 109, 114, 118
melancholy (*see also* Melancholi and Tungsind*), 5, 31–32, 48, 53–81, 124, 126–127, 129–130, 134, 157;
 —and despair, 87, 103;
 —of Johannes, 107, 110–111, 113–118
mood, 2–3, 28, 58, 61, 80, 120–134
Mozart, 62–63
mythology, 63(*n*24)

necessity, 52, 88–90, 130, 159;
 —despair of, 95–96, 117
negativity, 7, 27, 33
nothing, 5, 41, 49, 50, 112, 126
nothingness, 27, 38–39, 45, 47, 52, 128–129

Olsen, Regine, 72
original sin (*see also* Arvesynden*), 36–37, 82, 84
Otto, Rudolph, 49(*n*32)

INDEX

passion, 20–21, 28–29, 31, 46, 109, 128, 131
Pelagianism, 5
philosophy, 5, 28, 122, 136–140, 145, 157–161
Plato, 9, 70, 72, 109, 138–139, 157
Plotinus, 64
possibility, 5, 12, 23–24, 29, 37, 39(n13), 40–46, 48–50, 52, 60, 84–86, 88–90, 95, 101, 103–104, 121, 128–134;
—despair of, 93–95, 104, 116;
—of Johannes, 111–113, 116, 118–119
Protagoras, 13
pseudonymity, 4, 36
pseudonyms, 4, 34, 37–38, 45, 53, 54(n5), 78, 83, 85, 87, 106–107, 120–121, 144, 159
psychology, 1, 5, 35, 38, 51, 73, 75, 88–89, 101, 160

Quidam, 75–77

rationalism, 2,
reason, 2, 123
religious, the (*see also* the ethico-religious), 8, 24–25, 27, 31, 33, 47, 52, 70(n50), 75–77, 81, 83, 87, 103, 110, 116, 120–121, 124, 129, 131–134, 145, 150, 159–160
repetition, 32, 39(n13), 44, 72–74, 90, 101, 114, 120, 125, 156
resignation, 48, 121
Revelation (Christian), 5–6, 46, 84–85, 88, 95, 130, 146–148, 161
revelation, 44, 50, 52, 58–59, 71, 76, 132, 146, 156, 160
Romanticism, 3, 5, 24, 38, 45, 96, 103–104, 131, 134, 138(n5), 140
Romantics, the, 2, 6, 8–12, 23, 26–30, 92, 95, 104, 110–111, 117, 120, 134–135, 142–143, 148
Ryle, Gilbert, 123–124

Sartre, Jean-Paul, 49, 123
Schelling, 44(n20)
Schlegel, F., 9, 11, 24
self, the, 5, 28–29, 31, 64–66, 71–72, 80–81, 90–91, 125–128, 130–133, 135, 146, 149, 156, 160;
—and despair, 83, 87, 90–105;
—of Johannes, 112, 117

sin, 5, 27, 36, 39–43, 45, 49, 68, 84, 88, 99–101, 103, 130, 132, 153, 156;
—despair as, 90, 101, 104–105, 116–118;
—forgiveness of, 95, 100
sin-consciousness, 5, 12, 38, 40, 42–43, 101, 118, 121, 130–131;
—and despair, 83–84, 87, 90, 94, 96, 103

Socrates, 2, 8–15, 17, 19, 23, 25–26, 29(n69), 70, 99, 138–139, 151, 157, 160–161
Solger, 9
Solomon, 143
spirit, 11–13, 30, 38–43, 46–48, 50–52, 62–63, 65, 68–69, 72–73, 79, 83–84, 89–90, 96, 115, 121, 126–131, 133, 139, 155, 160
Stoicism, 145
subjectivity, 19–22, 30, 33–34, 50, 52, 121–122, 126–127, 132–133, 142,`146, 155, 160–161;
—of Johannes, 106–119
System, the (*see also* Hegelianism), 1, 22, 34, 36, 40, 138–139, 151

Tieck, 9
Tillich, Paul, 44(n20)
Tungsind, 5, 53, 55–56, 62, 64–66, 68–70, 72–77, 80, 84, 103, 127, 129–132, 150;
—of Johannes, 110, 113–116, 118

Victor Eremita, 56–59, 106–107, 148
Vigilius Haufniensis, 34, 36–38, 40–43, 45–49, 53, 84–85, 88, 111–112

will, the, 27, 29, 31, 40–42, 46, 51, 61–62, 67–69, 71, 80–81, 87, 91–92, 96–100, 115, 117–118, 120, 122, 141, 156;
—act of, 87, 98, 102, 110, 124–126, 130–131, 134;
—and Johannes, 110
William, *see* Judge William
Wittgenstein, Ludwig, 123–124
world-view (*see also* life-view), 28, 136, 147

Xenephon, 9

Printed in the USA
CPSIA information can be obtained
at www.ICGtesting.com
LVHW011138150324
774517LV00040B/1652